Lecture Notes in Artificial Intelligence   8178

Subseries of Lecture Notes in Computer Science

Longbing Cao   Hiroshi Motoda
Jaideep Srivastava   Ee-Peng Lim
Irwin King   Philip S. Yu   Wolfgang Nejdl
Guandong Xu   Gang Li   Ya Zhang (Eds.)

Behavior and Social Computing

International Workshop on Behavior and Social Informatics,
BSI 2013, Gold Coast, QLD, Australia, April 14, 2013 and
International Workshop on Behavior and Social Informatics
and Computing, BSIC 2013, Beijing, China, August 3-9, 2013
Revised Selected Papers

 Springer

Volume Editors

Longbing Cao, University of Technology, Sydney, Australia
E-mail: longbing.cao@uts.edu.au

Hiroshi Motoda, Osaka University, Japan
E-mail: motoda@ar.sanken.osaka-u.ac.jp

Jaideep Srivastava, University of Minnesota, Minneapolis, MN, USA
E-mail: srivasta@cs.umn.edu

Ee-Peng Lim, Singapore Management University
E-mail: eplim@smu.edu.sg

Irwin King, The Chinese University of Hong Kong
E-mail: king@cse.cuhk.edu.hk

Philip S. Yu, University of Illinois at Chicago, IL, USA
E-mail: psyu@cs.uic.edu

Wolfgang Nejdl, Leibniz Universität Hannover, Germany
E-mail: nejdl@kbs.uni-hannover.de

Guandong Xu, University of Technology, Sydney, NSW, Australia
E-mail: guandong.xu@uts.edu.au

Gang Li, Deakin University, Burwood, VIC, Australia
E-mail: gang.li@deakin.edu.au

Ya Zhang, Shanghai Jiao Tong University, China
E-mail: ya_zhang@sjtu.edu.cn

ISSN 0302-9743   e-ISSN 1611-3349
ISBN 978-3-319-04047-9   e-ISBN 978-3-319-04048-6
DOI 10.1007/978-3-319-04048-6
Springer Cham Heidelberg New York Dordrecht London

Library of Congress Control Number: 2013956132

CR Subject Classification (1998): I.2, J.4, H.4, H.3, H.5, C.2, H.2.8, F.4

LNCS Sublibrary: SL 7 – Artificial Intelligence

Typesetting: Camera-ready by author, data conversion by Scientific Publishing Services, Chennai, India
Printed on acid-free paper
Springer is part of Springer Science+Business Media (www.springer.com)

Preface

Behavior and social sciences are increasingly recognized as a key component in business intelligence and problem-solving. Behavior and social informatics and computing (BSIC) has emerged as a new scientific field that studies effective methodologies, techniques, and technical tools for representing, modeling, analyzing, understanding, and managing human behaviors and social characteristics, and for disclosing deep behavior and social intelligence for improved decision-making and business values.

This book constitutes the proceedings of the 2013 International Workshop on Behavior and Social Informatics and Computing (BSIC 2013) held in conjunction with IJCAI 2013 (Beijing, China); the 2013 International Workshop on Behavior and Social Informatics (BSI 2013) was held jointly with the Workshop on Understanding Collective Behaviors in Complex Networks (UCBCN 2013) in conjunction with PAKDD 2013 (Gold Coast, Australia).

The papers in this volume give an indication of recent advances in behavior and social informatics (BSI). It is an exciting and emerging interdisciplinary area in which a wide range of techniques and methods are being studied for behavior/social-oriented analyses including behavioral and social interaction and networks, behavioral/social patterns, behavioral/social impacts, the formation of behavioral/social-oriented groups and collective intelligence, and behavioral/social intelligence emergence.

The series of workshops aims to increase potential collaborations and partnerships by bringing together academic researchers and industry practitioners from data mining, statistics and analytics, business and marketing, finance and politics, and behavioral, social and psychological sciences with the objectives of presenting updated research efforts and progress on foundational and emerging interdisciplinary topics of BSI, exchanging new ideas, and identifying future research directions.

The two workshops received 58 submissions. Each submitted paper was reviewed by three members of the Program Committee. Following the independent review, there were discussions among the reviewers. When necessary, additional reviews were requested. A total of 23 papers were selected for these proceedings, yielding an acceptance rate of 40%.

In addition to accepted papers, we were honored with the presence of five outstanding keynote speakers, namely, Prof. Hiroshi Motoda and Prof. Yanchun Zhang for BSI-UCBCN 2013, and Prof. Daniel Zeng, Prof. Qiang Yang, Prof Irwin King, and Prof. Longbing Cao for BSIC 2013.

The success of this series of workshops depends largely on support and cooperation from many individuals and organizations. We would like to take this opportunity to thank the authors, the Program Committee members, external reviewers, and our volunteer students for offering their time and effort to make

this series of workshops successful and enjoyable. We extend our sincere grati-
tude to the IJCAI 2013 and PAKDD 2013 Conference Organizing Committees
for accepting our workshops in such premier venues. Last but not the least, we
would like to thank Springer for their assistance in publishing this proceedings
as a single volume in its LNAI series.

October 2013   Longbing Cao
                                                               Hiroshi Motoda
                                                           Jaideep Srivastava
                                                                 Ee-peng Lim
                                                                  Irwin King
                                                               Philip S. Yu
                                                              Wolfgan Nejdl
                                                              Guandong Xu
                                                                    Gang Li
                                                                   Ya Zhang

Organization

BSIC 2013/General Chairs

Philip S. Yu	University of Illinois at Chicago, USA
Wolfgan Nejdl	Leibniz University Hannover, Germany

BSIC 2013/Program Chairs

Longbing Cao	University of Technology, Sydney, Australia
Hiroshi Motoda	Osaka University and AFOSR/AOARD, Japan
Jaideep Srivastava	University of Minnesota, USA
Ee-peng Lim	Singapore Management University, Singapore
Irwin King	Chinese University of Hong Kong, Hong Kong, SAR China

BSIC 2013/Organizing Chairs

Guandong Xu	University of Technology, Sydney, Australia
Gang Li	Deakin University, Australia
Ya Zhang	Shanghai Jiaotong University, China

BSI-UCBCN 2013/General Chair

Philip S. Yu	University of Illinois at Chicago, USA

BSI-UCBCN 2013/Program Chairs

Longbing Cao	University of Technology, Sydney, Australia
Hiroshi Motoda	Osaka University and AFOSR/AOARD, Japan
Graham Williams	Australian Taxation Office, Australia
Irwin King	Chinese University of Hong Kong, Hong Kong, SAR China
Ya Zhang	Shanghai Jiaotong University, China

BSI-UCBCN 2013/Organizing Chairs

Gang Li	Deakin University, Australia
Guandong Xu	University of Technology, Sydney, Australia
Ya Zhang	Shanghai Jiaotong University, China

BSIC 2013/Steering Committee

Philip S. Yu	University of Illinois at Chicago, USA
Longbing Cao	University of Technology, Sydney, Australia
Hiroshi Motoda	Osaka University and AFOSR/AOARD, Japan
Qiang Yang	Hong Kong University of Science and Technology, SAR China
Huan Liu	Arizona State University, USA
V.S. Subrahmanian	University of Maryland, USA
Laks V.S. Lakshmanan	The university of British Columbia, Canada
Wolfgan Nejdl	Leibniz University Hannover, Germany

BSIC 2013/Program Committee Members

Palakorn Achananuparp	Singapore Management University, Singapore
Raian Ali	Bournemouth University, UK
Fred Amblard	CNRS IRIT - Université des Sciences Sociales Toulouse 1, France
Lashon Booker	The MITRE Corporation, Virginia
Yi Cai	South China University of Technology, China
Simon Caton	Karlsruhe Institute of Technology, Germany
Enhong Chen	University of Science and Technology of China, China
Soon Ae Chun	City University of New York, USA
Paolo Garza	Politecnico di Torino, Italy
Lilia Georgieva	Heriot-Watt University, Edinburgh, UK
Christos Grecos	University of West of Scotland, UK
Lynne Hall	University of Sunderland, UK
Ben He	University of Chinese Science Academy, China
Yeye He	Microsoft Research, USA
Panagiotis Karampelas	Hellenic American University, USA
Sang-Wook Kim	Hanyang University, Korea
Wookey Lee	Inha University, Korea
Carson K. Leung	University of Manitoba, Canada
Ruixuan Li	Huazhong University of Science and Technology, China
Lin Li	Wuhan University of Technology, China
Wenxin Liang	Dalian University of Technology, China
Peter Mutschke	GESIS-IZ, Germany
Federico Neri	Synthema, Italy
Dunlu Peng	University of Shanghai for Science and Technology, China
Weining Qian	East China Normal University, China
Juwel Rana	Lulea University of Technology, Sweden

Sherif Sakr   The University of New South Wales, Australia
Man-Kwan Shan   National Chengchi University, Taiwan
Haifeng Shen   Flinders University, Australia
Xiaolin Shi   Microsoft Corporation, USA
Mohammad Siddique   Fayetteville State University, USA
Kazutoshi Sumiya   University of Hyogo, Japan
Lynda Tamine   IRIT, France
Mehmet Tan   TOBB University of Economics and
                             Technology, Turkey
Abdullah Uz Tansel   City University of New York, USA
Xiaohui Tao   University of Southern Queensland, Australia
Damir Vandic   Erasmus University Rotterdam,
                             The Netherlands
Iraklis Varlamis   Harokopio University of Athens, Greece
Athanasios Vasilakos   National Technical University of Athens,
                             Greece
Jinlong Wang   Qingdao Technological University, China
Xufei Wang   Arizona State University, USA
Chaokun Wang   Tsinghua University, China
Xiaofeng Wang   Chinese Academy of Sciences, China
Zongda Wu   Wenzhou University, China
Shanchun Wu   HP Labs, USA
Rong Xie   Wuhan University, China
Kun Yue   Yunnan University, China
Xianchao Zhang   Dalian University of Technology, China
Jianwei Zhang   Kyoto Sangyo University, Japan
Yanchang Zhao   RDataMining.com, Australia
Minqi Zhou   East China Normal University, China
Jianke Zhu   Zhejiang University, China
Tingshao Zhu   Chinese Academy of Sciences, China
Yu Zong   West Anhui University, China

BSI-UCBCN 2013/Program Committee Members

Palakorn Achananuparp   Singapore Management University, Singapore
Raian Ali   Bournemouth University, UK
Toshiyuki Amagasa   University of Tsukuba, Japan
Fred Amblard   CNRS IRIT - Université des Sciences Sociales
                             Toulouse 1, France
James Bailey   University of Melbourne, Australia
Lashon Booker   The MITRE Corporation, USA
Yi Cai   South China University of Technology, China

Athanasios Vasilakos   National Technical University of Athens,
                                    Greece
Jinlong Wang   Qingdao Technological University, China
Xiaofeng Wang   Chinese Academy of Sciences, China
Chaokun Wang   Tsinghua University, China
Jianmin Wang   Tsinghua University, China
Yimin Wen   CCF, China
Zongda Wu   Wenzhou University, China
Jierui Xie   Oracle, USA
Ping Xiong   Zhongnan University of Economics and Law,
                                    China
Hui Xiong   Rutgers University, China
Eiko Yoneki   University of Cambridge, UK
Kun Yue   Yunnan University, China
Jianwei Zhang   Tsukuba University of Technology, Japan
Minqi Zhou   East China Normal University, China
Jianke Zhu   Zhejiang University, China
Tingshao Zhu   Chinese Academy of Sciences, China
Yu Zong   West Anhui University, China

Table of Contents

Part III: Socio-Behavioral Analytics

Mining Frequent Sequences Using Itemset-Based Extension

Ma Zhixin[1,*], Xu Yusheng[1], and Tharam S. Dillon[2]

[1] University of Padova, Italy
School of Information Science and Technology, Lanzhou University, Lanzhou, China
mazhx8616@gmail.com, xuyusheng@lzu.edu.cn
[2] School of Information System, Curtin University, Perth, Australia
tharam.dillon@cbs.curtin.edu.au

Abstract. In this paper, we systematically explore an itemset-based extension approach for generating candidate sequence which contributes to a better and more straightforward search space traversal performance than traditional item-based extension approach. Based on this candidate generation approach, we present FINDER, a novel algorithm for discovering the set of all frequent sequences. FINDER is composed of two separated steps. In the first step, all frequent itemsets are discovered and we can get great benefit from existing efficient itemset mining algorithms. In the second step, all frequent sequences with at least two frequent itemsets are detected by combining depth-first search and itemset-based extension candidate generation together. A vertical bitmap data representation is adopted for rapidly support counting reason. Several pruning strategies are used to reduce the search space and minimize cost of computation. An extensive set of experiments demonstrate the effectiveness and the linear scalability of proposed algorithm.

Keywords: Data Mining, Frequent Itemsets, Frequent Sequences, Algorithm.

1 Introduction

The sequences mining task, which discovers all frequent subsequences from a large sequence database, is an important data mining tool for behavior informatics and computing [Cao 2010; Cao and Yu 2012]. It has attracted considerable attention from database practitioners and researches because of its broad applications in many areas such as analysis of sales data, discovering of Web access patterns in Web-log dataset, extraction of Motifs from DNA sequence, analysis of medical database, identifying network alarm patterns, etc.

In the last decade, a number of algorithms have been proposed to deal with the problem of mining sequential patterns from sequence database. Most of them are based on Apriori property which states that any sub-pattern of a frequent pattern must be frequent. These Apriori-like algorithms utilize a bottom-up candidate generation-and-test method and a breadth-fist search space traverse strategy. In each candidate generation step, algorithm iteratively generate all candidate k-sequences from all frequent (k-1)-sequences. Because each candidate k-sequences has one more item than

L. Cao et al. (Eds.): BSIC/BSI 2013, LNAI 8178, pp. 1–9, 2013.
© Springer International Publishing Switzerland 2013

a frequent $(k-1)$-sequences, this candidate generation method can be considered as an item-based extension approach. In other words, all these algorithms deal with the problem of mining sequential patterns using an item-based viewpoint. The main bottleneck of these algorithms is that huge number of candidate sequences could be generated and the cost of candidate generation, test and support counting is very expensive. In fact, a lot of candidate sequences are infrequent or not exist in database. Furthermore, some algorithms require multiple full database-scans as the longest frequent sequence and the cost of I/O is very expensive, some approaches use very complicated internal data structures to maintain database in memory which add great space and computation overhead.

In this paper, we systematically explore an itemset-based extension approach for generating candidate sequence which contributes to a better and more straightforward search space traversal performance than traditional item-based extension approach. The general idea is outlined as follow: A candidate sequence can be generated by adding one frequent itemset into the end of a frequent sequence instead of adding one item into a frequent sequence each time. Since any candidates with infrequent itemsets are not generated, the number of candidates is reduced efficiently. Based on this candidate generation approach, we present a novel algorithm, called *FINDER* (**F**requent Sequence MIning usiNg Itemset-baseD Extension AppRoach), for discovering the set of all frequent sequences. FINDER is composed of two separated steps. In the first step, all frequent itemsets are discovered and we can get great benefit from existing efficient itemset mining algorithms [Burdick *et al.*, 2001]. In the second step, all frequent sequences with at least two frequent itemsets are detected by combining depth-first search and itemset-based extension candidate generation together. In addition, FINDER can reduce the search space and minimize cost of computation efficiently by using several pruning strategies.

2   Problem Statement and Related Works

Let $I=\{i_1, i_2, \ldots, i_m\}$ be a set of m distinct items comprising the alphabet. An *itemset e* $= \{i_1, i_2, \ldots, i_k\}$ is a non-empty unordered collection of items. Without loss of generality, we assume that items of an itemset are sorted in lexicographic order and denoted as $(i_1 i_2 \ldots i_k)$. A *sequence* $s = \{e_1, e_2, \ldots, e_n\}$ is an ordered list of itemsets and denoted as $(e_1 - e_2 - \ldots - e_n)$, where e_i is an itemset. An item can occur at most once in an itemset of a sequence, but can occur multiple times in different itemsets of a sequence. The number of instances of items in a sequence is called the *length* of sequence. Let $|e_i|$ refer to the number of items in itemset e_i, a sequence with length l is called *l-sequence*, where $l = \sum |e_i|$ and $1 \leq i \leq n$. For example, C-AB-A is a 4-sequence.

A sequence $s_1 = (a_1 - a_2 - \ldots - a_m)$ is said to *contained* in another sequence $s_2 = (b_1 - b_2 - \ldots - b_n)$ if and only if $\exists\ i_1, i_2, \ldots, i_m$, such that $1 \leq i_1 < i_2 < \ldots < i_m \leq n$, and $a_1 \subseteq b_{i1}, a_2 \subseteq b_{i2}, \ldots, a_m \subseteq b_{im}$. If s_1 is contained in s_2, s_1 is a *subsequence* of s_2 and s_2 is a *supersequence* of s_1.

Given a sequence database D, the *support count* of a sequence s, denoted as $\delta(s, D)$, is the total number of input-sequences in D which contain s. The *support* of s, denoted as *support(s)*, is the fraction of sequences in D that contain s. If the symbol $|D|$

denotes the number of sequences in D, $support(s) = \delta(s, D) / |D|$. Given a user-specified threshold min_sup, we say that a sequence s is *frequent* if $support(s)$ is greater than or equal to min_sup.

Given a database D of input-sequences and a user-specified threshold min_sup, the problem of sequence mining is to find all the frequent sequences in the database.

Since the problem of frequent sequence mining was first introduced in [Agrawal *et al.*, 1995], a large amount of studies have been done toward the development of efficient algorithms for solving this problem and its variations. In same work three algorithms are presented: AprioriAll, AprioriSome and DynamicSome for solving this problem. Note that these three algorithms utilize itemset to generate candidate sequence, but this idea is not adopted in later sequence mining algorithms. Srikant *et al.* [1996] generalized definitions of sequence mining to include time constrains, sliding time window, and user defined taxonomy. They also proposed GSP algorithms which outperformed AprioriAll by up to 20 times.

In [Zaki *et al.*, 2001], Zaki proposed SPADE algorithm which uses a vertical id-list database format for efficient joining operation and a lattice-theoretic approach to decompose the original search into small pieces so that all working id-list can be load into memory. Pei et al. [2004] proposed PrefixSpan which utilizes a pattern-growth approach instead of refinement of the candidate generation-and-test approach. PrefixSpan recursively projects a sequence database into a set of smaller projected sequence databases and grows sequential patterns in each projected database by exploring only locally frequent fragment. A memory-based pseudo-projection technique is applied to reduce the number of physical projected databases to be generated. Ayres et al. [2002] presented SPAM which integrates a depth-first traversal of the search space with some efficient pruning mechanisms. In addition, SPAM utilizes vertical bitmap representation for candidate generation and rapid support counting. Spade, PrefixSpan and SPAM are considered as the three fastest algorithms that mine sequential patterns. Previously, Tan and Dillon et al. , [2006] presented SEQUEST which uses a Direct Memory Access Strips (DMA-Strips) structure to efficiently enumerate candidate subsequence. A unique property of DMA-Strips is that it ensures all enumerated subsequences are valid in the sense that they exist in the database, and no extra work is required to prune invalid candidate sequences.

3   An Itemset-Based Extension Approach

Definition 1. Let e_1 and e_2 be two itemsets. If e_1 is a subset of e_2, then e_1 is a *subitemset* of e_2 and e_2 is a *superitemset* of e_1.

Definition 2. The number of itemsets in a sequence is called the *size* of sequence. A sequence with k itemsets is called k'-*sequence*.

For example, each itemset is a $1'$-sequence because its size is 1, sequence (AC-CD) is a $2'$-sequence because its size is 2. Note that the *size* of a sequence is different from the *length* of a sequence.

Definition 3. Given sequence database D, a user-specified threshold min_sup, we say that an itemset e is *frequent* if $support(e)$ is greater than or equal to min_sup. The set of all frequent itemsets is denoted as *FE* .

Definition 4. A frequent sequence of size k is called a *frequent k'-sequence*.

The *lexicographic subset tree* is presented originally by Rymon [1992] and extended to describe the framework of sequence lattice in SPAM [Ayres *et al.*, 2002]. All sequences can be arranged in a lexicographic sequence tree whose root is null sequence labeled with $\varnothing$ and each node in tree represents a sequence. Each lower level *k* in tree contains all of k-sequences which are ordered lexicographically. Each node is recursively generated from its parent node by using a sequence-extension step or an itemset-extension step. The sequence-extension step is the process of generating a sequence-extended sequence which is generated by adding a new itemset consisting of a single item to the end of its parent's sequence. The itemset-extension step is the process of generating itemset-extended sequence which is a sequence generated by adding an item into the last itemset in the parent's sequence.   For example, Figure 1 shows the complete lexicographic sequence tree for two items, *A* and *B*, given that the maximum size of a sequence is three.

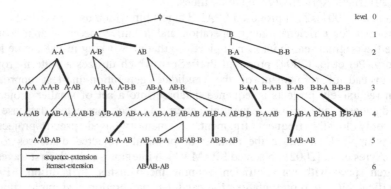

Fig. 1. Example of the lexicographic sequence tree

Definition 5. Given a *k'*-sequence s_1 and a *(k+1)'*-sequence s_2. If s_2 can be generated by adding an itemset *e* to the end of sequence s_1, we say that s_2 is an *itemset-based extension sequence* of s_1, denoted as $s_2 = s_1 \oplus e$.   For example, sequence (AB-C-BD) is an itemset-based extension sequence of (AB-C).

From this definition, each sequence can be considered as an itemset-based extension sequence. So, we can enumerate all sequences in lattice and organize lexicographic sequence tree by using an *itemset-based extension approach*. First, all itemsets are generated from the set of items and kept in an *itemset-list* by lexicographical order. The root of tree is null sequence labeled with ϕ and each node in tree represents a sequence. Each lower level *k* contains nodes of all *k'*-sequences. The level 1 of tree contains nodes of all itemsets (1'-sequences) in itemset-list. In level *k*, each node is an itemset-based extension sequence of its parent node in level *(k-1)*. All these nodes of *k'*-sequence are generated by iteratively adding an itemset from itemset-list to the end of its parent node in level *(k-1)*. We refer to lexicographic sequence tree organized in this itemset-based extension manner as *itemset-based lexicographic sequence tree* (abbr. *itemset-based tree*). Theoretically, an itemset-based tree is infinite. But in practice, it is finite because the maximal size of sequences in an input database is limited.

For example, given the maximum size of a sequence is three, figure 3 shows the complete itemset-based tree for two item A and B. Contrasting figure 2 with figure 1, itemset-based tree is more straightforward than lexicographic sequence tree. It gives us a new and straightforward viewpoint to analyzing the problem of sequence mining.

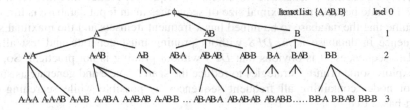

Fig. 2. Example of the lexicographic sequence tree

4 The FINDER Algorithm

Since all frequent sequences in a database can be considered as two types: frequent itemset (frequent 1'-sequenc) and frequent sequence with at least two frequent itemsets (frequent k'-sequence, k>1), the problem of frequent sequences mining can be divided into two sub-problems: one is to find all frequent itemsets, the other is to find all frequent k'-sequences where k>1. The first sub-problem is equal to the problem of mining frequent itemset and can be solved by using existing efficient frequent itemset mining approaches. If all frequent itemsets are known, the itemset-based extension approach can be used to enumerate candidate sequences. The general idea is outlined as follow: A candidate k'-sequence is generated by adding one frequent itemset into the end of a frequent $(k-1)$'- sequence. The sub-problem of find all frequent k'-sequences can be seemed as a process of generating and test candidate sequences by traversing the itemset-based tree discussed above.

```
FINDER (min_sup, D)

(1)  Finding F1;
//   F1 is the set of all frequent items;
(2)  Finding EL;
//   EL is the set of all frequent events;
(3)  FS= EL;
//   FS is the set of all frequent sequences;
(4)  for  each event e_i ∈ EL do
(5)      DFS(e_i, EL)


DFS(n, EL)
// without pruning strategies

(1)  for  each event e_i ∈ EL do
(2)      s = n ⊕ e_i;
(3)      if  support(s) ≥ min_sup then
(4)          FS = FS ∪ {s};
(5)      DFS(s, EL)
```

Fig. 3. Pseudo-code of FINDER

Figure 3 shows the high level structure of FINDER algorithm which is composed of three main steps: 1) Finding the set of all frequent items (1-sequences) F_1. 2) Finding the set of all frequent itemsets ($1'$-sequences) FE. 3) Finding all frequent k'-sequences, where $k>1$, by using procedure DFS which repeats depth-first search recursively on *each* n's itemset-based extension sequence. Notice that this recursive process is finite because the maximal size of sequences in an input database is limited.

Assume that the database to be mined has k frequent itemsets and the maximal size of sequence in database is m. DFS without pruning must generate and test all m^k candidate sequences. It is obvious that DFS without pruning is not practical. So, we must explore some pruning strategies to reduce the search space and generate as small a set of nodes containing all frequent sequences as possible while searching the itemset-based tree.

Definition 6. In the itemset-based tree, each node n is associated with one *itemset list*, denoted by EL, which is the set of frequent itemsets that are considered for a possible itemset-based extension of node n. All itemsets in EL are kept in lexicographic order.

Definition 7. Given a node n and its itemset list $EL=\{e_1,e_2,...,e_k\}$. An itemset e_i is said to be *a frequent extension itemset* of n if $e_i \in EL$ and $support(n \oplus e_i) \geq min\_sup$. An itemset e_j is said to be *an infrequent extension itemset* of n if $e_j \in EL$ and $support(n \oplus e_j)<min\_sup$. The *frequent extension itemsets list* (abbr. *FEL*) of n is the set of all n's frequent extension itemsets.

Pruning strategy 1(abbr. *PS1*). In the itemset-based tree, if a node n is not frequent, then all its children are not frequent and can be trimmed off.

Pruning strategy 2(abbr. *PS2*). Given a node n and its $EL=\{e_1,e_2,...,e_k\}$. Each $e_i \in EL$ is checked iteratively. If one frequent extension itemset e_i is found, we scan the rest itemsets in EL and find each e_j which is a subset of e_i. Since e_j is a frequent extension itemset, sequence $(n \oplus e_j)$ can be inserted into the set of all frequent sequences directly without further testing.

Pruning strategy 3(abbr. *PS3*). Given a node n and its $EL=\{e_1,e_2,...,e_k\}$. Each $e_i \in EL$ is checked iteratively. If one infrequent extension itemset e_i is found, we scan the rest itemsets in EL and trim off all itemsets which are superitemsets of e_i.

Pruning strategy 4(abbr. *PS4*). Given a node n and its itemset list $EL=\{e_1,e_2,...,e_k\}$. Each $e_i \in EL$ is checked iteratively and the frequent extension itemsets list *FEL* is generated. We can use the *FEL* as n's children's EL.

Figure 4 shows the pseudo-code of procedure DFS with all pruning strategies discussed above.

5   Experimental Results

In this section, we study the performance of proposed FINDER algorithms by comparing it with SPADE and SPAM. The experiments were performed on a 1.7GHz Pentium 4 PC with 512MB main memory, running Microsoft Windows 2003 server.

DFS(n, EL)
// with pruning strategies

```
(1)    FEL={ }
(2)    for each event e_i∈ EL do
(3)        if support(n ⊕ e_i) ≥ min_sup then
(4)            FS=FS ∪ {n ⊕ e_i}; FEL=FEL ∪ e_i;
(5)            for each e_j∈ EL and j>i do
(6)                if e_j⊆ e_i then
(7)                    FS= FS ∪ {n ⊕ e_i};
                       FEL= FEL ∪ {e_j};
                       EL=EL-(e_j);
(8)        if support(n ⊕ e_i)<min_sup then
(9)            for each e_j∈ EL and j>i do
(10)               if e_i⊆ e_j then
(11)                   EL=EL-(e_j);
(12)   for each  e_i∈ FEL do
(14)       s= n ⊕ e_i ;
```

Fig. 4. Pseudeo-code of DFS with pruning

We obtained the source code of SPADE and SPAM from their authors' websites. All three algorithms are written in C++, and compiled using g++ with option -03. Same as SPAM, all synthetic datasets are generated by using the IBM AssocGen program [Agrawal *et al.*, 1995] which takes the parameters listed in Table 1.

Table 1. Parameters used in dataset generation

Option	Description
D	Number of customers
C	Average transactions per customer
T	Average items per transaction
S	Average length of maximal pattern

We compared FINDER with SPADE and SPAM on several synthetic datasets for various minimum support values.

The results of these tests are shown in Figures 5 which clearly shows that FINDER outperforms SPADE by about a factor of average 1.5 on small datasets and better than an order of magnitude for reasonably large datasets. There are several reasons why FINDER outperforms SPADE: 1) FINDER uses itemset-based extension approach for generating candidate sequence which insures no candidate with infrequent itemsets is generated, the number of candidates is reduced efficiently. 2) Since FINDER discovers all frequent itemsets in the first step, we can get great benefit from existing efficient itemset mining algorithms. 3) FINDER adopts vertical bitmap representation of data structure which performs counting process in an extremely efficient manner.

The Figures 5 also shows that SPAM outperforms FINDER. For each dataset, SPAM is about twice as fast as FINDER at lower values of support and two algorithms have nearly equal performance at higher values of support. The primary reason is due to space requirement problem of FINDER. Assume that the database to be mined has n different items, there would be 2^n-1 different possible frequent itemsets in database. It is obvious that keeping all bitmaps of frequent itemsets in memory is not practical. In implementation of FINDER, only bitmaps of each item are kept in main memory, each bitmap of frequent itemset is generated and released dynamically. Because same bitmap of a frequent itemset should be generated several times, the costs of runtime are increased accordingly.

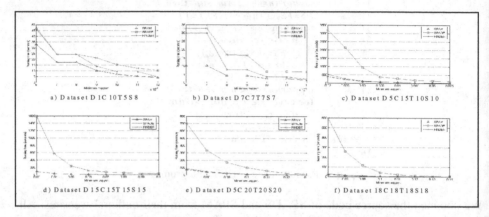

a) Dataset D 1C 10T 5S 8   b) Dataset D 7C 7T 7S 7   c) Dataset D 5C 15T 10S 10

d) Dataset D 15C 15T 15S 15   e) Dataset D 5C 20T 20S 20   f) Dataset 18C 18T 18S 18

Fig. 5. Execution times on different synthetic datasets for various minimum support values

We study the scale-up performance of algorithms as several parameters in dataset generation were varied. For each test, one parameter was varied and the others were kept fixed. The parameters that we varied were number of customers, average transactions per customer, average items per transaction and average length of maximal pattern. The results of tests are shown in Figure 6. It can be easily observed that the FINDER scales linearly with four varying parameters.

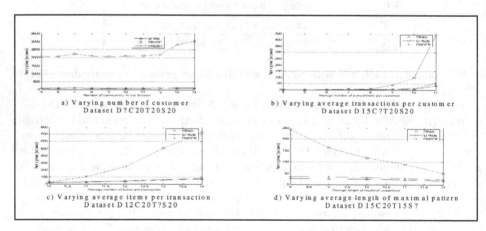

a) Varying number of customer
Dataset D 7C 20T 20S 20

b) Varying average transactions per customer
Dataset D 15C 7T 20S 20

c) Varying average items per transaction
Dataset D 12C 20T 7S 20

d) Varying average length of maximal pattern
Dataset D 15C 20T 15S 7

Fig. 6. Scale-up with varying parameters of dataset

6   Conclusion

In this paper, we systematically explore an itemset-based extension approach for generating candidate sequence. Based on this approach, a novel algorithm for discovering the set of all frequent sequences is presented which can reduce the search space and minimize cost of computation efficiently by using several efficient pruning strategies.

The itemset-based extension approach opens several research opportunities and future work will be done in various directions. First, we are studying how to discover maximal or closed sequential patterns by using proposed approach. Second, we are investigating how to apply this approach to incremental mining of sequential patterns. In addition, extending FINDER for sequence mining on uncertain dataset is also considered.

References

1. Agrawal, R., Srikant, R.: Mining Sequential Patterns. In: Proc. of 11th Int'l Conf. on Data Engineering, pp. 3–14 (March 1995)
2. Ayres, J., Gehrke, J., Yiu, T., Flannick, J.: Sequential Pattern Mining Using a Bitmap Representation. In: Proc. of ACM SIGKDD Conf. on Knowledge Discovery and Data Mining, pp. 429–435 (2002)
3. Burdick, D., Calimlim, M., Gehrke, J.: MAFIA: A maximal frequent itemset algorithm for transactional databases. In: Proc. of 17th Int'l Conf. on Data Engineering, pp. 443–452 (2001)
4. Cao, L.: In-depth Behavior Understanding and Use: the Behavior Informatics Approach. Information Science 180(17), 3067–3085 (2010)
5. Cao, L., Yu, P. (eds.): Behavior Computing: Modeling, Analysis, Mining and Decision. Springer (2012)
6. Pei, J., Han, J., Mortazavi-Asi, B., Wang, J., Pinto, H., Chen, Q.: Mining Sequential Patterns by Pattern-growth: The PrefixSpan Approach. IEEE Transactions on Knowlede and Data Engineering 16, 1–17 (2004)
7. Rymon, R.: Search through systematic set enumeration. In: Proc. of 3rd Int'l Conf. on Principles of Knowledge Representation and Reasoning, pp. 539–550 (1992)
8. Srikant, R., Agrawal, R.: Mining Sequential Patterns: Generalizations and Performance Improvements. In: Proc. of 15th Int'l Conf. on Extending Database Technology, pp. 3–17 (1996)
9. Zaki, M.J.: SPADE: An Efficient Algorithms for Mining Frequent Sequences. Machine Learning 40, 31–60 (2001)
10. Tan, H., Dillon, T., Hadzic, F., Chang, E.: SEQUEST: Mining frequent subsequences using DMA Strips. In: Proc. of Data Mining & Information Engineering 2006 (2006)

Network Flow Based Collective Behavior Analysis

Yuting Hu[*], Rong Xie, and Wenjun Zhang

Institute of Image Communication and Network Engineering
Shanghai Key Lab of Digital Media Processing and Transmission
Shanghai Jiao Tong University, Shanghai
{huyuting,xierong,zhangwenjun}@sjtu.edu.cn

Abstract. With the large-scale activities increasing gradually, the intelligent video surveillance system becomes more and more popular and important. The trajectory identification and behavior analysis are very important techniques for the intelligent video surveillance system. This paper focuses on the trajectory identification and behavior analysis framework for video surveillance system. The framework is implemented on footbridge video and queuing video of Shanghai World Expo 2010 video surveillance system. The experimental results show the efficiency of our proposed framework.

Keywords: trajectory identification (TI), behavior analysis, integer programming (IP), trajectory merging and matching.

1   Introduction

With the large-scale activities increasing gradually, the intelligent video surveillance system becomes more and more popular and important. It can intelligently detect some potentially dangerous conditions such as overcrowded and unplanned gatherings in crowded scenes, like theme park and subway station. The video surveillance system generates huge amount of video data which become awkward to work with using the hazardous work, physical labor, and repetitive tasks. To detect the abnormal events and even predict the user's upcoming actions using the video data generated by the surveillance system, the trajectory identification and behavior analysis are very important techniques. We focus on the trajectory identification and behavior analysis framework for video surveillance system.

Previous works about trajectory identification and tracking have mainly come from wireless sensor networks and computer vision. In computer vision filed, although tracking has been applied to the crowded situation [1, 2], it is hard for multiple cameras to achieve relay tracking of multiple users because of limitation of camera. In collaborative wireless sensor networks, general methods can rely on learning algorithms about searched trajectory history and observation data for user habitat recognition [3]; general methods can also rely on a pure theoretical or experimental-proven approach such as filtering algorithms [4] and the cluster-track algorithm [5].

---

[*] Corresponding author.

L. Cao et al. (Eds.): BSIC/BSI 2013, LNAI 8178, pp. 10–19, 2013.

Besides, the TI problem can be defined as a global optimization problem. Recently, an integer programming (IP) based multiple users trajectory identification (TI) method with binary sensors is proposed [6]. The TI algorithms with binary sensor network cannot be used directly in collective behavior analysis for video surveillance systems because people number detected by each camera sensor is much bigger than binary value.

To solve the problem mentioned above, in this paper, we propose a trajectory identification and behavior analysis framework in video surveillance system: first, zone partition is done to a group of video frames and a camera sensor network is formed by counting pedestrians in each zone; then trajectory identification and behavior analysis are done about the camera sensor network. To illustrate the effectiveness of our algorithm, we implement the proposed framework on Shanghai Expo surveillance video data. This paper is organized as follows. Section 2 first describes the trajectory identification and behavior analysis framework. Section 3 shows the experimental result on Shanghai Expo surveillance video data. Section 4 gives the conclusion.

2   Framework Description

Fig. 1 shows the trajectory identification and behavior analysis framework. First, video processing methods are used on video data to model a camera sensor network. Secondly, an optimization method is utilized to identify the hidden trajectories hidden behind the camera sensor network. Thirdly, behavior analysis is done by use of trajectory merging and similarity matching.

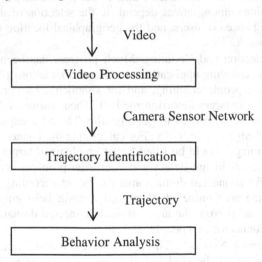

Fig. 1. Framework Diagram

2.1   Video Processing

Fig. 2 shows the steps of video processing.

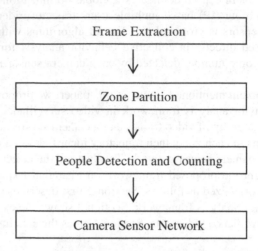

Fig. 2. Video Processing

- Frame Extraction. Through the video surveillance system, a group of continuous video frames can be obtained. In order to analyze how the trajectories of users evokes the observation results in the camera sensor network, we extract some video frames from the original video with a sampling time interval, Δt. The selection of Δt depends on real applications.
- Zone Partition. Each extracted frame is partitioned into a few zones. The connectivity relations among zones depend on the selection of the sampling interval Δt, the walking speed of users, and the geographical location of sensors in the camera sensor network.
- People Detection and Counting. Much progress has been made in detection and tracking for counting applications in crowded situations [7, 8]. Target detection is the basic for people counting, and for simplicity, background subtraction can be used as a basic target detection method. Then, various edge operators like canny edge operator can be used to get a profile. The edge expansion helps to solve the problem of edge discontinuity. For calculating the connected domain area, the target in the image should be filled based on obtained target profile. Taking into account the small image defect and occlusion problem in the counting process, a threshold for connected domain area can be set according to real applications. For example, the area value of connected domain belonging to [S1_min, S1_max] counts for one person; the area value of connected domain belonging to [S2_min, S2_max] counts for two people, and etc.
- Camera Sensor Network. Through a time window sliding strategy, the camera sensor network can be modeled. We assume there are m sensors, n users, and the length of the window is T. The observational data from m counting sensors is the set of non-negative integer time sequences $\{S_{it}, i = 1, \cdots, m; t = 1, \cdots, T\}$, which denotes the number of targets detected by sensor i at time t. Our objective is to recover trajectory sequences $\{P_{tj}, t = 1, \cdots, T; j = 1, \cdots, n\}$, which denotes the

location of user j at time t in the same environment. The next work is to analyze how user trajectories evoke the activation pattern in the camera sensor network.

2.2   Trajectory Identification

To solve the TI problem, integer programming is chosen in this paper. The pedestrian number flowing from one sensor to another can be regarded as a network flow problem using $Ax = b$, A is a network flow matrix and b is a column vector. If the network flow matrix A is a unimodular matrix and A and b are both integer, every equation $Ax = b$ has an integer solution [9]. Therefore, our TI problem as a linear integer programming problem, can be solved efficiently due to characteristics in network flow issue.

Assuming that the camera sensor network has been obtained by steps mentioned above, some assumptions are needed to make the IP based TI problem well defined:

- High density of camera sensors: any user will be detected by one and the only one camera sensor at any time.
- Time window sliding: the total number of users is a constant value and each user is always present inside the sliding time window.

To set up a connection between $\{S_{it}\}$ and $\{P_{tj}\}$, we introduce a binary variable $\{X_{itj}, i = 1, \cdots, m; t = 1, \cdots, T; j = 1, \cdots, n\}$, which indicates whether user j appears in sensor i at time t. The obtained solution $\{X_{itj}\}$ can be rewritten with the trajectory sequence $\{P_{tj}\}$ easily. The trajectory identification problem can be written as an IP problem.

$$\sum_{i=1}^{m} X_{itj} = 1 \tag{1}$$

$$\sum_{j=1}^{n} X_{itj} = S_{it} \tag{2}$$

$$\forall(i_1, i_2) \in \Omega, \ x_{i_1,t,j} + x_{i_2,t+1,j} \leq 1 \tag{3}$$

We have the following remarks:

- Constraint (1) ensures the assumption of high density of camera sensors mentioned above.
- Constraint (2) ensures the sum of users is equal to the observation data in the camera sensor network.
- For constraint (3), Ω is a set whose elements are pairs of non-reachable camera sensors and Ω has some relation with the deployment of camera sensors, the sampling time interval and the walking speed of pedestrians.

2.3   Behavior Analysis

Trajectory pattern mining has been researched [10, 11,12]. To analyze collective behavior after the pedestrian trajectories are estimated, we can make behavior analysis by trajectory merging and similarity matching. Some relevant work has been done on clustering users' trajectories [13]. Two trajectory sequences may not be totally the same at every time during the time interval, but they may have something in common such as shared locations or similar transition time from one location to another. If some trajectory sequences are similar, they are merged to a group; if a trajectory cannot find its belonging group, it can be regarded as an outlier. The operations of trajectory merging and similarity matching used in this paper can be summarized as follows.

A computed trajectory can be written as: $s_0(\Delta t_0) \rightarrow s_1(\Delta t_1) \rightarrow \cdots \rightarrow s_k \Delta t_k$, where k represents the total number of locations included in a trajectory; s_k represents the kth sensor present in a trajectory; Δt_k represents the stay time at sensor s_k. Compare two trajectories $seq_1[a_0, a_1, \cdots, a_k]$ (stay time: Δt_{x_seq1}) and $seq_2[b_0, b_1, \cdots, b_k]$ (stay time: Δt_{x_seq2}), seq_1 and seq_2 are similar when satisfying the following conditions:

- $\forall 1 \leq x \leq k a_x = b_x$;
- $\forall 1 \leq x \leq k, |\Delta t_{x\_seq1} - \Delta t_{x\_seq2}|/\max(\Delta t_{x\_seq1}, \Delta t_{x\_seq2}) \leq p$.

where $p \in (0,1)$ is a time difference ratio threshold.

3   Testing Examples

Shanghai World Expo 2010 is a typical example about collective behavior analysis in video surveillance system. In Expo video surveillance system, footbridge video and queuing video are two typical examples about walking and queuing pattern. The framework mentioned above is implemented on Expo video data to show its efficiency. It is interesting to observe the patterns of trajectories for different days and different time periods so that we can allocate the bus stations more efficiently or improve the customer satisfaction in queuing system for large-scale activities.

 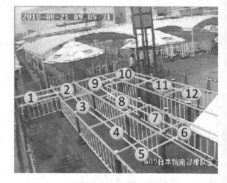

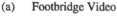

(a)   Footbridge Video   (b) Queuing Video

Fig. 3. Zone Layout in Video

Table 1. Example 1

(a)   Ground truth.

User	t=1	2	3	4	5	6
P_1	2	2	2	2	2	2
P_2	7	5	5	3	3	3
P_3	7	5	5	3	3	3
P_4	8	6	4	4	4	2
P_5	8	6	4	4	4	2

(b)   Camera Sensor Network.

User	t=1	2	3	4	5	6
S_1	0	0	0	0	0	0
S_2	1	1	1	1	1	3
S_3	0	0	0	2	2	2
S_4	0	0	2	2	2	0
S_5	0	2	2	0	0	0
S_6	0	2	0	0	0	0
S_7	2	0	0	0	0	0
S_8	2	0	0	0	0	0

(c)   Estimated trajectories.

User	t=1	2	3	4	5	6
P_1'	2	2	2	②	4	2
P_2'	7	5	5	3	3	3
P_3'	7	5	5	3	3	3
P_4'	8	6	4	4	4	2
P_5'	8	6	4	④	2	2

Fig. 3(a) shows a network of 8 camera sensor nodes in the footbridge video, as well as the connectivity relations of camera sensors. The sampling time interval is 2 seconds. We set m = 8, n = 5 and T = 6. The ground truth is shown in Table 1. (a) and camera sensor network is modeled in Table 1. (b). Applying the proposed framework, the estimated trajectories are presented in Table 1. (c), which are almost identical with the ground truth. The little difference between our experimental result and the ground truth is due to the not unique solutions for this problem. We will explain this adversary condition later on.

Fig. 3(b) shows a network of 12 camera sensor nodes in the queuing video, together with the connectivity relations of camera sensors. We set m = 12, n = 6 and T = 3. The ground truth is shown in Table 2. (a) and camera sensor data is shown in Table 2. (b). Applying the proposed framework, the estimated trajectories are presented in Table 2. (c), which are identical with the ground truth.

Table 2 Example 2

(a) Ground truth.

User	t=1	2	3
P_1	1	2	3
P_2	2	3	4
P_3	3	4	5
P_4	4	5	6
P_5	6	7	8
P_6	7	8	9

(a) Camera Sensor Network.

User	t=1	2	3
S_1	1	0	0
S_2	1	1	0
S_3	1	1	1
S_4	1	1	1
S_5	0	1	1
S_6	1	0	1
S_7	1	1	0
S_8	0	1	1
S_9	0	0	1
S_{10}	0	0	0
S_{11}	0	0	0
S_{12}	0	0	0

(b) Estimated trajectories.

User	t=1	2	3
P_1'	4	5	6
P_2'	7	8	9
P_3'	2	3	4
P_4'	6	7	8
P_5'	1	2	3
P_6'	3	4	5

Fig. 4(a) and Fig. 4(b) show the computed trajectories for different time periods in not too crowded people and it is interesting to observe about conventional route and to detect outlier by using trajectory merging and similarity matching. Each polyline represents one trajectory sequence. Most trajectories have high repetition, i.e., same trajectory by different users at different times. The blue line represents the conventional trajectory. The darker the polyline is, the higher is the repetition. The red line indicates the abnormal trajectory or the trajectory with low repetition. Fig. 4(c) shows abnormal behavior detection like finding running pedestrians; Fig. 4(d) shows abnormal behavior detection in queuing video like people towards opposite walking direction.

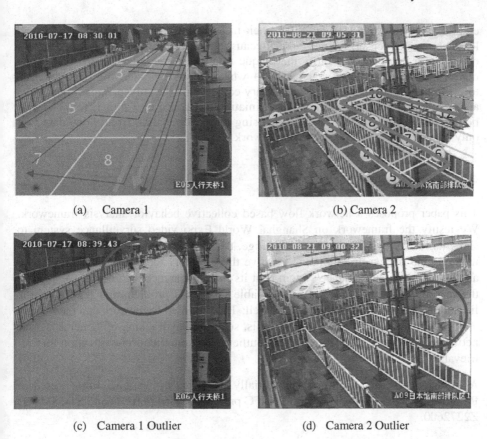

(a)   Camera 1   (b) Camera 2

(c)   Camera 1 Outlier   (d)   Camera 2 Outlier

Fig. 4. Experimental Result on Video Surveillance Video at Shanghai Expo Site

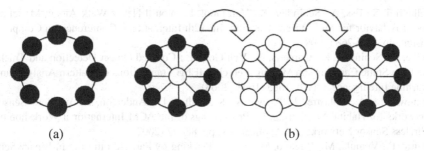

(a)   (b)

Fig. 5. Not Unique Cases

However, some adversary cases should be discussed. In Fig. 5(a), eight groups with the same size are observed by 8 sensors respectively at time t, which are marked by solid black circles in the graph. At the next time $t + 1$, they are observed again by the same eight sensors. Due to the connectivity among sensors, we do not have any method to identify whether the true trajectories are clockwise or counterclockwise. Fig. 5(b) shows another adversary case. Eight groups with the same size are observed by eight sensors at time t. At time t + 1, their trajectories cross in the center sensor and leave the center sensor at time t + 2. Because the center sensor is connected to any other sensor, we cannot identify the unique true trajectories like {which one of the outer-ring sensors → the center sensor → which one of the outer-ring sensors}. Due to many possible solutions, some adversary cases cannot be solved. This limitation is also the reason for our experimental estimation difference in Table 1. (c). The proposed framework will be improved by using more information from video data (not only the number of people) in the future work.

4   Conclusion

This paper proposes a network flow based collective behavior analysis framework. We testify the framework on Shanghai World Expo video surveillance system to show its feasibility. To our best knowledge, the idea of combining video processing methods and integer programming to solve the trajectory identification and behavior analysis in video surveillance system is at its first appearance. Moreover, we analyze the reason why IP approach is well suitable for the TI problem and points out the limitation of the proposed approach as well. The proposed framework can have many applications in collective behavior analysis, such as relay tracking of cameras, sensor network deployment, crowd event and outlier detection, video classification and retrieval, etc.

Acknowledgement. This work was partially supported by National Basic Research Program of China (2010CB731406), NSFC project (NO. 61221001) and STCSM12D Z2272600.

References

1. Pellegrini, S., Ess, A., Schindler, K., Van Gool, L.: You'll Never Walk Alone: Modeling Social Behavior for Multi-target Tracking. In: 12th International Conference on Computer Vision, pp. 261–268 (2009)
2. Leibe, B., Schindler, K., Cornelis, N., Van Gool, L.: Coupled Object Detection and Tracking from Static Cameras and Moving Vehicles. IEEE Transactions on Pattern Analysis and Machine Intelligence 30(10), 1683–1698 (2008)
3. Mainwaring, A., Polastre, J., Szewczyk, R., Culler, D., Anderson, J.: Wireless Sensor Networks for Habitat Monitoring. In: Proceedings of the ACM International Workshop on Wireless Sensor Networks and Applications, pp. 88–97 (2002)
4. Djuric, P., Vemula, M., Bugallo, M.: Target Tracking by Particle Filtering in Binary Sensor Networks. IEEE Transactions on Signal Processing 56(6), 2229–2238 (2008)
5. Singh, J., Kumar, R., Madhow, U., Suri, S., Cagley, R.: Multiple-target Tracking with Binary Proximity Sensors. ACM Transactions on Sensor Networks 8(1) (2011)
6. Wang, C., Huo, X., Song, W.Z.: An Integer Programming Approach for Multiple-target Trajectory Identification with Binary Proximity Sensors. In: Annals of Operations Research (2012) (submitted)

7. Sidla, O., Lypetskyy, Y., Brändle, N., Seer, S.: Pedestrian Detection and Tracking for Counting Applications in Crowded Situations. In: IEEE International Conference on Video and Signal Based Surveillance 2006. AVSS (2006)
8. Kong, D., Gray, D., Tao, H.: Counting Pedestrians in Crowds Using Viewpoint Invariant Training. In: British Machine Vision Conference (2005)
9. Unimodular matrix, http://en.wikipedia.org/wiki/Unimodular_matrix
10. Giannotti, F., Nanni, M., Pinelli, F., Pedreschi, D.: Trajectory Pattern Mining. In: Proceedings of the ACM SIGKDD International Conference on Knowledge Discovery and Data Mining, pp. 330–339 (2007)
11. Cao, L.: In-depth Behavior Understanding and Use: the Behavior Informatics Approach. Information Science 180(17), 3067–3085 (2010)
12. Zheng, Y., Zhang, L.X., Xie, X., Ma, W.Y.: Mining Interesting Locations and Travel Sequences from GPS Trajectories. In: Proceedings of the 18th International World Wide Web Conference, pp. 791–800 (2009)
13. Hu, L., Chen, J., Shen, S.Y., Huang, J.: Recommendation Algorithm Research Based on Clustering Users' Trajectories. In: Proceedings of the 34th International ACM SIGIR Conference on Research and Development in Information Retrieval, pp. 305–314 (2011)

Design, Conduct and Analysis of a Biased Voting Experiment on Human Behavior

Cong Zhao, Guangzhong Sun, and Ye Tian

University of Science and Technology of China, China
congzhao@mail.ustc.edu.cn, {gzsun,yetian}@ustc.edu.cn

Abstract. To explore whether and how different social activities and phenomena, network structures and incentive machanisms could influent human behavior in social networks, Prof. Kearns and his colleagues conducted a series of human participated behavior experiments [3]. Recently, we recurred one of those experiments called biased voting to verify whether and how the factors work on Chinese students. In this paper, we presented not only on the difference we found in the result, but also the design and preparation of the experiment to make some contributions to researchers who are interested in such experiments. We shared our source code and experiment data so that new experiments can be conducted quickly and easily.

1 Introduction

This paper reported on a biased voting experiment we recurred which is one of seven social network behavior experiments the Prof. Kearns has conducted [3]. There are works such as [5, 6] focused on how and whether network structure could influence human behavior [8] in social network as well as works such as [7] focused on the social phenomen (minority power). The biased voting experiment Prof. Kearns conducted [1] was participated by 36 human subjects and each one can only accesses a local view of network structure in order to explore whether and how different social activities and phenomena, network structures and incentive machanisms could influent human behavior in a nearly real social network.

There is a significant literature on the spread of opinion in social networks, for example [9, 10 and 11]. The biased voting process can be regard as a kind of decision making activity that contains conflict between personal preferences and the collective benefits. Only everybody ended in consensus choice, everyone would got payoff. This process can be compared to the Democratic Party leader election [2]. Members should reach a consensus in limited time to make sure the profit of the party although members may intent to vote different candidates who can bring benefit to him or her originally.

The repeated experiment was to verify result on subjects who grown up under different background (including the culture, politics and education) with the subjects in Prof. Kearns's experiments. This paper was dedicated to show a full picture of how

L. Cao et al. (Eds.): BSIC/BSI 2013, LNAI 8178, pp. 20–29, 2013.
© Springer International Publishing Switzerland 2013

we design, run and analyse a behavior experiment in social network area. It didn't refer too much detail about the experiment itself. We strongly recommand you read Prof. Kearns's paper [1] before continue.

The main contributions of this paper are as below:

- It's helpful for other researchers to quickly build platform of this experiment by deploying our shared source code and experiment's data.
- Other researchers would benefit from our consideration of designing and preparation of experiment described comprehensively in this paper to conduct similar experiments.
- Kearns's result [1] showed both the phenomena, network structures and incentive mechanism influenced result. Authors of paper [5] found network structures made no significant effect. This paper provided more evidence for network structure and incentive mechanism made little difference on performance in our experiments.

This paper was organized as follows. Section 2 reviews our consideration of designing and preparation of experiment in detail. Section 3 introduces the method we adopted to handle data and analyzed result of this experiment, followed by conclusions and future work in Section 4.

2   Experiments Designing and Preparation

The scale, phenomena (says cohesion and minority power) and incentive mechanisms (strong/weak symmetric and asymmetric) of our experiment were similar with Kearns's [2009]. The network structures were also categorized as Prof. Kearns's but not exactly similar. It was illustrated in section of "Data process and result analysis". We made a lot of mistakes in early design stage. By discussion, we drew out a final scheme which works well but not perfect. In this section, I described our discussion and consideration during the designing and preparation stage hoping which would be useful to others.

2.1   Platform Selection

Prof. Kearns's experiments [1] were hosted in PC platform. Subjects participanted them in front of PCs and through brower softwares. To scaling up the number of subjects who would participant the experiments and support some asynchronous experiments such as the bargaining experiment hosted by Prof. Kearns [4], we developed an android App client.

In trial stage of this experiment, although we have considered the App would be disturbed by users' phone call or SMS and let all participants open their phones' airmode. It still turned out there were a lot of push notifications appeared on users' mobiles phone which disturbed the experiment.

After the unsuccessful trial, we decided to transplant the client to PC platform. To minimize transplant cost, we made an environment independent android virtual machine and customed ROM which pre-installed our client App. It was the stability of PC platform ensured the success of our second experiment.

2.2   Incentive Mechanism

Due to our experiments budget was limited, we couldn't copy Prof. Kearns's experiment [1] completely. If we simply set a total budget then hand out the money according to everyone's total scores after experiment, there was an obsolete dominent priority stratergy said the earliest man who made his fortune would try to prevent later experiments reaching to consensus so that keep his benefit maximzed.

To achieve a positive inspire at the same time avoid dominent priority stratergy exists. We adopted the incentive mechanism form of Prof. Kearns's experiments [1] but scaled down the payoff by 18 times. That means, the expectation payoff of each person was about thirty RMB yuan if all voting in this experiment ended in consensus (we emphasized this point before experiment to inspire subjects).

2.3   Subjects Selection

Prof. Kearns's experiments [1] were made up of 36 undergraduate students from his course about social network, we think of that was a perfect subjects source. They had conformably time (the course time) to participate experiments and good understand of the background of experiments. Last but not the least; they both had positive motivation to throw them into experiments.

In both the two experiments we were not so luck in aspect of subjects. In the unsuccessful trial, we advertised our call for volunteer in school's bbs before two weeks of experiment, but only eighteen persons signed up to participate it voluntarily. So we gave up finding volunteer, instead, my supervisor convened 36 graduate students from the National High Performance Computing Center (Hefei, China).

2.4   Software

In order to scale up the experiment easily, we developed an android app as client which communicates with server runs on JVM through the TCP protocol. The server end logged users' behavior during the experiment in detail such as: "INFO 14:45:34,452 - Game0: Player6 (test11) choose Red."

Subjects made their choice on their mobile phones or android emulator which has been pre-installed the client app on personal computers. As figure 1 shows, the center circle stand for current player and circles around it represent his or her "neighbors". Edges between connected neighbors are also shown. The integers denoting how many neighbors each neighbor has. Vertex colors are the current color choices of the subjects, which can be changed at any time using the buttons at the bottom. The subject's payoffs for the experiment are shown (in this case 1.5 points for global red consensus, 0.5 point for blue). There are two progress bars. The one above indicated how long has passed. The one below shows a simple global quantity measuring the larger fraction of edges in the network with the same color.

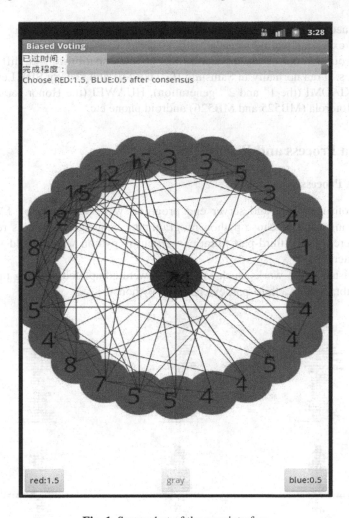

Fig. 1. Screenshot of the user interface

For more details about the programs, please dive into our source code on GitHub[1].

2.5   Hardware

The server end program was hosted on an assembled PC whose operation system was Ubuntu 12.04 32-bit. It was equipped with the Intel Core 2 Duo E4500 CPU and 2GB memory. It worked well for this task and no crash happened during the two experiments.

We have tried two kind of router says TP-Link mini router[2] and ordinary TP-Link router[3]. It turned out the former cannot hold 36 devices simultaneously. After 30

---

[1] http://goo.gl/MmDuY
[2] http://goo.gl/R6Gj5

devices connected, no devices could connected to it successfully anymore.   The latter one showed excellent quality instead.

It turned out that our client application has good compatibility with different Android devices. It ran normally in Samsung (Galaxy SIII and Galaxy SII), Lenovo (the K series), XIAOMI (the 1st and 2nd generation), HUAWEI (the Honor series), HTC, Sony and Motorola (MB525 and MB526) android phone etc.

3   Data Process and Result Analysis

3.1   Data Process

Although both the client and server end programs were developed by JAVA programming language, we chose python programming language to process result data for there were a lot of third-part libraries written by python which could visualized data conveniently.

All the visualization works, such as figure 2, were completed utilizing the famous matplotpy library, also a third-part extension to python.

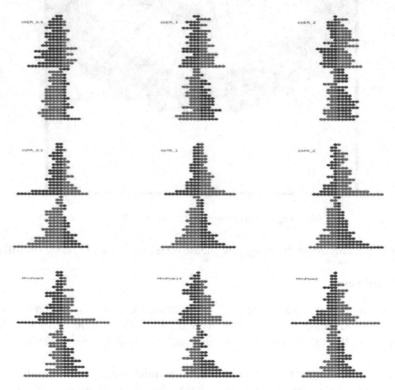

Fig. 2. Visualization of netowrk and incentive structures

---

[3] http://goo.gl/i4w3x

3.2   Result Analysis

Collective Behavior. The most intuitive results was that the collective performance appeared to very different with Kearns's [1]. In his paper, there were 55 experiments ended in global consensus within 1 min but only 15 experiments reached consensus in our experiments. The mean completion time of the successful experiments being 46.1s (standard deviation 10.4s). We compared the result with Kearns's from three aspects: the phenomenal category, the network structure and the incentive mechanism.

In Prof. Kearns's result, both the phenomena experiments reflected and the network structure influenced collective performance in a variety of notable ways. From the aspect of the phenomenon category, the cohesion experiments (31 out of 54 success) were more harder than minority power experiments (24 out of 27 success). Out result showed apparent performance difference according to the phenomenon categories too. For the cohesion experiments, 15% (8 out of 54) successes achieved while for the minority experiments, 26% (7 out of 27) success achieved. But there was an interesting difference to Prof. Kearns's result [1]. Among all 24 of the successfully completed Minority Power experiments in Prof. Kearns's experiments, the global consensus reached was the preferred color of the well-connected minority. While our result shows that, about 57% (4 out of 7) successful minority experiments ended in color red which is not preferred by the minority group. More detailed statistics is show in table 1 and table 2.

Table 1. Statictics of count of successful experiments of Prof. Kearns

Phenomen / Network	Cohesion	Minority	Total
ER	11/27(0.41)	-	11/27(0.41)
PA	20/27(0.74)	24/27(0.89)	44/54(0.81)
Total	31/54(0.57)	24/27(0.89)	55/81(0.68)

Table 2. Statictics of count of successful experiments of us

Phenomen / Network	Cohesion	Minority	Total
ER	5/27(0.19)	-	5/27(0.19)
PA	3/27(0.11)	7/27(0.26)	10/54(0.19)
Total	8/54(0.15)	7/27(0.26)	15/81(0.19)

In Prof. Kearns's result [1], a significant distinction existed between the two network structures. It was easily observed from table 1 that the success ratio of Erdos-Renyi experiments (11 out of 27) was half of preferential attachment experiments' (44 out of 54). But our result showed no significant difference between the two network structures. Furthermore, we set different inter- and intra-connectivity ratio to divide the 54 cohesion experiments into 3 groups whose intra- and inter-connectivity ratio were 0.5, 1 and 2 respectively and get the same result trend with Prof. Kearns's experiments [1]. The cohesion performance improved systematically as inner-group edges were replaced by inter-group edges. Out of our 8 successful cohesion experiments, 2 experiments whose intra- and inter-connectivity rate were 0.5 and 2 experiments whose rate were 1.0. Half of successful cohesion experiments had twice inter-connectivity than the intra-connectivity.

The incentive mechanisms make slight difference of the success rate in our experiments but keep consistent with the trend of Prof. Kearns's result [1]. Refer the table 3 to get more information about the success rate under different incentive mechanism.

Table 3. Success rate under different incentive mechanism in our and Prof. Kearns's experiments respectivily

Experiments / Incentive	Our	Prof. Kearns's
Strong Symmetric	4/27(0.15)	14/27(0.52)
Weak Symmetric	5/27(0.19)	19/27(0.70)
Asymmetric	6/27(0.22)	22/27(0.81)

We plotted the dynamics for all 81 games in figure 3. For each netowrk and incentive structure there was a set of axes with 3 plots corresponding to the 3 trials of those structures. Each plot showed the number of players choosing the eventual collective consensus or majority color minus the number of players choosing the opposite color(y axis) at each moment of time in the experiment(x axis). All plots start at 0 before any color choices have been made; plots reaching a value of 36 within 60 s were those that succeeded in reaching unanimous consensus. Negative values indicated moments where the current majority color was the opposite of its eventual value.

Plots were grouped by network structure first (Cohesion experiments with Erdos-Renyi connectivity in A; Cohesion experiments with preferential attachment connectivity in B; Minority Power experiments in C), and then labeled with details on the network and incentive structure. Within the Cohesion experiments, inter-group connectivity increases from left to right; within the Minority Power experiments, the minority size was decreasing from left to right. Several distinctive effects of network structure on the dynamics could be observed. Many Cohesion experiments spent a significant period "wandering" far from the eventual consensus solution. In contrast, Minority Power experiments invariably experience an initial rush into negative territory as the majority select their preferred color, but were then quickly influenced by the well-connected minority. Several instances of rather sudden convergence to the final color could also be seen, even after long periods of near-consensus to the opposite color.

In conclusion, our experiments result showed two significant differences with Prof. Kearns's experiments. First and the most important, the overall performance was lower than Prof. Kearns's. Secondly, the network structure and incentive mechanism made little difference in experiments results.

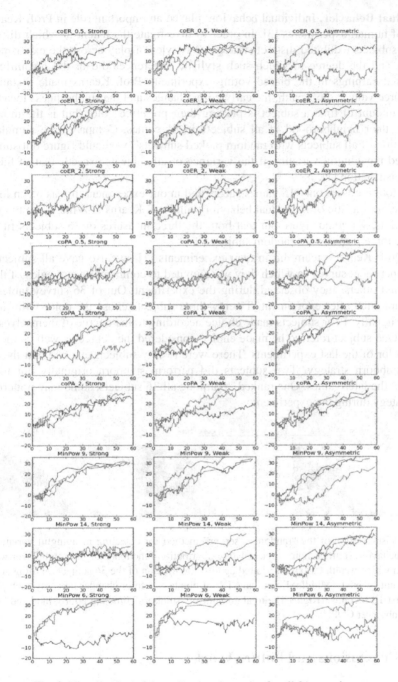

Fig. 3. Visualization of the collective dynamics for all 81 experiments

Individual Behavior. Individual behaviors played an important role in Prof. Kearns's series of human experiments [3]. In order to investigate the extent to which different human subjects exhibited distinct strategies or styles of play across the experimental session, and the degree to which such stylistic differences did or did not influence individual earnings in the biased voting experiment, Prof. Kearns made a statistics about three values: the wealth, the early color changes and the stubbornness measured by the amount of time a subject is playing their preferred color, but is the minority color in their neighborhood of all subjects in 81 games. Compared the cumulative distribution of all subjects with random picked subjects', we could figure out subjects exhibited meaningful variation if the variance of all subjects exceeds that of the ob-server distribution [1].

Due to there were only 15 games succeeded in our experiment, it was mean less to compare the statistic of individual behavior with Prof. Kearns's. While from the visu-alized plots, we could figure out that both the three measures of 36 subjects fit well with the three measures of random subjects.

As Prof. Kearns's team did in their experiments [1], we also gave all subjects an after experiment survey in which they were invited to comment on strategies of them-selves and others' they observed during the experiment. Out of 36 survey tables, 31 were submitted after experiment. Twenty-three subjects chose the color with higher score originally. Four subjects made choice according to the degree of themselves and others. One subject referred he made choice considered the degree as well as the ma-jority color of the last experiments. There were twenty subjects claimed that they did adopt stubborn strategy. Two subjects did perform stubborn originally but follow others in the later games. One ranked 26 among all 36 subjects, so he may not consist this strategy during the experiment.

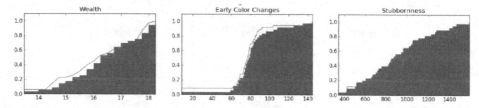

Fig. 4. Visualization of the "random observer" method for detecting meaningful variation in subject behavior. (Left) Empirical cumulative distribution function(CDF) of total player wealth (blue), in which wealth (x axis) is plotted against the fraction of the 36 subjects earning at least that amount (y axis). (Middle) Empirical CDF of number of color changes taken by each player in the first 10 seconds. (Right) The total amount of "stubborn" time are poorly modeled by the random observer CDF.

4   Conclusions and Future Work

In this paper, we conducted a comprehensive description of our experiment. Com-pared wich the mobile phone, PC platform worked more stable to host the experiment. Subjects who with positive motivation achieve good performance. We gave an outline of archtecture and programming language we used. In our experiments, the phenomena did influence the performance like Prof. Kearns's while the network structure didn't make much sense.

Since we have transplanted client of Prof. Kearns' experiments from PC to Android and open sourced our code, it's easy to scaling up the experiments. One reasonable method we have considered was provide this game to students along with a social network related online open course, just like the interesting experiments in game theory class on the Coursera.

Acknowledgment. This work is supported by the National Natural Science Foundation of China under the grant No. 61033009 and No. 61202405. It is also supported by the Anhui Natural Science Foundation under the grant No. 1208085QF106.

References

1. Kearns, M., Judd, S., Tan, J., Wortman, J.: Behavioral experiments on biased voting in networks. Proceedings of the National Academy of Sciences 106(5), 1347–1352 (2009)
2. Kearns, M., Tan, J.: Biased voting and the democratic primary problem. In: Papadimitriou, C., Zhang, S. (eds.) WINE 2008. LNCS, vol. 5385, pp. 639–652. Springer, Heidelberg (2008)
3. Kearns, M.: Experiments in social computation. Communications of the ACM 55(10), 56–67 (2012)
4. Chakraborty, T., Judd, S., Kearns, M., Tan, J.: A behavioral study of bargaining in social networks. In: Proceedings of the 11th ACM Conference on Electronic Commerce, pp. 243–252. ACM (2010)
5. Suri, S., Watts, D.J.: Cooperation and contagion in web-based, networked public goods experiments. PLoS One 6(3), e16836 (2011)
6. Centola, D.: The spread of behavior in an online social network experiment. Science 329(5996), 1194–1197 (2010)
7. Xie, J., Sreenivasan, S., Korniss, G., Zhang, W., Lim, C., Szymanski, B.K.: Social consensus through the influence of committed minorities. Physical Review E 84(1), 011130 (2011)
8. Cao, L.: In-depth Behavior Understanding and Use: the Behavior Informatics Approach. Information Science 180(17), 3067–3085 (2010)
9. Kleinberg, J.: Cascading behavior in networks: Algorithmic and economic issues. Algorithmic Game Theory 24, 613–632 (2007)
10. Granovetter, M.: Threshold models of collective behavior. American Journal of Sociology, 1420–1443 (1978)
11. Schelling, T.C.: Micromotives and Macrobehavior (1978)

Using Mobile Phone Location Data for Urban Activity Analysis

Rong Xie[1,2], Huizheng Xu[1], and Yang Yue[3,4]

[1] International School of Software, Wuhan University,
430079 Wuhan, China
[2] Shenzhen Key Laboratory of High Performance Data Mining
518055 Shenzhen, China
[3] Shenzhen University, Shenzhen, China
[4] State Key Lab of Information Engineering in Surveying, Mapping and Remote
Sensing, Wuhan University, Wuhan 430079, China
{xierong,yueyang}@whu.edu.cn, xhz.hehe@gmail.com

Abstract. Mobile phone data record people's calling logs in everyday life, which reflecting their custom, pattern and lifestyle. In this paper, we present approaches to urban activity analysis from real mobile phone location data, including individual activity analysis and group activity analysis, which can be applied to the field of urban planning and management.

Keywords: Mobile phone location data, Data mining, Individual activity analysis, Group activity analysis.

1 Introduction

Mobile devices, such as mobile phones and other hand-held devices, are growing popularity. Particularly in cities, people are becoming increasingly dependent on mobile devices, so that mobile devices have become the necessities of human daily life.

Mobile phone data record people's calling logs in everyday life, which reflecting their custom, pattern and lifestyle. Study on urban activity is becoming an important challenging research, which can be applied to the field of urban planning and management. The Reality Mining project [1], as the first step for the research of mobile phone data mining, provides a new thinking way. They introduce a system for sensing complex social systems with data collected from 100 mobile phones over 9 months to recognize social patterns in daily user activity, infer relationships, identify socially significant locations, and model organizational rhythms. Since the year of 2008, research on mobile phone location-based individual behavior patterns mining have been gradually expanding [2]. [3] studies trajectories of 100,000 anonymized mobile phone users during six-month period and find a high regularity degree in human trajectories contrasting with estimation by prevailing Lévy flight and random walk models. [4] provides a complete framework-Mobility Profiler for discovering cellphone users' frequent mobility patterns and profiles from raw cell tower connection data. They use

L. Cao et al. (Eds.): BSIC/BSI 2013, LNAI 8178, pp. 30–43, 2013.
© Springer International Publishing Switzerland 2013

real-world cellphone log data to demonstrate their framework. Based on 226 daily GPS traces of 101 subjects, [5] develops a mobility model that captures the effect of human mobility patterns characterized by some fundamental statistical functions. [6] proposes a MAST (Movement, Action, and Situation over Time) probabilistic model for using mobile phone sensors to analyze and predict user behavior patterns. To study pattern mining in human dynamics, [7] studies spatiotemporal human dynamics as well as social interactions. They investigate the patterns in anomalous events, which can be useful in real-time detection of emergency situation. At the individual level, they find that the interevent time of consecutive calls can be described by heavy-tailed distribution. For urban analysis, most studies focus on urban activities, urban dynamics and urban monitoring. In the Mobile Landscapes project, [8] analyzes coverage map that users use mobile phone at different time period in one day at Milan, Italy, and other metropolitan areas, showing spatio-temporal density maps of urban activities and their evolution. [9] develops an activity-aware map that describes the most probable activity associated with a specific area of space based on POIs from a large mobile phone data of nearly one million records of users in the central Metro-Boston area. They find a strong correlation in daily activity patterns within the group of people who share a common work area's profile. [10] explores how researchers might be able to use data for an entire metropolitan region to analyze urban dynamics. [11] presents a new real-time urban monitoring platform and its application to the City of Rome. However, in the current research, there is relatively few commercial software or application systems to fully meet the requirements of effectively mining these behavioral characteristics. Since all location logs of mobile phone data are in low level data units, it is difficult to access meaningful information about activities of mobile users directly [4]. Some challenges exist in the urban activity analysis from mobile phone location data. Focusing on it, this paper aims to study the approaches to activity analysis in cities.

The rest of the paper is organized as follows. The next section explains our methodology and data preparation. Section 3 and Section 4 present individual activity analysis and group activity analysis, respectively. Related work is discussed in Section 5. Conclusion and future work are finally given in Section 6.

2   Preliminaries

2.1   Methodology

First, we handle preprocessing on individual dataset and group dataset, respectively, to obtain data storage and data structure. Second, information is extracted from individual dataset to identify individual activities and comparative analysis among individuals' activities. For group activity analysis, we narrow and determine the case study scope by K-means algorithm. Combined with individual activity analysis, group activity regularity is finally discovered using DBScan algorithm.

2.2   Data Preparation

Raw data in our research are from mobile users' calling logs in Kunming City, China, which are divided into two separate parts. 15 mobile users' records during September 1 to September 30, 2010 are selected for the analysis of individual activity. The other is 350 mobile users' records on August 1, 2010 for group activity analysis. In order to distinguish these two datasets, we name the former as individual dataset and the latter as group dataset. The raw dataset, including active record ID, date, time, user ID and geographic information, is described as shown in Table 1.

Table 1. Raw data set

Field	Description
Active record ID	Each record has a unique ID, a continuous sequence of real numbers.
Date	Date when data are recorded, in format of *yyyy/mm/dd*.
Time	Time when data are recorded, in format of *hh:mm:ss*.
User ID	Uniquely identification of user. To protect user's privacy, 5 digits are intercepted from the middle of user's mobile phone number.
Geographic information	User's geographic location when activity log is generated, which is divided into two columns, i.e. large area ID and base station ID.

3   Individual Activity Analysis

We propose an approach to individual activity analysis as follows. First, find user's staying location in activity, and get his/her periodical patterns. Second, contrast individual's daily activities to observe stability and difference of these activities. Then, horizontally contrast different individuals to get similarity and difference among individuals' activities.

3.1   Spatio-Temporal Hotspot Sequence

Mobile phone data are generated depending on a user's activities, which are random. Mobile phone may be used frequently during a short time period, or it may be idle in a long time which makes the data discrete. To generate meaningful hotspot sequence, we should make tags for each location to determine whether we finally retain or remove these locations and define their attributes, such as home, workplace and leisure place etc. The steps are tag identification, tag merge and tag deletion.

Tag Identification. Every location is identified by a tag, which is a vector, corresponding to the database field <*lac*, *cid*, *tag*, *num*>, i.e. region ID, base station ID, tag value and number of occurrences. When time elapses, location may vary. When a new location appears, it will be tagged in sequence and stored in the database. *tag* is set to 1. If the next occurrence of location has been already existed in the database, *num* will add 1.

Tag Merge. Mobile phone data are generally located by base station. When there is a user's activity, issued in the same location, signal can be sometimes received by different base stations. So, there may have two base stations alternately in the record in a short time period. We call it shocking pair. As interval of each concussion is only a few seconds, and the original value is returned after a few seconds, such phenomenon is obvious and easy to identify. We can detect shocking pair as follows. Set time threshold as T and frequency threshold as N. If the number of occurrences of two locations is more than N at time T, then determine these two locations as a shocking pair. For example, if there is a sequence $\{A, B, A, C, A, B\}$ at $T=30$ seconds and $N=2$, the frequency of A and B exceeds N, then A and B is a shocking pair. Shocking pair can be described as a vector V: $<A: \{lac_1, cid_1, tag_1, n_1\}, B: \{lac_2, cid_2, tag_2, n_2\}>$, A and B in V have the same geographic location. We deal with shocking pair by the following way. If the tag value of A in the database is not equal to the tag value of B, then compare the tag values and replace the large one to the small one; otherwise, keep it unchanged.

Tag Deletion. All tags can be divided into two categories by the number of occurrences as follows, i.e. high-frequency and low frequency. Get the average value of all tags. Tags, whose frequency is greater than the average, shall be gathered in hot group; otherwise in noise group. Then divide one day into 24 hours, to check the data for each hour. Tag with the highest frequency in an hour is regarded as a hotspot. Store a record of the hotspot into the database, with attribute tag ID, user ID, date and time, and number of activities. Here, tag ID can be empty, which means that user does not stay at any hotspot in an hour. Number of activities also can be empty, meaning that user have no activity. There should be 24 records for each user in a day, representing the user's activities within a day. But these records should remove shocking pairs and noise points, to form a hotspot sequence.

3.2   Stability and Periodicity of Individual Activities

Individual activity includes activity hotspot and activity intensity. Its stability is defined as personal periodical activities, repeatedly in daily. For example, people usually stay at home in early morning and at night, work between 9-12am and 2-5pm.

Based on hotspot sequence generation, we can handle stability analysis of individual activities. For example, we analyze user 90865's hotspot sequence on 3 Mondays of September (i.e. September 6, September 13 and September 20, 2010) as shown in Figure 1, where the horizontal axis is the time of 24 hours in a day; the vertical axis is the number of activities. Color in the figure indicates tag of hotspot.

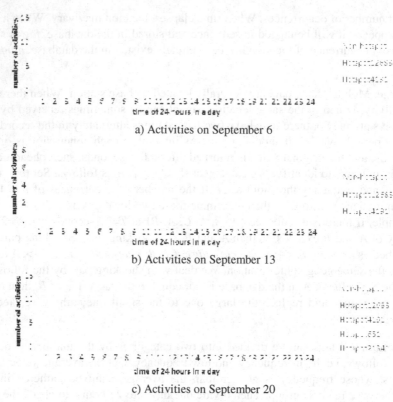

a) Activities on September 6

b) Activities on September 13

c) Activities on September 20

Fig. 1. Activities of user 90865 on Monday

These figures can interpret stability and difference of individual activity. User 90865 uses mobile phone very irregularly. In Figure 1a), except in the morning, only a small amount of activities are recorded. Statistically, there are blank activity logs in 9 hours. In Figure 1b), no record is generated in the morning, but a lot of records in the afternoon. From Figure 1c), the user used mobile phone for whole day, and went to hotspot 651 and 21341. Therefore, frequency that this user uses mobile phone is strongly random, that is, activities in a day are uneven, and number of activities is uncertain at the same time at different date.

Besides, individual activities in the temporal and spatial properties also have differences. Comparing Figure 1a) and Figure 1b), the time of the first appearance in blue column is different, one at 10:00am; another at 9:00am. For the last time in blue column, one is at 2:00pm; another at 4:00pm. From Figure 1c), there are two new staying hotspots. i.e. yellow column and purple column. Therefore, user 90865's activities in time and space have differences: 1) dividing line of activity hotspot is not constant; 2) daily activities are also different.

Stability of individual activities is represented that the frequency of activity in a day is always less at both ends but more in the middle, which showing that the user's daily activities are similar. In addition, hotspot sequence also has a high similarity. To be observed easily, we further handle data abstraction and remove the impact of data. A colored timeline comparison is shown in Figure 2.

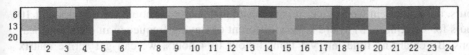

Fig. 2. Location information comparison of user 90865 within 3 days

From Figure 2, individual activity in time and space is stable. Brown zone appears in both ends, and blue and green zone are staggered in the middle. Occasional differences in purple and yellow zone do not affect the stability of individual activities. Blank zone means there is no user's activity record during the time period. So, we can consider that blank zone is the default that the user still stays at the last location. The optimization is shown in Figure 3.

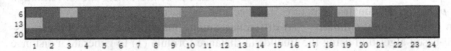

Fig. 3. Location information comparison of user 90865 within 3 days after filling the blank

Figure 3 shows spatial and temporal stability of the individual activities. All data remains in brown zone at 1:00-8:00am. Blue and green alternating region happens to be the most active period people make activities from 9:00am to 7:00pm. General type of hotspot can be inferred as follows. Most areas (brown zone) at night are for residential; while the areas (blue zone) in day are workplaces. As people do not always stay in office location all the time at working hours, maybe having lunch break or visiting customers, there may be a large amount of non-hotspots, representing on the road or temporary destinations.

3.3   Similarity and Difference among Individuals' Activities

In order to analyze similarity and difference of activity among individuals, we select user 90865, 91861 and 91895 as objects, named p_1, p_2, p_3. Three users' data performance on Tuesday, September 21, 2010 is shown in Figure 4.

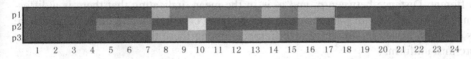

Fig. 4. Location comparison among user 90865, 91861, 91895 after filling the blank

It is shown that, there is a greater difference in comparison chart among individuals' activity and comparison chart of individual itself. 1) Comparing to individual's activity, there are obvious differences at boundary of hotspot among individuals. Between p_1 and p_3, user p_1 goes home at 5:00pm; user p_3 at 10:00pm, the gap is 5 hours. For individual contrast, the gap is only 1 hour or so. 2) Time length of staying at different locations for each person is quite different. User p_2 stays at home for up to 18 hours, but 4 hours in workplace. It is opposite that user p_3 at home for 9 hours, but 10 hours for workplace. 3) There is very different of staying frequency in different locations. By enlarging time interval from 1 hour to 4 hours, we can get active matrix shown in Table 2, here 0 for home and 1 for workplace.

Table 2. Datamation of users' location

p_1	0	0	1	1	0	0
p_2	0	1	0	0	0	0
p_3	0	0	1	1	1	0

From Table 2, activities of user p_1 are regular, showing a symmetrical structure. User p_2 is the most irregular, only the second term is 1, the others are 0. Although user p_3 has an asymmetric structure, it has certain regularity.

In order to study similarity and difference among individuals, we propose a distance-based algorithm using the Euclidean distance formula (1) to generate a distance matrix among p_1, p_2, p_3. Calculate distance between the multi-dimensional vectors, and analyze the dissimilarity between the data objects.

$$d(x, y) = \sqrt{\sum_{k=1}^{n}(x_k - y_k)^2} \tag{1}$$

When two users' activities are identical, as we know, distance will be 0. As long as there is a difference, distance value d will be between 1 and 2.45. Table 3 gives three users' distance matrix.

Table 3. Users' distance matrix

	p_1	p_2	p_3
p_1	0	1.73	1
p_2	1.73	0	2
p_3	1	2	0

From Table 3, p_1 and p_3 is the nearest, which means behavior patterns of p_1 and p_3 are similar. Distance between p_2 and p_3 is 2, showing that their behavior patterns are different. Distance between p_1 and p_2 is in the mean, indicating that there is a difference between behavior patterns of p_1 and p_2, but a certain inherent correlation. There is no more biased in similarity or difference among these three users, their activities are thus uniform.

In general, individuals' activities have the spatio-temporal characteristic of similarity, as well as difference, but similarity and difference are uniformly distributed. Such individual activity analysis provides the support for group activity analysis.

4   Group Activity Analysis

We propose an approach to group activity analysis as follows. First, determine base station distribution in city. Second, identify geographic boundary of spatio-temporal flow of urban populations, and then get the regularity of urban activities.

4.1 Base Station Distribution

Geographic information of active records in the database is closely related to the base station location of a user's activity. We regard the geographical location of the original activity log data as a foreign key to the activated base station table. The procedure is shown below to identify the activated base stations.

```
procedure findCell(File originalFile)
    do List<RawRecord> list ← Read originalFile;
    for i=0 to size of list
        RawRecord rec• (RawRecord)list.get(i);
        do if rec == null
            then continue the loop;
            else if <rec.lac, rec.cid> do not exist in DB
                then Position po ← GoogleAPI(lac,cid);
                    do if co == null
                        then continue the loop;
                        else do insert co into DB;
            pid ← the id of po found in DB;
            do insert <rec, pid> into DB;
end.
```

There are a total of 10,250 active records and 1,380 base stations in the generated data and 8,870 data are recorded in the activated base station.

After reading database, we can get the total number of activities recorded by the activated base station, to observe activity regulation of base stations. Figure 5 shows the results; here horizontal axis represents the number of base stations in database. If base station is activated sooner, the number is smaller. Vertical axis represents the total number of activities recorded by base station. Base station on hotspot can be activated early. Base stations, which are activated sooner, thus receive more activities.

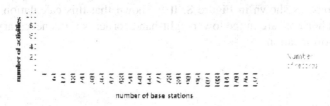

number of base stations

Fig. 5. Base station activity chart

In addition, we can analyze the number of bases stations which have the same number of records, shown in Figure 6. The horizontal axis in Figure 6 is the vertical axis in Figure 5 For instance, height of the column, whose abscissa is 1, is 381, representing that there are 381 base stations received 1 activity record on August 1. There are total 63 points on the horizontal axis in Figure 6. The height of each point is at least 1. We can see from the figure that the number of most locations is not high; while less activity with high number. Urban activity is generally hot or non-hot, and hot activities tend to be concentrated in a few locations.

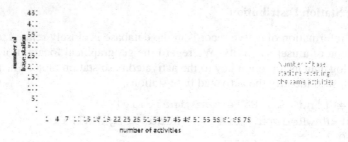

Fig. 6. Relationship chart between the number of activities and the number of base stations

As height value in the right half of Figure 6 is too small to display on the map, we make optimization as follows. Divide the abscissa into 10 parts and weighted sum these data, that is, ordinate equals to the number of times × the number of base stations. The results are shown in Figure 7, which are clearer than in Figure 6.

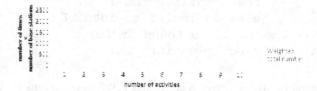

Fig. 7. Weighted sum chart

4.2   Geographic Boundary

Hotspots are in general a small part of the total number of base stations. Scattered non-hotspots usually have a great impact on data mining, so it is required to narrow the scope of the study. Firstly, we find the minimum range of the map that can cover all base stations, as shown in Figure 8. It is shown that this calculation is not very accurate, real hotspots are in the lower right-hand corner, so it is necessary to process data with far-off location.

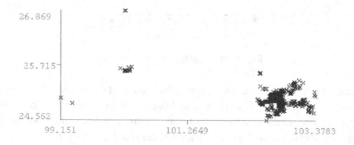

Fig. 8. Geographical distribution of base station

We propose a clustering method based on *K*-Means algorithm, making clusters on base stations, and secondary clustering on the filtering results.

For the first clustering, exclude alienation points within the study area which have great impact on data observation. And then make partition for the first results; remove sparse areas to get the ideal targets for group activity analysis. In the paper, data are divided into three clusters, shown in Table 4 and Figure 9.

Table 4. Clustering results

Attribute	Full Data	0(blue)	1(red)	2(green)
	(1379)	(168)-12%	(24)-2%	(1187)-86%
Centroids	102.7147	103.116	100.1647	102.7094
	25.0326	25.0424	25.7638	25.0164

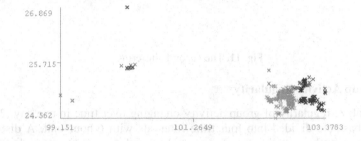

Fig. 9. Clustering results

From the clustering results, cluster 2 is the cluster with the excluded alienation points, showing the obvious progress in Figure 10.

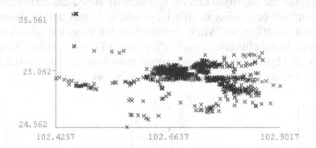

Fig. 10. Clustering after excluding sparse points

Comparing Figure 10 with Figure 9, new data are intensive than the original data. But there are still some alienation points within the compression range. In order to get discrimination of these alienated areas and intensive regions, we use K-Means algorithm to make clusters for them again. The second clustering will divide the first clustering results into four clusters, shown in Table 5 and Figure 11.

From Table 5 and Figure 11, the region indicated in cluster 3 is very sparse, not meeting the requirements of the study. The other three clusters show relatively good. Cluster 0 is the most intensive, which is the best object for analysis.

Table 5. The second clustering

Attribute	Full Data	0(dark blue)	1(red)	2(green)	3(light blue)
	(1185)	(571)-48%	(209)-18%	(208)-29%	(46)-5%
Centroids	102.7093	102.6722	102.8024	102.7497	102.5213
	25.0163	25.0394	24.8854	25.0632	24.9886

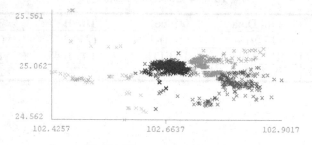

Fig. 11. The second clustering

4.3   Group Activity Regularity

We can analyze regularity of group activity changing over time in one day. 24 hours in the database are divided into four time intervals with 6-hour unit. A distribution view of activated base station can be created at each time interval, including base station geographic ID, latitude, longitude and number of activated times.

In order to analyze variation within a day, data are clustered again to find intensive points and sparse points. *K*-Means algorithm can create data block, but cannot represent the hierarchical relationship of clusters, as well as clusters with different sizes. It is needed to distinguish the density. *DBScan* is a density-based clustering method, whose clustering is traditional center-based, that is, counting points within the region in *Eps* radius to get density distribution. When a point does not meet the minimum distance, it will not be counted in the clustering results. We use *DBScan* algorithm to get clustering results as shown in Figure 12, here color represents density. The darker shows in the figure, the higher density is. Sparse dots are shown in dark blue.

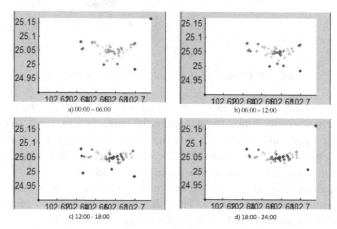

Fig. 12. Activity density chart under remote observation

As we can see from Figure 12, activity is low from 0:00 to 6:00, the rest has high-density activities. Urban group activities are in general stability, having high similarity. In addition, modern urban human habits have been a great change. It is evident that there are a large number of activities between 6:00pm-0:00am, and the intensity is almost no difference in daytime. But the number of outside points marked blue is significantly reduced in that period in suburbs.

We can further analyze the detailed chart of group activity. Removing the records of outside points marked by *DBScan* algorithm, and increasing the accuracy of clustering, we can highlight hot group activities to get activity density chart under near observation, shown in Figure 13.

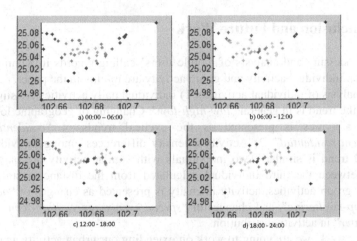

Fig. 13. Activity density chart under near observation

Most dots are outside points between 00:00-06:00 in Figure 13a). Although these outside points are activated, they are not active. Except outside points, hot degree of the rest points is very slight. The hottest points are in orange. However, in Figure 13c), the hottest spots are almost black. Group activities in the early morning are very week in line with reality. In addition to the heat chat with other charts differ in early morning, distribution of the data are dispersed but uniform. Through analysis of individual activity, it is observed that main locations of individuals recorded are at home in the early morning.

Between 06:00-12:00, urban activity has started to strengthen gradually. The city has an obvious change in activity hotspot. Deep blue is transformed into light blue. The number of red and yellow dots is increased. The red hot center is expanding. Human activity gradually recovers during 06:00-12:00, and reaches the peak at 12:00-18:00. In Figure 13c), outline of hot center becomes clear, and multiple thermal centers are appeared. Brown and red dots are obviously increased; while orange and yellow dots are diminishing. It is shown group is aggregated in the afternoon, which is actually the period of main activity in city.

Activities in city began to disperse between 18:00-24:00, but still be concentrated around the city center. Brown dots are reduced to only one, which is the city center.

For the others, red dots are slightly reduced, orange and yellow dots are increased, and are all scattered around the center of city. From individual activity analysis, most people are actually at home or enjoy entertainment.

Group activities have a strong correlation with individual activities, which also have the same periodicity as the individual. Changes in the activity intensity are periodic, from downturn to recovery, and then from recovery to the summit, and finally retained sweltering. Cyclical phenomenon of activity distribution is uniformly dispersed at the beginning, and then slowly moves closer to the center, and finally disperse. It shows that there is a strong liquidity and cyclical change in the intensity of urban activities.

5   Conclusion and Future Work

Through processing and analysis of mobile users' calling records in Kunming City, China, urban individual activity and group activity are mining in the paper.

In the analysis of individual activities, 1) individual daily activities are slightly different, but the trend is in general "*low-high-low*". Changing of geographic location of individual activities is presented as the cyclical trends of "*residential-work-entertainment-residential*". 2) Activity intensity differences among individuals, but the general trend is similar. Two individuals with similar activity are maybe quite different between the third individual calculated from the distance results. In the analysis of group activities, activity intensity is presented as changes of "*downturn-recovery-top-sweltering*", and changes of "*spread evenly-aggregation- concentrated-around center*" in activity distribution.

As future work, we are going to work on extending our urban activity analysis, including, 1) Extend the scope of time from week to monthly and annual to discover individual's activity patterns and background information. 2) Determining different characteristics of different hotspots to distinguish and discover hotspots in cities.

Acknowledgment. This work is supported by National Nature Science Foundation of China under grant no. 41231171. The authors would like to thank Xiaoqing Zou at Kunming University of Science and Technology, Kunming, China for providing us with mobile phone data.

References

1. Eagle, N., Pentland, A.S.: Reality Mining: Sensing Complex Social Systems. Personal and Ubiquitous Computing 10(4), 255–268 (2006)
2. Cao, L.: In-depth Behavior Understanding and Use: the Behavior Informatics Approach. Information Science 180(17), 3067–3085 (2010)
3. González, M.C., Hidalgo, C.A., Barabási, A.L.: Understanding Individual Human Mobility Patterns. Letters 453(5), 779–782 (2008)
4. Bayir, M.A., Demirbas, M., Eagle, N.: Discovering Spatiotemporal Mobility Profiles of Cellphone Users. In: Proceedings of IEEE International Symposium on a World of Wireless, Mobile and Multimedia Networks & Workshops, pp. 1–9 (2009)

5. Lee, K., Hong, S., Kim, S.J., Rhee, I., Chong, S.: SLAW: A New Mobility Model for Human Walks. In: INFOCOM 2009, pp. 855–864. IEEE Press, New York (2009)
6. Song, J., Tang, E.Y., Liu, L.: User Behavior Pattern Analysis and Prediction Based on Mobile Phone Sensors. In: Ding, C., Shao, Z., Zheng, R. (eds.) NPC 2010. LNCS, vol. 6289, pp. 177–189. Springer, Heidelberg (2010)
7. Candia, J., González, M.C., Wang, P., Schoenharl, T., Madey, G., Barabási, A.L.: Uncovering Individual and Collective Human Dynamics from Mobile Phone Records. Journal of Physicsa: Mathematical and Theoretical 41, 1–11 (2008)
8. Ratti, C., Pulselli, R.M., Williams, S., Frenchman, D.: Mobile Landscapes: Using Location Data from Cell Phones for Urban Analysis. Environment and Planning B: Planning and Design 33, 727–748 (2006)
9. Phithakkitnukoon, S., Horanont, T., Di Lorenzo, G., Shibasaki, R., Ratti, C.: Activity-Aware Map: Identifying Human Daily Activity Pattern Using Mobile Phone Data. In: Salah, A.A., Gevers, T., Sebe, N., Vinciarelli, A. (eds.) HBU 2010. LNCS, vol. 6219, pp. 14–25. Springer, Heidelberg (2010)
10. Reades, J., Calabrese, F., Sevtsuk, A., Ratti, C.: Cellular Census: Explorations in Urban Data Collection. Pervasive Computing 6(3), 10–18 (2007)
11. Calabrese, F., Colonna, M., Lovisolo, P., Parata, D., Ratti, C.: Real-Time Urban Monitoring using Cell Phones: A Case Study in Rome. IEEE Transactions on Intelligent Transporation Systems 12(1), 141–151 (2011)

Dynamic User Behavior-Based Piracy Propagation Monitoring in Wireless Peer-to-Peer Networks

Benke Qu[1], Wenjia Niu[2], Tianqing Zhu[3], Lei Wu[1], Shijun Liu[1], and Na Wang[4]

[1] School of Computer Science & Technology, Shandong University, Jinan, China
qubenke2013@gmail.com, {i_lily,lsj}@sdu.edu.cn
[2] Institute of Information Engineering, Chinese Academy of Sciences, Beijing, China
nwj6688@gmail.com
[3] School of Information Technology, Deakin University, VIC 3125, Australia
ztianqin@deakin.edu.au
[4] East China Institute of Computer Science, Shanghai, China
naseberry@gmail.com

Abstract. Wireless peer-to-peer (P2P) networks such as ad hoc networks, have reviewed considerable attention due to their potential content sharing applications in the civilian environment. Unfortunately, because of fast and effective content sharing without strict authorization mechanism, wireless P2P networks are abused and suffer from massive copyright infringement problems. To solve this problem, piracy propagation monitoring becomes very necessary. In general, user behaviors should be employed as the base to construct piracy distribution, further predict and analyze the piracy propagation. However, some dynamic user behaviors such as the migration from download to upload, which embody important knowledge on behavior threat, have been largely ignored. In this paper, an approach to monitoring piracy propagation based on dynamic user behavior is proposed, in which fuzzy logic is applied to quantitatively model the behavior threat and piracy propagation ability. Furthermore, a new clustering algorithm named \emph{REGKM} is proposed for piracy propagation analysis.

Keywords: Dynamic User Behavior, Wireless P2P Networks, Content Similarity, Piracy Propagation Monitoring.

1 Introduction

Wireless peer-to-peer (P2P) networks have been extensively applied widely, such as Dartmouth College's Mature Campus-wide Network [1], CodeTorrent [2] and LPG [3]. The popularity of this hybrid network lies in its decentralized nature and thus its cost-effectiveness in large file delivering to massive number of users. These two characteristics make it convenient for various applications to directly communicate with each other without the aid of central nodes and improve the scalability and sustainability of P2P networks. Especially, any peer can serve as a content provider, which improves the content availability and guarantees faster delivering.

However, like other P2P networks, uncontrolled sharing of pirated contents would also lead to a rampant piracy propagation problem in wireless P2P networks without

L. Cao et al. (Eds.): BSIC/BSI 2013, LNAI 8178, pp. 44–55, 2013.

strict content authorization and third-party supervision. Furthermore, peers in the hybrid network may easily access their nearby wi-fi hot points. This highly dynamic nature has further aggravated the problem and made it even harder to track than normal P2P networks. Thus we need to migrate necessary propagation monitoring work from P2P networks to wireless P2P networks, so that it can keep track of piracy propagation and unfold its panorama for future supervision's reference.

The graph-based method [4] is an intuitive monitoring for content. It fully exploits the semantic link to built smart heuristic rules and develops effective propagation prediction [5, 6, 7]. As a novel and popular method in P2P monitoring, the content similarity graph (CSG) [8, 9, 10, 12, 13] mines and constructs the content relation. The similarity between two contents can be well calculated by the number of the users that upload or download both two contents at one time. Hence, based on CSG, how to further study the piracy's influence sphere and predict the possible "infecting" tracks, is a very natural idea.

However, the direct CSG usage would result in a noticeable problem in piracy monitoring applications: CSG's construction is mainly based on a network snapshot at a given time and the statistics of users' contents ownership. It fails to take account of the dynamic user behavior for which the instantaneous changes can instantly vibrate the piracy propagation. For instance, in a turbulent wireless P2P network, users can be randomly in or out. Moreover, when they stay in the network, they may casually or frequently upload or download contents within the network. Such casual or frequent characteristic can pose a direct influence on the threatening ability of users' sharing behavior and the propagating ability of shared pirated contents.

Hence, CSG would not be fit for the instability nature of the wireless P2P network, and decrease the timeliness and accuracy of piracy monitoring. This paper aims to make three contributions on the piracy monitoring:

- In view of the dynamic characteristic of user behavior [11], we propose a fine-granularity dynamic user behavior (DUB) model, which characterizes four dynamic attributes that are closely related with user behavior to subtly depict the instantaneous behavior characteristics.
- We introduce the user behavior threat (UBT) and the piracy propagation ability (PPA) for piracy propagation prediction. UBT stands for the threat extent of user distributing contents, while PPA indicates the piracy propagation ability. Fuzzy rules are designed to quantify the UBT and PPA.
- A new clustering algorithm REGKM is developed by utilizing the PPA and the PPA difference. It can effective improve the piracy monitoring.

The rest of this paper is organized as follows. Section 2 discusses the detailed approach of dynamic user behavior-based piracy propagation monitoring. Section 3 illustrates the whole monitoring process for piracy propagation followed by experimental evaluations in Section 4. Section 5 concludes this paper.

2   Modeling Dynamic Behaviors and Piracy Propagation

In this section, in order to portray a peer's behavior in the wireless P2P network, a dynamic user behavior (DUB) model is firstly given. Next, the DUB model is leveraged to help define and quantify the user behavior threat (UBT), which works as an indicator for the gravity of a user sharing pirated products. In the end, the piracy propagating ability (PPA) is retrieved via UBT to demonstrate the propagation potential of the pirated products during the sharing process driven by users in the wireless P2P network.

2.1 DUB Characterization

In general, we have four observations: 1) in terms of driving piracy propagation, uploading behavior is more threatening than downloading behavior; 2) the longer user does with piracy, the more threatening the user behavior is; 3) a higher velocity of the user behavior means more menaces in his/her driving piracy propagation; 4) a user habitually stays in the wireless P2P network does more harm than a casual one. To illustrate these points, first, uploading a pirated product actually can be viewed as a one-to-many mapping process, in which the uploader provides the pirated content to many distributed downloaders, while a downloader just downloads his own share of the pirated content from the uploader, which can be viewed as a one-to-one mapping process. The sphere of influence of the two process are obviously different and thus the distinction of the gravity of user behavior is proven. Next, the faster, longer and more frequent sharing process is definitely more threatening.

Those four dimensions are combined together to vividly illustrate the gravity of a user's sharing behavior in the wireless P2P network. So, based on the above statement, DUB will contain four attributes: state, duration, velocity and type, and the model is represented as:

$$DUB_i=\{B(i,j), i \in E, j \in C\} \tag{1}$$

$$B(i,j)=(B_{up}(i,j), B_{down}(i,j)) \tag{2}$$

$$B_{up}(i,j)=(state(i,j), duration(i,j), velocity(i,j), type(i,j)) \tag{3}$$

$$B_{down}(i,j)=(state(i,j), duration(i,j), velocity(i,j), type(i,j)) \tag{4}$$

In the above model, i represents an element of user set E, and j represents an element of data set C which is directly related with user i. DUB_i stands for the dynamic user behavior of user i. B(i,j) shows a relationship between i and j, which means user i uploads or downloads j. $B_{up}(i,j)$ stands for user i uploading content j, while $B_{down}(i,j)$ stands for user i downloading content j. B(i,j) means user i's behavior is the union of download behavior and upload behavior. The state(i,j) stands for the current state of user i uploads/downloads content j. The duration(i,j) stands for duration of user i uploads/downloads content j in the last time period t, whose length can works as a coefficient to be customized. The velocity(i,j) stands for the instantaneous speed of user i uploads/downloads content j. The type(i,j) illustrates whether user i occasionally or frequently downloads/uploads content j in the   time period t.

2.2   UBT and PPA Calculation

UBT can be calculated as follows:

$$UBT(i) = \omega_{up} \cdot UBT_{up}(i) + \omega_{down} \cdot UBT_{down}(i), \tag{5}$$

$$UBT_{up}(i) = \sum_{i \in U, j \in C, (i,j) \in E} \omega_{j_{up}} \cdot ubt_{up}(i, j), \tag{6}$$

$$UBT_{down}(i) = \sum_{i \in U, j \in C, (i,j) \in E} \omega_{j_{down}} \cdot ubt_{down}(i, j), \tag{7}$$

$$ubt_{up}(i, j) = state(i, j) \cdot velocity(i, j) \cdot duration(i, j) \cdot type(i, j), \tag{8}$$

$$ubt_{down}(i, j) = state(i, j) \cdot velocity(i, j) \cdot duration(i, j) \cdot type(i, j) \tag{9}$$

UBT(i) stands for the user i's total UBT. UBT_{up}(i) and UBT_{down}(i) stand for uploading and downloading UBTs respectively.   Because whether user behavior is dominated by uploading or downloading can vastly sway UBT, we will assign ω_{up} and ω_{down} with different weights, i.e., up-UBT with $\omega_{up} \in [0.5,1]$, down-UBT with $\omega_{down} \in [0,0.5]$, and $\omega_{up} + \omega_{down} = 1$.   The total UBT is a weighted sum of up-UBT and down-UBT.

Piracy propagation simultaneously may change along with users' DUB and one user's UBT conceivably affects the PPAs of the contents he uploads and downloads. The PPA will be calculated as follows.

$$PPA(j) = \sum_{i \in U, (i,j) \in E} \omega_i \cdot UBT(i) \tag{10}$$

We can see that PPA is a weighted sum of UBTs. Conceivably, users with higher UBTs impose a greater influence on the determination of contents' PPAs. Therefore, PPA is defined as a weighted sum of its involving users' UBTs. So it's indispensable to define a hierarchy of UBTs and their corresponding weights of different levels. We classify the UBT into four levels. Their hierarchy and weights are illustrated in Table 1 below.

Table 1. UBT and their corresponding weights

UBT interval	UBT hierarchy	UBT weight
[0,0.25]	"LOW"	0.1
(0.25,0.5]	"MEDIUM"	0.2
(0.5,0.75]	"HIGH"	0.3
(0.75,1]	"WARNING"	0.4

Additionally, a threat distribution vector T, is created for one content, recording the UBTs of users related with this content. In order to make PPA help find contents much more related with the known pirated content, we define PPA difference to tell the similarity of two contents' PPA, as is shown in Equation (11) below.

$$pd = \frac{\sum_{i=1}^{k}(k-i+1)\lambda_i}{\sum_{i=1}^{k}i} \tag{11}$$

Suppose the known pirated content's threat distribution vector is $T_i=(UBT_1, UBT_2,...,UBT_n)$, and the threat distribution vector of the unknown content to be tested is expressed as $T_i=(UBT'_1, UBT'_2,...,UBT'_n)$. The difference between UBT_i and UBT'_i can be calculated by the relative error coefficient λ_i.

$$\lambda_i = \left| \frac{UBT_i' - UBT_i}{UBT_i} \right| \tag{12}$$

Much smaller coefficients play trivial roles in the calculation of pd but increase the time and amount of calculation, so we only deal with those significant coefficients. First, we shuffle those significant coefficients from large to small, select the first k to form the error coefficient vector $v=(\lambda_1, \lambda_2,...\lambda_k)$. Then, a weighted average calculation is applied to the elements of v to obtain pd. It is noteworthy that the weighted average calculation employs different weights. Here, we will assign larger weights to relative error coefficients to stress the larger coefficients' contributions to the ultimate result.

The interval of pd is $[0, +\infty)$ and the smaller pd is, the more similar between two PPAs is. If and only if pd $=0$, the two contents' PPAs are just the same.

3   Monitoring Process for Piracy Propagation

3.1   Node Ability Calculation Module

Based on UBT and PPA, the piracy propagation monitoring process can be developed as is shown in Fig. 1.

As Fig. 1 shows, during the data-preprocessing phase, the filtrations are carried out twice on the coarse dataset, leaving behind the significant user dataset, content dataset and their relationship dataset that will be leveraged for the construction of user-content bipartite graph. Next, we insert a node ability calculation module between the data preprocessing module and post-construction process. This node ability calculation module executes the calculation on UBT and PPA. Then "paint" the content node with different colors according to the different PPAs, so as to visually exhibit contents' PPAs and their distributions. If a region crowded with red nodes may demonstrate that pirated contents in this area are overwhelming, and by clicking one node in this picture, DUBs related with this content are visually cataloged.

In the node ability calculation module, user dataset is processed and utilized to obtain users' UBTs. With UBT fully prepared, the calculation of PPA, which is the weighted sum of UBTs, follows. Then UBTs and PPAs, acting as additive attributes, get attached to corresponding nodes. In the process of vertical layering sub-module that belongs to the node ability calculation module, CSG nodes are layered according to a PPA stratification strategy.

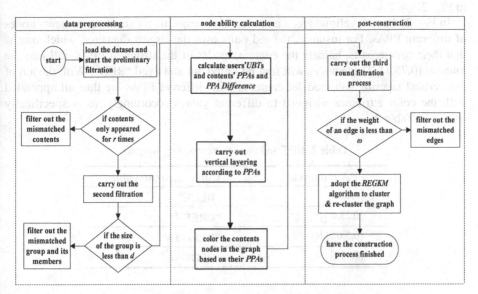

Fig. 1. The overall monitoring process of piracy propagation

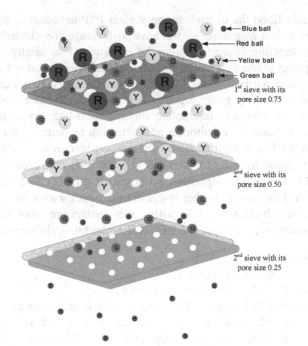

Fig. 2. Vertical layering sub-module

Figuratively, three sieves with their sieve pores of different sizes are vertically located. The diameters of the sieve pores are determined via extended systematic logs and statistics on the contents' PPAs. The vertical layering process is vividly illustrated in Fig. 2.

In Fig. 2, the red, yellow, green and blue balls respectively stand for contents nodes of different PPAs. For instance, the red balls own the largest diameter, which means that their counterparts, namely the contents nodes of the strongest PPAs, fall into the interval [0.75,1]. These nodes will first be sifted out and dyed "RED". With the aid of the vertical layering sub-module, contents with different PPAs are thus all appended with the color attributes assigned to different values accordingly, as is specifically shown in Table 2.

Table 2. UBT and their corresponding weights

PPA interval	Color attribute values
$[0,0.25]$	"BLUE"
$(0.25,0.5]$	"GREEN"
$(0.5,0.75]$	"YELLOW"
$(0.75,1]$	"RED"

3.2   REGKM Algorithm for Reclustering

To mechanically flood the overwhelmingly giant P2P networks to single out the pirated contents is just awesome, so we have to leverage the clustering algorithm to condense the detecting amount of potential contents while ideally guaranteeing the detection of piracy contents. So after the node ability calculation is finished, the clustering process necessarily follows. In the last module, carrying out an effective clustering process would help group together nodes that share more similar propagation characteristics and thus help interpolate missing metadata, revise those misspelled metadata and facilitate the monitoring and detection of potential piratets concealing themselves in the P2P networks. Based on the consideration of PPA difference, we develop a new algorithm—Reinforced GKM (REGKM) that intensifies the previous GKM (Graphic k-medoids) algorithm proposed in [8]. REGKM makes full use of PPAs and PPA difference to further re-cluster the nodes within the same cluster into two independent sub-clusters. PPAs within sub-clusters are much more similar, but vary greatly among sub-clusters. The REGKM algorithm is shown below.

```
REGKM(G,k,m)
//G is CSG's data structure;
//k stands for k cluster centers;
//m is the default min distance between cluster centers
Randomly select k nodes in the node set of G(V,E) as ini-
tial cluster centers and the minimum distance between two
of the k centers should not be less than m, namely ∀d_{ij}>m
```

```
for every node v∈V do
    Calculate the distance between v and every cluster
    center, namely d₁~dₖ;
    Select the 2 nearest clusters: cluster i and j
    if |dᵢ - dⱼ| >δ do  //δ is the threshold in the
                       //realistic system
        v joins the nearer cluster of i and j
    else
        v joins the cluster of a smaller size of i and j
end for
Recalculate k cluster centers c₁~cₖ as the final centers of
the k new clusters respectively
for every cluster C do //C is one of the k new clusters
    Randomly select 2 nodes in C as the initial subclus
    ter center α, β
    repeat
        for every node γ∈C do
            Calculate the PPA difference dₐ between γ and
            α and PPA difference d_β between γ and β
            if dₐ > d_β do
                γ joins α
            else
                γ joins β
        end for
        Recalculate the cluster centers of the two respec
        tive subclusters
    until two subclusters are stable
endfor
```

Distinct from the previous GKM algorithm, "distance", which is measured in the re-clustering part of REGKM, directly evolves from the PPA difference of contents. The smaller PPA difference is, the smaller distance between two contents. Thus, leveraging PPAs and PPA difference, a re-clustering is carried out, which results in subclusters whose members own much more similar PPAs. Details about the REGKM algorithm are shown below.

Step1. Randomly select k content nodes in the CSG as the initial cluster centers. By the way, in the CSG, content nodes have been colored according to their PPAs;

Step2. Calculate the distance between any two nodes of the k initial centers and tell whether the retrieved distance is greater than the threshold of the system. If not, go back to Step 1 and select another k nodes;

Step3. For every node *i* in the CSG, calculate and sort the distances between i and the k centers using the Dijkstra algorithm;

Step4. Single out the first two minimum distances and the corresponding two nearest clusters;

Step5. Tell whether the difference of the two distances is less than the default threshold. That is, to determine whether they are roughly of the same length. If yes, node i will join the cluster with a smaller size. Or else, node i will join the nearest cluster;

Step6. iterate Step3~5 until all nodes   in the CSG find their groups. Recalculate the centers of the newly formed k groups and the new k centers will be final cluster centers. It's noteworthy that on account of the overwhelming size of the CSG and the existence of popular contents, nodes will conceivably grow around those popular content nodes and thus a relatively k steady clusters, so it's appropriate to just carry out once the above process;

Step7. For every cluster, randomly select two subcluster centers;

Step8. Calculate the PPAs from any node to the two subcluster centers and classify it to a subcluster with a bigger PPA;

Step9. For every cluster, iterate Step7~8 until two stable subclusters.

By discriminating the twin sub-clusters in the REGKM algorithm, it would further faciliate fine-granularity piracy propagation monitoring and analysis.

4   Experimental Evaluation

In this section we define **piracy content percentage** to quantitatively illustrate the effect of the REGKM algorithm in terms of clustering the suspected pirated contents. This index indicates the amount of piracy contents in the formed clusters retrieved by the REGKM algorithm. A bigger index showcases a finer effect. To activate the REGKM algorithm, we firstly make use of FreePastry [14] to construct a P2P overlay environment in which we have M computers join the overlay, simulate and analyze their upload/download behavior, retrieve the piracy propagation regularity in the P2P network, carry out the REGKM algorithm and thus calculate the piracy content percentage in the cluster.

Initially, we have M computers upload or download N contents. During the simulation process, each user will select a certain content to upload or download with a given probability. In addition, the "type" attribute of user behavior indicates a user may be likely to follow his own habit and has an obvious inclination to upload/download a specific kind of contents. If a user is found to prefer to upload/download pirated content according to the historical statistics, it is of higher probability for him to continue to upload/download piracy contents in the future. Hence, in order to simulate the actual user behavior in the P2P overlay, we calculate the *percentage of the pirated contents* in a user's historical uploaded/downloaded contents and thus dynamically adjust the probability of his uploading/downloading piracy contents in the future.

In order to make our experiment moderately long enough so as to efficiently and effectively observe a more conspicuous change of our result, in our experiment, we set M to 30,000 and N to 2,000,000. For each uploading/downloading behavior, the "velocity" is randomly set to [20, 150], "duration" is randomly set to [5, 30] and "type" is calculated based on the historical inclination of that user's upload/download. Then, we do several experiments with initial   5%, 10%, 15% and 20% percents of pirated contents in the P2P overlay respectively. If we manually detect every possible content circulating in the P2P overlay and single out the pirated contents, we have to mechnically the dectection process for 2,000,000 times, so the workload will increase *linearly* with the increase of the contents sent into the P2P networks. A bad idea! While leveraging the proposed REGKM algorithm, we can simply single out the most suspected cluster, in which red nodes dominate, and effectively detect the condensed amount of nodes. Thus, the efficiency and effectiveness of the piracy detection work get vastly boosted. The experimental results are collectively shown in Fig.3.

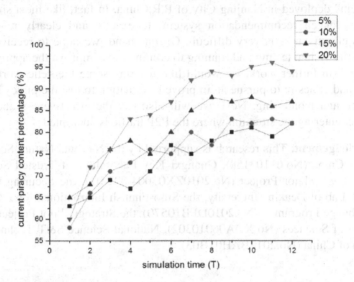

Fig. 3. Performance analysis of proposed piracy propagation monitoring approach

In Fig. 3, X-axis is the simulation time with the unit of T (the running period of our proposed approach in the P2P overlay), and Y-axis indicates the highest piracy rate among our most suspected CSG cluster. As we can see in Fig. 3, the piracy content percentage in our CSG cluster is far above the average percentage (95%-20%, 86%-15%, 83%-10%, and 80%-5%). Take the 80%-5% for example. Initially, 10,0000 piract contents are sent into the P2P overlay. Without the aid of the REGKM algorithm, we have to manually detect the overall 2,000,000 contents so as to find the 100,000 (2,000,000 * 5%) piracy content. While leveraging the REGKM algorithm, after sometime, we have successfully clustered 80% piracy contents in the most suspected cluster. If the cluster owns 150,000 content nodes, we then can simply detect the 100,000 most suspected nodes and single out 80, 000 piracy contents. As seen from the example, the detection work gets obvious simplified. So, by carrying out the overall piracy propagation monitoring process proposed in our approach, pirated contents can get vastly clustered together. It is to be noted that, when the initial piracy rate is 20%, pirated contents account for 95% of the overall contents in the most suspected CSG cluster. So, our approach will acquire a better performance and effectively inhibit the rampant growth of the pirated contents in P2P when they are inclined to overwhelm the network.

5   Conclusion

In this paper, we propose a dynamic user behavior-based monitoring approach for piracy propagation. Based on the characterization on dynamic user behavior, UBT and PPA can be quantified for predict piracy propagation. Furthermore, utilizing the PPA difference to design a new clustering algorithm REGKM is first proposed by us in piracy propagation monitoring.

Fortunately, this approach has already been embedded into our "copyright monitoring system" deployed in Nanjing City of P.R.China. In fact, like most similarity and prediction-related recommendation system, to exactly and clearly reveal the approach's effectiveness is very difficult. On one hand, we hope to receive rich feedbacks in the system testing and running to continuously improve the approach. On the other hand, in further work, we would like to bring some theoretic work from psychology and ethics in to pursue an improved evaluation to test the piracy propagation prediction and monitoring. Next, we will also test the effectiveness and efficiency when encountering the situation where the P2P traffic is encrypted.

Acknowledgement. This research is supported by the National Nature Science Foundation of China (No.61103158), Guangxi Key Laboratory of Trusted Software, the National S&T Major Project (No.2010ZX03004-002-01), the Securing CyberSpace Research Lab of Deakin University, the Sino-Finnish International S&T Cooperation and Exchange Program   (No.2010DFB10570), the Strategic Pilot Project of Chinese Academy of Sciences (No.XDA06010302), National Science S&T Technology Pillar Program of China (No.2012BAH01B03).

References

1. Henderson, T., Kotz, D., Abyzov, I.: The changing usage of a mature campus-wide wireless network. In: ACM MobiCom, pp. 187–201 (2004)
2. Karagiannis, G., Altintas, O., Ekici, E., Heijenk, G., Jarupan, B., Lin, K., Weil, T.: Vehicular Networking: A survey and tutorial on requirements, architectures, challenges, standards and solutions. IEEE Communications Surveys & Tutorials 13(4), 584–616 (2011)
3. Chen, W., Cai, S.: Ad Hoc peer-to-peer network architecture for vehicle safety communications. IEEE Communications Magazine 43(4), 100–107 (2005)
4. Schenker, A.: Graph-theoretic techniques for web content mining. World Scientific Publishing (2005)
5. Hassanzadeh, O., Lim, L., Kementsietsidis, A., Lim, L., Miller, R.J., Wang, M.: A declarative framework for semantic link discovery over relational data. In: Proceedings of 18th World Wide Web Conference, pp. 1027–1036 (2009)
6. Liu, J., Zhuge, H.: A semantic-link-based infrastructure for web service discovery in p2p networks. Special Interest Tracks and Posters of the 14th International Conference on World Wide Web, pp. 940–941 (2005)
7. Zhuge, H.: Communities and emerging semantics in semantic link network: Discovery and learning. IEEE Transactions on Knowledge and Data Engineering 21(6), 785–799 (2009)
8. Shavitt, Y., Weinsberg, E., Weinsberg, U.: Mining musical from large-scale peer-to-peer networks. IEEE Multimedia 18(1), 14–23 (2011)

9. Schenker, A.: Graph-theoretic techniques for web content mining. World Scientific Publishing (2005)
10. Kosala, R., Blockeel, H.: Web mining research: a survey. ACM SIGKDD Explorations Newsletter 2(1), 1–15 (2000)
11. Cao, L.: In-depth Behavior Understanding and Use: the Behavior Informatics Approach. Information Science 180(17), 3067–3085 (2010)
12. Mobasher, B., Dai, H., Luo, T., Nakagawa, M.: Discovery and evaluation of aggregate usage profiles for web personalization. Data Mining and Knowledge Discovery 6(1), 61–82 (2002)
13. Chatterjee, A., Raghavan, P.: Similarity graph neighborhoods for enhanced supervised classification. Procedia Computer Science 9, 577–586 (2012)

World Expo Problem and Its Mixed Integer Programming Based Solution

Hongteng Xu[1], Dixin Luo[1], Xiaoming Huo[2], and Xiaokang Yang[1]

[1] Institute of Image Communication, Shanghai Jiao Tong University, Shanghai, China
[2] School of Industrial and Systems Engineering,
Georgia Institute of Technology, Atlanta U.S.A.
{hongtengxu,luodixin,xkyang}@sjtu.edu.cn,
xiaoming@isye.gatech.edu

Abstract. In this paper, we introduce an interesting "World Expo problem", which aims to identify and track multiple targets in a sensor network, and propose a solution to this problem based on the mixed integer programming. Compared with traditional tracking problem in the sensor network, the World Expo problem has following two features. Firstly, the target in the network is not limited to single individuals. It can also be a group composed of multiple individuals with same path in the network, which implies that multiple targets can share the same path and be detected by the same sensor at the same time. Moreover, both the size and the number of groups are unknown. Secondly, differing from traditional sensor networks, the sensor network in the World Expo problem usually is sparse. These two features increase the difficulty in identification and tracking. To solve the aforementioned problem, we analyze the solvability of this problem and come up with a mixed integer programming based algorithm. The simulation result shows that our method has good performances and is robust to errors in the data.

Keywords: Social Collective Behavior, Sensor Networks, Path Identification, Integer Programming.

1 Introduction

In this paper, we focus on solving a problem described as follows. In a social collective site, such as the field of World Expo, there are hundreds and thousands of tourists visiting the field. From the open time of the place to the close time, we can record the number of visitor in each pavilion of the Expo by surveillant cameras, tickets or ID cards at each time point. In the end of the day, we will further get the total number of tourists from the record of entrances or exits. According to the total number of tourists and the observational data of each pavilion, can we estimate the paths of tourists? We will call this problem the "World Expo problem", because this problem was motivated by visitors tracking problem in the World Expo.

1.1 Previous Work

This problem is inspired by the object tracking problem, which has been researched for many years. Many works have been done from different viewpoints. In the computer vi-

L. Cao et al. (Eds.): BSIC/BSI 2013, LNAI 8178, pp. 56–67, 2013.
© Springer International Publishing Switzerland 2013

sion field, object detection and tracking is achieved from video data, seeing the works in [1–5]. However, because of the perspective limitation of camera, the video based tracking is difficult to apply to large-scale scene. In the work of [1, 2, 5], the camera is fixed in a local, simple scene. Although [3, 4] achieve tracking in the crowded situation, it is still difficult to achieve relay tracking by multiple cameras. Besides computer vision, tracking is also widely researched in social computation and modeling field [6–10]. A common feature of these works is that they achieve object tracking based on an effective sensor network.

In fact, the World Expo problem can be viewed as an extension of target identification problem in the sensor network. Target identification is an essential problem in the sensor network, especially in the binary sensor network. When it comes to single target situation, this problem is a pure tracking problem and many algorithms can achieve good results, such as Kalman filtering in [11], the particle filtering in [12] and the maximum posteriori (MAP) algorithm in [13]. In binary sensor network, HMM has been used to track users [14]. A series of rigorous theories on the single target tracking with binary proximity networks are given in [15–18] and large-scale experiments are given in [19, 20]. In multiple target situation, the problem becomes more complicated. In [21], a multiple targets tracking algorithm in a 1-D binary network is given. In 2-D binary network, an integer programming approach for multiple targets identification is proposed in [22]. Moreover, [23] gives an analysis on the solvability of multiple targets identification in 2-D binary network, which gives sufficient conditions on when a path identification problem is solvable.

1.2   Our Work

World Expo problem is different from traditional multiple targets identification problem. Firstly, the sensor network in World Expo problem is not binary, the observation we get is the number of target in the region of each sensor. Secondly, taking the sensor network as a graph, each sensor is a vertex of the graph and the connected path between two sensors is the edge of two vertices. The work in [23] is based on two assumptions: 1) two distinct targets cannot share the same vertex (in other words, be detected by the same sensor) at the same time; 2) two distinct targets cannot share the same edge. It is obvious that neither of these two assumption is true in World Expo problem—it is very likely that several tourists go in company and share the same path. World Expo problem is a new identification problem. Solving this problem is very meaningful to analyze the collective behavior in social events [3, 24, 5, 10, 4].

To solve World Expo problem, we give the impossibility condition of this problem and propose an algorithm based on the mixed integer programming. By introducing a new concept called "group", we reduce the dimension of the problem greatly, which reduces the computational complexity of the algorithm. Moreover, by designing a path clustering post-processing method, the proposed algorithm is robust to the error of the observation data.

The rest of the paper is organized as follows. The graphic model of World Expo problem is described in Section 2. In Section 3, we improve the model and the corresponding algorithm to overcome the difficulty from practical applications, which makes the algorithm not only feasible to sparse sensor networks but also robust to error data.

In Section 4, we gives simulation result in test model and analyze the solvability of the proposed method. Finally, conclusion is provided in Section 5.

2   The Graphics Model of the World Expo Problem

2.1   Problem Statement

In World Expo problem, we can define a field F, which represents the region where a sensor network reside on. The sensor network can be represented by a graph $G = (V, E)$, $V = \{v_i\}_{i=1}^I$ is the set of vertices in G, which corresponds to the sensor set $\{i\}_{i=1}^I$; E is the corresponding edge set of G. If v_i and $v_{i'}(i \neq i')$ can be connected directly without passing any other vertices, then $(v_i, v_i') \in E$. To each vertex v_i, we define a field R_i corresponding to the available detection region of sensor i. In an ideal sensor network, we have

$$R_i \cap R_{i'} = \phi, \quad i \neq i', \quad \text{and} \quad \bigcup_{i=1}^I R_i = F, \tag{1}$$

which means that the sensing regions of these sensors in the network are disjoint to each other while the network covers the whole field. We use the ideal sensor network in this section for the convenience of modeling. In the next section, the assumption will be relaxed to obey practical situation. Furthermore, each vertex v_i has a set D_i, which includes all the vertices not directly connecting to v_i. In the graph G, some vertices are the entrances of G while some others are the exits. When $t = 1$, all of the N targets are in the set of entrance vertices V_{en} and begin to move in the graph in the next time. When $t = T$, all of the targets are in the set of exits V_{ex}. Figure 1 gives an illustration of graph G.

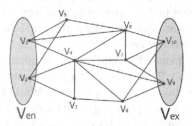

Fig. 1. An illustration of the graph of sensor network

The vertices of the above group can be pavilions in a world expo site. The organizer may know the queue length as well as the number of visitors who entered each pavilion. However their identifications are unknown. Ven and Vex corresponds to the entrances and exists of the site.

Assume that there are N targets moving in G, which correspond to N paths denoted as $\{P_n\}_{n=1}^N$. Each path P_n is a sequence $\{p_{nt}\}_{t=1}^T$, where $t = 1, ..., T$ is the time sequence. The observation data is the number of target in each vertex at each time denoted as $\{c_{it}, i = 1, ..., I, t = 1, ..., T\}$. If v_i is a pavilion, then c_{it} is the number of visitors who have toured this pavilion; if v_i is an entrance (or exit), c_{it} is the number of visitors who enter (exit) from this gate. Our aim is to estimate the path of each target from observation data; i.e., through observable c_{it}'s, we want to recover p_{nt}'s.

For achieve this aim, we need to introduce a binary variable x_{int} defined as follows

$$x_{int} = \begin{cases} 1, & p_{nt} = v_i, \\ 0, & \text{otherwise.} \end{cases} \tag{2}$$

From the definition, we can find that x_{int} is an indicator representing whether target n appears in vertex v_i at time t. It is easy to find that if x_{int} is estimated accurately, we will have $\sum_{n=1}^{N} x_{int} = c_{it}$. Then we can replace estimating P_n by getting x_{int} through the following dichotomous integer programming.

$$\sum_{i=1}^{I} \sum_{t=1}^{T} \left| \sum_{n=1}^{N} x_{int} - c_{it} \right| \tag{3}$$

$$s.t. \quad x_{int} = 0 \quad \text{or} \quad 1, \tag{4}$$

$$-x_{int} + x_{in,t+1} \leq 0, \quad v_i \in V_{en}, \tag{5}$$

$$x_{int} - x_{in,t+1} \leq 0, \quad v_i \in V_{ex}, \tag{6}$$

$$x_{int} = 0, \quad \text{if} \quad c_{it} = 0, \tag{7}$$

$$\sum_{i=1}^{I} x_{int} = 1, \quad n = 1, .., N, \quad t = 1, ..., T. \tag{8}$$

$$x_{int} + x_{i'n,t+1} \leq 1, \quad v_{i'} \in D_i. \tag{9}$$

Here, (3) is objective function, which represents the residual between observation data and our estimation result. (4) is the binary constraint of x_{int}. (5) is the entrance constraint of x_{int}. It means that if a target leaves one of the entrance, it will not go back to any entrance vertex during the recording time. Similarly, (6) is the exit constraint of x_{int}. When a target goes into one of the exit, it cannot leave it any more. Constraint (7) means that when observation data $c_{it} = 0$, no target appears in v_i at time t. (8) is an occupation constraint implying that one target can occupy only one vertex at a time. Constraint (9) is a little complicated. It requires that a target in vertex v_i can only transfer to the vertex directly connected with v_i in the next time.

Although this integer programming seems to be available to World Expo problem, it has some difficulties to practical situation. To World Expo problem, the number of targets in the graph is always very large, which influences the efficiency of solving this problem. Besides this difficulty, a more serious problem is that the solution of the optimization problem is usually not unique based on the theory in [23]. In [23], the distinct targets are not allowed to share the same vertex at the same time while World Expo problem does not have such a constraint. The aforementioned integer programming approach is just a starting point. We will incorporate other considerations, in order to come up with a more practical approach. We need to do some modifications to the algorithm, which is achieved by introducing a new concept called "group".

2.2 From Multi-targets to Multi-groups

It is a common phenomenon in social behavior that people prefer to go in company with their families, friends, or join in a tour group when they visit some places. In other words, there always has multiple targets sharing same path in a World Expo problem. According to this universal fact, we propose the concept, "group", which represents a set of targets moving together. By introducing this concept, the previous multiple targets identification problem becomes a multiple groups identification problem.

Assume there are J groups in the graph G, and the size of the group j is denoted as m_j, which is the number of targets in the group. In practical situation, we can know neither the actual number nor the actual size of group in the graph, but it is obvious that if two groups have same path, we can merge them together. So, on the condition of meeting observation data, the number of group should be as small as possible to avoid redundancy. This requirement is very significant, which can be the objective function of the modified optimization problem. In such situation, the original variable x_{int} is modified to x_{ijt}. Moreover, we need to introduce a new variable y_j as following shows

$$y_j = \begin{cases} 1, & m_j \neq 0, \\ 0, & m_j = 0. \end{cases} \tag{10}$$

As we have said, we do not know the actual number of group, so the J we assume is always larger than the actual number[1]. y_j is an indicator helping us to index redundant groups. Based on the analysis above, the modification as follows.

$$\min \sum_{j=1}^{J} y_j \tag{11}$$

$$s.t. \quad x_{ijt} = 0 \quad \text{or} \quad 1, \tag{12}$$

$$y_j = 0 \quad \text{or} \quad 1, \tag{13}$$

$$-x_{ijt} + x_{ij,t+1} \leq 0, \quad v_i \in V_{en}, \tag{14}$$

$$x_{ijt} - x_{ij,t+1} \leq 0, \quad v_i \in V_{ex}, \tag{15}$$

$$x_{ijt} + x_{i'j,t+1} \leq 1, \quad v_{i'} \in D_i, \tag{16}$$

$$x_{ijt} \leq y_j, \tag{17}$$

$$\sum_{i=1}^{I} x_{ijt} = y_j, \tag{18}$$

$$\sum_{j=1}^{J} m_j = N, \tag{19}$$

$$\sum_{j=1}^{J} m_j x_{ijt} = c_{it}. \tag{20}$$

Here (11) is the objective function to minimize the number of group. (14, 15, 16) are similar to (5, 6, 9), which make constraints on the entry, leaving and transfer of each group in the graph. The differences between current optimization problem and the original one are shown in the additional constraints. (17, 18) are the occupation constraints of group to identify the path of a group, as long as it is present. Differing from the occupation constraint (8), the upper bound of each x_{ijt} is not 1 but y_j. (19) ensures that the sum of the group size is equal to the number of targets. (20) requires the configuration of the size and the number of group meeting the observation data. It is easy to

---

[1] It should be noted that although J is larger than actual group number, it is much smaller than the number of target, N.

find that this constraint is the objective function in original optimization problem. In the modified problem, it becomes a strict constraint, which increases the accuracy of solution.

A difficulty to solve the optimization problem above by integer programming is that (20) includes the multiplication of variables. To overcome this difficulty, we need to further modified the problem as following shows

$$\min \sum_{j=1}^{J} y_j - \alpha \sum_{i=1}^{I} \sum_{j=1}^{J} \sum_{t=1}^{T} H_{ijt} \tag{21}$$

$$s.t. \quad x_{ijt} = 0 \quad \text{or} \quad 1, \tag{22}$$

$$y_j = 0 \quad \text{or} \quad 1, \tag{23}$$

$$-x_{ijt} + x_{ij,t+1} \leq 0, \quad v_i \in V_{en}, \tag{24}$$

$$x_{ijt} - x_{ij,t+1} \leq 0, \quad v_i \in V_{ex}, \tag{25}$$

$$x_{ijt} + x_{i'j,t+1} \leq 1, \quad v_{i'} \in D_i, \tag{26}$$

$$x_{ijt} \leq y_j, \tag{27}$$

$$\sum_{i=1}^{I} x_{ijt} = y_j, \tag{28}$$

$$\sum_{j=1}^{J} H_{ijt} \leq c_{it}, \quad H_{ijt} \in Z_+ \tag{29}$$

$$H_{ijt} \leq m_j, \tag{30}$$

$$H_{ijt} \leq N \cdot x_{ijt}, \tag{31}$$

$$\sum_{j=1}^{J} m_j = N. \tag{32}$$

Here (20) is replaced by three additive constraints (29, 30, 31), and the objective function is added a penalty term. $\alpha > 0$ is the weight of penalty term. The key idea is to introduce a new positive integer variable H_{ijt}. If $x_{ijt} = 0$, then (31) will impose $H_{ijt} = 0$. If $x_{ijt} = 1$, then because of (29, 30) and the penalty term of objective function, we hope to achieve $H_{ijt} = m_j$.

Overall, (21-32) give the mixed integer programming approach for World Expo problem in an ideal sensor network. $\{x_{ijt}\}_{i,t}$ gives the path P_j of group j while m_j is the size of the group. In the next section, we will do further improvement for applying the method in real situation.

3   Improvements for Practical Applications

3.1   Introduce a Super Vertex

In the former section, we come up with an algorithm to identify groups in an ideal sensor network. In practical situation, however, the sensor network is not ideal. Actually, to World Expo problem the common situation of sensor network is sparse as follows

$$R_i \cap R_{i'} = \phi, \quad i \neq i', \quad \text{and} \quad \bigcup_{i=1}^{I} R_i \subsetneq F. \tag{33}$$

It means that the sensors are disjoint but the sum of regions of sensors cannot cover the whole field. As a result, sometimes the sensor network can only detect part of a group. In such situation, the sum of observation data in time t is less than N. We have $\sum_{i=1}^{I} c_{it} \leq N, t = 2, ..., T - 1^2$. To make the algorithm available to real application, we need to make a little change on the graph G.

Define a super vertex S, which directly connects to all the vertices of G. After adding S, a new graph G' is gotten as Figure 2 shows. We can assume that the undetected targets all go to the super vertex at each time. Denote the residual data denoted as r_{St}, we have $r_{S1} = r_{ST} = 0$, and $r_{St} = N - \sum_{i=1}^{I} c_{it}$. According to the residual data, we can find the maximum one, which is denoted as $r_{St_{\max}}$. Then, we can apply the mixed integer programming approach on G' and corresponding data as follows.

$$\min \sum_{j=1}^{J'} y_j - \alpha \sum_{i=1}^{I'} \sum_{j=1}^{J'} \sum_{t=1}^{T} H_{ijt} \tag{34}$$

$$s.t. \quad x_{ijt} = 0 \quad or \quad 1, \tag{35}$$

$$y_j = 0 \quad or \quad 1, \tag{36}$$

$$-x_{ijt} + x_{ij,t+1} \leq 0, \quad v_i \in V_{en}, \tag{37}$$

$$x_{ijt} - x_{ij,t+1} \leq 0, \quad v_i \in V_{ex}, \tag{38}$$

$$x_{ijt} + x_{i'j,t+1} \leq 1, \quad v_{i'} \in D_i, \tag{39}$$

$$x_{ijt} \leq y_j, \tag{40}$$

$$\sum_{i-1}^{I'} x_{ijt} = y_j, \tag{41}$$

$$\sum_{j=1}^{J'} H_{ijt} \leq c_{it}, \quad H_{ijt} \in Z_+ \tag{42}$$

$$H_{ijt} \leq m_j, \tag{43}$$

$$H_{ijt} \leq N x_{ijt}, \tag{44}$$

$$\sum_{j=1}^{J'} m_j = N, \tag{45}$$

$$x_{Sjt_{\max}} = 1, \quad j = J + 1, ..., J', \tag{46}$$

$$m_j = 1, \quad j = J + 1, ..., J'. \tag{47}$$

Here $I' = I + 1$ because of taking S into consideration, and $J' = J + r_{St_{\max}}$. Besides the original assumed J groups, the additional constraints (46, 47) introduce another $r_{St_{\max}}$ groups. Each of these groups has only one target and all of them are not always able to be detected by the sensor network. As a result, the solution gotten by (35-47) is different from the ground truth, so we need to apply a post-processing strategy to merge the additional $r_{St_{\max}}$ groups into the assumed J groups.

3.2 The Strategy of Path Clustering

The groups and corresponding paths gotten by (35-47), $\{(m_j, P_j)\}_{j=1}^{J}$ can be classified into two classes C_1 and C_2. If $S \in P_j$ and $m_j = 1$, then $(m_j, P_j) \in C_1$. Otherwise, $(m_j, P_j) \in C_2$. If a group belongs to C_1, it means that it sometimes is not detected by the sensor network. Such a group should be merged into the group belonging to C_2.

---

[2] Here we assume that the N is a known variable, which can be gotten by the data in V_{en} or V_{ex}.

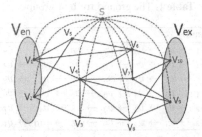

Fig. 2. The graph G' after adding super vertex S

What we want to do is to design a clustering strategy to merge the groups in C_1 with those in C_2 rightly.

To achieve this aim, we need to define a new operator "$\oplus$" between different paths P_j and $P_{j'}$, as follows.

$$P_{jt} \oplus P_{j't} = \sum_{t=1}^{T} p_{jt} \oplus p_{j't}, \tag{48}$$

$$p_{jt} \oplus p_{j't} = \begin{cases} 1, & p_{jt} = p_{j't}, \\ -1, & p_{jt} \neq p_{j't}, \\ 0, & p_{jt} \quad \text{or} \quad p_{j't} = S. \end{cases} \tag{49}$$

The principle of our clustering strategy is merging the group in C_1 to the group in C_2 with maximum value of "$\oplus$" value. The detail of the strategy as follows.

To each group j' in C_1: 1) calculate $P_{jt} \oplus P_{j't}$ with every group j in C_2;
2) find the group j having maximum value of $P_{jt} \oplus P_{j't}$;
3) achieve merging: $(m_j, P_j) = (m_j + m_{j'}, P_j)$, delete $(m_{j'}, P_{j'})$.

4 Experiments

4.1 Simulation Results

To demonstrate the feasibility and the robustness of the proposed method, we test the proposed method on an ideal sensor network and a sparse one, respectively. The ideal sensor network is defined as (1), which ensures each target can be detected by one sensor at each time. The sparse sensor network is defined as (33) so that the target may not be detected all the time. The graph of the two networks is described in Figure 2. In the model, there exists 6 groups moving in the graph, and the time sequence is $t = 1, ..., 8$. The ground truth of the sizes and the paths of groups is displayed in Table 1. The observational data c_{it} in ideal sensor network and sparse sensor network are shown in Table 2.

In the experiment, the we assume that the group number $J = 10$, which is larger than the actual number. After applying (21-32), we get the solution in Table 3. The parameter α is set as $J/(NT)$, which makes the penalty term comparable to the sum of y_j. From Table 3, we can find that the result gotten by proposed algorithm is equal

Table 1. The ground truth of groups

size	path
$m_1 = 5$	$v_1 \to v_6 \to v_4 \to v_7 \to v_6 \to v_4 \to v_8 \to v_{10}$
$m_2 = 7$	$v_1 \to v_1 \to v_5 \to v_6 \to v_4 \to v_3 \to v_8 \to v_{10}$
$m_3 = 8$	$v_1 \to v_1 \to v_1 \to v_4 \to v_3 \to v_8 \to v_8 \to v_9$
$m_4 = 10$	$v_1 \to v_5 \to v_5 \to v_6 \to v_4 \to v_9 \to v_9 \to v_9$
$m_5 = 12$	$v_2 \to v_4 \to v_3 \to v_3 \to v_8 \to v_4 \to v_7 \to v_{10}$
$m_6 = 13$	$v_2 \to v_3 \to v_4 \to v_6 \to v_6 \to v_{10} \to v_{10} \to v_{10}$

Table 2. The observational data in ideal sensor network (left) and sparse sensor network (right)

Ideal	v_1	v_2	v_3	v_4	v_5	v_6	v_7	v_8	v_9	v_{10}	S	Sparse	v_1	v_2	v_3	v_4	v_5	v_6	v_7	v_8	v_9	v_{10}	S
t_1	30	25	0	0	0	0	0	0	0	0	0	t_1	30	25	0	0	0	0	0	0	0	0	0
t_2	15	0	13	12	10	5	0	0	0	0	0	t_2	15	0	13	12	9	3	0	0	0	0	3
t_3	8	0	12	18	17	0	0	0	0	0	0	t_3	8	0	12	16	16	0	0	0	0	0	3
t_4	0	0	12	8	0	30	5	0	0	0	0	t_4	0	0	12	8	0	29	5	0	0	0	1
t_5	0	0	8	17	0	18	0	12	0	0	0	t_5	0	0	7	16	0	17	0	11	0	0	4
t_6	0	0	7	17	0	0	0	8	10	13	0	t_6	0	0	6	17	0	0	0	7	9	12	4
t_7	0	0	0	0	0	0	12	20	10	13	0	t_7	0	0	0	0	0	0	11	19	9	12	4
t_8	0	0	0	0	0	0	0	0	18	37	0	t_8	0	0	0	0	0	0	0	0	18	37	0

Table 3. The simulation results in the ideal sensor network

size	path
$m_i = 0, \quad i = 1 - 4$	
$m_5 = 5$	$v_1 \to v_6 \to v_4 \to v_7 \to v_6 \to v_4 \to v_8 \to v_{10}$
$m_6 = 7$	$v_1 \to v_1 \to v_5 \to v_6 \to v_4 \to v_3 \to v_8 \to v_{10}$
$m_7 = 8$	$v_1 \to v_1 \to v_1 \to v_4 \to v_3 \to v_8 \to v_8 \to v_9$
$m_8 = 10$	$v_1 \to v_5 \to v_5 \to v_6 \to v_4 \to v_9 \to v_9 \to v_9$
$m_9 = 12$	$v_2 \to v_4 \to v_3 \to v_3 \to v_8 \to v_4 \to v_7 \to v_{10}$
$m_{10} = 13$	$v_2 \to v_3 \to v_4 \to v_6 \to v_6 \to v_{10} \to v_{10} \to v_{10}$

Table 4. The simulation results in the sparse sensor network

size	path
$m_1 = 1$	$v_2 \to S \to S \to v_3 \to S \to S \to S \to v_9$
$m_2 = 1$	$v_1 \to S \to S \to S \to S \to S \to S \to v_9$
$m_3 = 1$	$v_1 \to v_1 \to v_1 \to v_4 \to S \to S \to S \to v_9$
$m_4 = 1$	$v_2 \to S \to S \to v_6 \to S \to S \to S \to v_9$
$m_1 = 5$	$v_1 \to v_6 \to v_4 \to v_7 \to v_6 \to v_4 \to v_8 \to v_{10}$
$m_2 = 7$	$v_1 \to v_1 \to v_5 \to v_6 \to v_4 \to v_3 \to v_8 \to v_{10}$
$m_3 = 7$	$v_1 \to v_1 \to v_1 \to v_4 \to v_3 \to v_8 \to v_8 \to v_9$
$m_4 = 9$	$v_1 \to v_5 \to v_5 \to v_6 \to v_4 \to v_9 \to v_9 \to v_9$
$m_5 = 11$	$v_2 \to v_4 \to v_4 \to v_6 \to v_6 \to v_4 \to v_7 \to v_{10}$
$m_6 = 12$	$v_2 \to v_3 \to v_3 \to v_6 \to v_6 \to v_{10} \to v_{10} \to v_{10}$

to the ground truth, which proves the feasibility of our method. It should be mentioned that compared with the original binary programming in Section 2.1, the dimension of the problem reduces from $N \times I \times T$ to $2J \times (I \times T + 1)$. Because $J \ll N$, the algorithm is accelerated.

On the other hand, in a sparse sensor network, the observation data is not completed. So the vertex S is used. From the right part of Table 2 we can find that $r_{St_{max}} = 4$, so the assumed group number is $J' = 14$. After applying (35-47), the initial solution is reported in Table 4[3]. With the help of the proposed clustering strategy, we get the final solution in Table 5.

The vertices in the brackets are ground truth. We can find that most of paths are estimated accurately, which proves the robustness of the proposed method. However, the reason for the errors in the final result is interesting, which reveals an adversary case of World Expo problem.

Table 5. The simulation results in the sparse sensor network

size	path						
$m_1 = 5$	$v_1 \to v_6 \to v_4$	$\to v_7$	$\to v_6$	$\to v_4$	$\to v_8$	$\to v_{10}$
$m_2 = 7$	$v_1 \to v_1 \to v_5$	$\to v_6$	$\to v_4$	$\to v_3$	$\to v_8$	$\to v_{10}$
$m_3 = 8$	$v_1 \to v_1 \to v_1$	$\to v_4$	$\to v_3$	$\to v_8$	$\to v_8$	$\to v_9$
$m_4 = 10$	$v_1 \to v_5 \to v_5$	$\to v_6$	$\to v_4$	$\to v_9$	$\to v_9$	$\to v_9$
$m_5 = 12$	$v_2 \to v_4 \to v_4(v_3)$	$\to v_6(v_3)$	$\to v_6(v_8)$	$\to v_4$	$\to v_7$	$\to v_{10}$
$m_6 = 13$	$v_2 \to v_3 \to v_3(v_4)$	$\to v_6$	$\to v_6$	$\to v_{10}$	$\to v_{10}$	$\to v_{10}$

4.2   An Adversary Case of World Expo Problem

From the experimental results above, we can find that the proposed method can achieve good identification results in the multi-target situation. However, it should be mentioned that in the two situations illustrated in Figure 3 World Expo Problem dose not have unique solution.

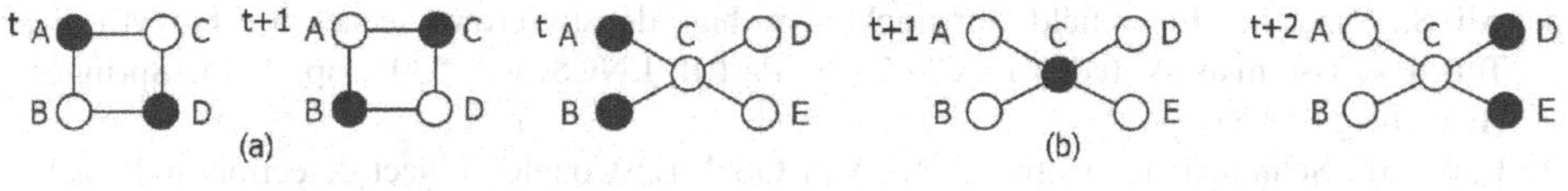

Fig. 3. Two situations leading to non-unique solution of World Expo problem

In Figure 3(a), two groups with the same size are observed by sensor A and D respectively at time t, which are marked by solid blue circles in the graph. At the next time $t + 1$, they are observed by sensor B and C. Because A is connected to B and C, and so is D, we do not have any method to identify whether the true paths are $\{A \to C, D \to B\}$ or $\{A \to B, D \to C\}$. Similarly in Figure 3(b), two groups with the same size are observed by sensor A and B at time t. At time $t + 1$, their

---

[3] In Table 4 and 5, the groups with 0 size are not shown.

paths cross in the sensor C and leave to C and D respectively at time $t + 2$. Because C is connected to A, B, C and D, we cannot identify whether the true paths are $\{A \to C \to D, B \to C \to E\}$ or $\{A \to C \to E, B \to C \to C\}$.

These two situations can be extended to the case that multiple groups with same size. It can be regarded as the worst case of World Expo problem. In such situations, the problem is impossible to be solved because we have multiple solutions while have no method to identify the truth. In fact, these conclusions are a generalization of the theory in [23]. [23] discusses the impossibility of multiple targets identification in binary sensor network, which is a special case with group size equals to 1. This limitation is the reason for the estimation error in Table VI, because the initial result before path clustering has groups with same size crossing together.

5   Conclusion

In this paper, we define a generalized multiple targets identification problem called World Expo problem, which is an important issue of social behavior analysis and sensor network. To solve this problem, we come up with a mixed integer programming approach, which is based on the fact that multiple targets share the same path in the problem. We design a path clustering strategy as the post-processing, which increases the robustness of the proposed method in sparse sensor network. Moreover, according to the feature of World Expo problem, we analyze an adversary case of World Expo problem and point out the limitation of the proposed method. In the future, we will further study the integer programming approach for World Expo problem and try to find the sufficient condition for the solvability of the problem.

References

1. Han, M., Xu, W., Tao, H., Gong, Y.: An algorithm for multiple object trajectory tracking. In: CVPR, pp. 864–871 (2004)
2. Saisan, P., Medasani, S., Owechko, Y.: Multi-view classifier swarms for pedestrian detection and tracking. In: CVPR, pp. 18 (2005)
3. Ali, S., Shah, M.: Floor fields for tracking in high density crowd scenes. In: Forsyth, D., Torr, P., Zisserman, A. (eds.) ECCV 2008, Part II. LNCS, vol. 5303, pp. 1–14. Springer, Heidelberg (2008)
4. Leibe, B., Schindler, K., Cornelis, N., Van Gool, L.: Coupled object detection and tracking from static cameras and moving vehicles. IEEE Transactions on Pattern Analysis and Machine Intelligence 30(10), 1683–1698 (2008)
5. Pellegrini, S., Ess, A., Schindler, K., van Gool, L.: You'll never walk alone: Modeling social behavior for multi-target tracking. In: ICCV, pp. 261–268 (2009)
6. Eagle, N., Pentland, A.: Reality mining: Sensing complex social system. Personal and Ubiquitous Computing 10(4), 255–268 (2006)
7. Celikoglu, H.B., Cigizoglu, H.K.: Public transportation trip flow modeling with generalized regression neural networks. Advances in Engineering Software 38, 71–79 (2007)
8. Vinciarelli, A., Pantic, M., Bourlard, H., Pentland, A.: Social signal processing: State-of-the-art and future perspectives of an emerging domain. In: Proceedings of the ACM International Conference on Multimedia, Vancouver, Canada, pp. 1061–1070 (2008)

9. Cristani, M., Murino, V., Vinciarelli, A.: Socially intelligent surveillance and monitoring: Analysing social dimensions of physical space. In: Proceedings of International Workshop on Society Intelligent Surveillance and Monitoring, San Francisco, USA, pp. 51–58 (2010)
10. Pickard, G., Pan, W., et al.: Time-critical social mobilization. Science 334(6055), 509–512 (2011)
11. Olfati-Saber, R.: Distributed kalman filtering for sensor networks. In: 46th IEEE Conference on Decision and Control, pp. 5492–5498 (2007)
12. Djuric, P., Vemula, M., Bugallo, M.: Target tracking by particle filtering in binary sensor networks. IEEE Transactions on Signal Processing 56(6), 2229–2238 (2008)
13. Oh, S., Sastry, S.: Tracking on a graph. In: Fourth International Symposium on Information Processing in Sensor Networks (IPSN), pp. 195–202 (2005)
14. De, D., Song, W.Z., Xu, M., Cook, D., Huo, X.: Real-time tracking of motion trajectories from anonymous binary sensing in smart environments. In: The 32nd International Conference on Distributed Computing Systems (2012)
15. Shrivastava, N., Madhow, R.M.U., Suri, S.: Target tracking with binary proximity sensors: fundamental limits, minimal descriptions, and algorithms. In: 4th International Conference on Embedded Networked Sensor Systems, pp. 251–264 (2006)
16. Crespi, V., Cybenko, G., Jiang, G.: The theory of trackability with applications to sensor networks. ACM Transactions on Sensor Networks (TOSN) 4(3), 16 (2008)
17. Shrivastava, N., Mudumbai, R., Madhow, U., Suri, S.: Target tracking with binary proximity sensors. ACM Transactions on Sensor Networks (TOSN) 5(4), 30 (2009)
18. Lazos, L., Poovendran, R., Ritcey, J.: Analytic evaluation of target detection in heterogeneous wireless sensor networks. ACM Transactions on Sensor Networks (TOSN) 5(2), 18 (2009)
19. Arora, A., Ramnath, R., et al.: Exscal: elements of an extreme scale wireless sensor network. In: 11th IEEE International Conference on Embedded and Real-Time Computing Systems and Applications, pp. 102–108 (2005)
20. Arora, A., Dutta, P., et al.: A line in the sand: a wireless sensor network for target detection, classification, and tracking. Computer Networks 46(5), 605–634 (2004)
21. Singh, J., Madhow, U., Kumar, R., Suri, S., Cagley, R.: Tracking multiple targets using binary proximity sensors. In: 6th International Conference on Information Processing in Sensor Networks, pp. 529–538 (2007)
22. Wang, C., Huo, X., Song, W.Z.: An integer programming approach for multiple-target trajectory identification with binary proximity sensors. Annals of Operations Research (2012) (submitted)
23. Busnel, Y., Querzoni, L., Baldoni, R., Bertier, M., Kermarrec, A.: Analysis of deterministic tracking of multiple objects using a binary sensor network. ACM Transactions on Sensor Networks (TOSN) 42(4), 8 (2011)
24. Cao, L.: In-depth behavior understanding and use: the behavior informatics approach. Information Sciences 180(17), 3067–3085 (2010)

Semantic Change Computation: A Successive Approach

Xuri Tang[1], Weiguang Qu[2], and Xiaohe Chen[3]

[1] Foreign Language School,
HuaZhong University of Science and Technology, Wuhan 430074, China
xrtang@hust.edu.cn
[2] School of Computer Science, Nanjing Normal University, Nanjing 210023, China
wgqu_nj@163.com
[3] School of Chinese Language and Literature,
Nanjing Normal University, Nanjing 210023, China
chenxiaohe5209@126.com

Abstract. The prevalence of creativity in the emergent online media language calls for more effective computational approach to semantic change. This paper advocates the successive view of semantic change and proposes a successive framework for automatic semantic change detection. The framework measures Word Status of a word in a time unit with entropy, forms a time series data with the Word Statuses obtained from successive time units, and applies curve-fitting to obtain change pattern over the time series data. Experiments with the framework show that change pattern, the speed of change in particular, can be successfully related to classical semantic change categories such as broadening, narrowing, new word coining, metaphorical change, and metonymic change. By transforming the task of semantic computation into change pattern detection, the framework makes a plausible platform for semantic change investigation.

1 Introduction

The realm of Computational Linguistics has witnessed a recent upsurge of interest in semantic change computation [1–9], due to the growing demand from emergent online services over internet, such as microblog, e-commerce, online advertising, and social networking etc. The language used in these services has been coining terms and introducing playful variations into established ones at no parallel rate in contemporary language use[10, p.67]. Accordingly, Natural Language Processing tasks associated with these services, including those basic tasks such as syntactic parsing and word sense disambiguation, and higher level applications such as automatic translation and dialogue systems, need access to the knowledge of semantic change. In addition, studies in lexicography also need a tool to help to pin down semantic change so that new senses can be more quickly accounted for in dictionaries.

The phenomenon can be illustrated with Example 1[1], which shows a metaphorical semantic change of the Chinese word *toumin*. In 1951, the word generally meant "*transparent*", a property of glass, water and other physical objects. But in 2001 it is observed

---

[1] Examples in the paper are all taken from the Chinese newspaper *People's Daily*. Numbers in the bracket denote the years.

L. Cao et al. (Eds.): BSIC/BSI 2013, LNAI 8178, pp. 68–81, 2013.

to acquire a new sense (*"overt"*) used for semantic domains such as market, government and legislation etc., which are generally abstract. In semantics, this phenomenon is studied in Semasiology, which takes interest in the Lexeme(L)-Meaning(M) pair and "investigates what changes did meaning M of L undergo [11, p.25] ".

Example 1

a. *Toumin* de beizi li zhen man jiu. (1951)

  The *transparent* glass is filled with liquor.

b. Shichang jinji yinggai changdao *toumin* xiaofei. (2001)

  Overt consumption should be advocated in market economy.

Studies on semantic change computation are observed to be still at a primal stage, with several issues waiting to be further explored. Researches are still divergent in understanding the basic nature of the task. The dominant view regards semantic change as a juxtapositional phenomena, as is in [12, 4, 2, 5], assuming that semantic change is the comparison and contrast of the word usage in two corpora of different periods of time. The other view, found in [9, 6, 8, 7], believes that semantic change is successively diachronic by nature and is embodied as a trend of change which is only detectable on corpora divided into temporally ordered stages, with or without gap in between. In addition, Automation of semantic change detection is only reported in a few works, with limited scale and coverage. For instance, [8] employs Semantic Density Analysis to check the validity of two types of semantic change, namely narrowing and broadening, on 4 words; [13] compares point-wise mutual information of 8 words in three corpora for categorization of amelioration and pejoration. Models which are capable of accommodating large scale semantic change detection and categorization are needed.

Based on the belief that semantic change is a process of successive and diachronic innovation over a span of time, this paper proposes a successive framework which automatically classifies a word into those established categories in theoretical semantic change studies, such as changed, unchanged, broadening, narrowing, newly coined words, metaphorical change, metonymic change and so on. Such a framework builds the connections between semantic change and behavior informatics and computing [14]. The framework employs Word-Context Model for sense representation, characterizes word usage within a period with entropy-based concept of Word Status, and applies curve-fitting for trend detection. With analyses on the parameters that constitute the trend, words' semantic change are categorized into different types. The plausible experiment results show that the framework can be used as a feasible platform for large scale investigation of word-based semantic change.

2 Successive View of Semantic Change

The metaphysical understanding on semantic change as a succession is inherited from [15], which defines the concept as below:

> "The thing changes from q_1 to q_2" is completely analyzable into a statement of the kind "There is a certain series of successive events so interrelated that it counts as the history of a certain thing [X], e_1 and e_2 are two successive adjoined phases in this series and e_1 has Q in the form q_1, while e_2 has Q in the form q_2 ..." [15, p.297]

Studies on this understanding possess two distinctive features, as compared with juxtaposition view of semantic change. The first lies in the type of data used for investigation. Successive view considers linguistic data from the successive stages over a historical period of time. Thus to account for the semantic change of words like *toumin*, a successive sequence of data (depicted in Figure 1) collected from corpora ranging from 1951 to 2001 should be investigated. But the juxtaposition view may just focus on two or more individual years, which may or may not be adjacent. In this aspect, the advantage of successive view over juxtaposition view is obvious, as the former gives a detailed and faithfully record of the phenomenon. The second distinctive feature is more important. As is discussed in [16], it is possible for successive view of semantic change to reveal the intimate inter-connection by spatial, causal and other relations between the successive members, which gives it the power to portray the pattern of change for a word. This can't be done with juxtaposition view. It has omitted a lot details in-between and its ability to detect change pattern is weak.

$$q_{1951}, \quad q_{1952}, \cdots q_{1959}, \cdots q_{2001}$$

Fig. 1. Successive View of Semantic Change

Studies like [9, 6, 8, 7] opt for this view of change. But they use the successive data only for human analyses or evaluation purposes, not for automatic detection. For example, [7] adopts methods from Information Visualization and Visual Analytics to visualize the context in which the words occur so as to guide researches by generating new hypotheses about development of semantic change; [6] makes use of correlations between frequency change and some ranking to look for some trend of change; [8] plots the sequence of change between the rise of semantic density and the percentage of use measured by human beings to show the feasibility of semantic density based approach. This usage of human analyses can be illustrated in Figure 2. The principle of uniformitarianism [17, 18] allows for confident prediction that the word is undergoing a change, but it does not tell the type of change it is undergoing, nor relate the type of change to the change in its inner semantic structure. This paper believes that successive view of semantic change can be further exploited to infer inner structural change of the word and predict its tendency in future by examining the process in details.

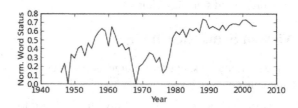

Fig. 2. Semantic Change of *toumin* in about 60 Years. Normalized Word Status of Y-axis is explained in Section 3.1.

3 Successive Semantic Change Computation

Based on the successive view of semantic change, this section constructs a framework to characterize the change pattern and relates the type of change to change in inner structures. The framework, depicted in Figure 3, is word oriented. It takes as input three things: the word to be studied, the historical time span under investigation, and the corpora. To start with, the corpora should be firstly divided in a successive mode into a series, with each two adjoining time units in temporal order. For each time-unit corpus, the concept of Word Status is proposed to denote the state-of-affairs of the word's inner semantic structure in the time unit, which is measured quantitatively with sense entropy. The Word Statuses over all time-unit corpora are then obtained and formed into a time series data. The Change Pattern Detection is then performed over the time series data to obtain parameters that characterize the trend of change, which are then used for categorization. Due to the fact that Word Status is a reflection of the word's inner sense structure, and that the word's inner sense structure is associated with word's denotation, the obtained trend of change has to be denotation-related, which is useful in predicting how the word is used. The components of Time-Unit Based Word Status Measurement and Word change Pattern Detection are explained in this section. Denotation-Related Word Change Categorization is illustrated in section 4.

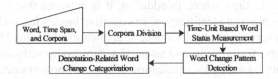

Fig. 3. Successive Semantic Change Computation Framework

3.1 Time-Unit Based Word Status Measurement

Semantic change is the change in a word's inner semantic structure and outward usage of the senses, called Word Status in this paper. For a target word T, two important issues needs to be considered to obtain its Word Status: (1) representation of senses for T and (2) accounting for usage of the senses in a time-unit corpus.

Sense Representation. This paper represents word senses with Word-Context Model, one of the subtypes of Vector Space Models [19]. The model is an explicit form of the Distributional Hypothesis, originating from [20–23], in which word senses are distinguished and represented by the context in which it occurs. According to the model, a sense of a word in a sentence can be a tuple $c =< T, W_{max} >$, in which T is the target word and W_{max} is the co-occurring word with the strongest association strength within a window size of ± 9 in the sentence. To better represent the denotation of the word, this paper has narrowed the "Word" into "Noun" and employs the Noun-Word-Context model, denoted by a tuple $< T, N_{max} >$, to represent the target word's senses in every sentences in corpora. In the tuple, N_{max} is the noun with the maximum association strength. The association strength is computed via Likelihood Ratio Test [24], the method of which is widely used for collocation extraction. Formula 1 gives the null hypothesis for the distributions of two words, and Formula 2 gives the alternative hypothesis.

$$H_1 : p = P(w_2|w_1) = P(w_2| \sim w_1) \tag{1}$$

$$H_2 : p_1 = P(w_2|w_1), p_2 = P(w_2| \sim w_1), p1 \neq p2 \tag{2}$$

Example 2
a. *Toumin* de *beizi* li zhen man jiu. (1951)
   $<$*toumin, beizi*$> \rightarrow$ TRANSPARENT
b. Shichang jinji yinggai changdao *toumin xiaofei*. (2001)
   $<$*toumin, xiaofei*$> \rightarrow$ OVERT

The choice of Noun-Word-Context model is based on the fact that the change in denotation is often reflected in the change of semantic domain, which is generally denoted by a noun. Take again *toumin* for example. The change of its application domain from "physical materials" to "spiritual world" is denoted by the noun *beizi(glass)* in Example 2a and the noun *xinling(soul)* in Example 2b. Thus the change of denotation is reflected by change in nouns in the context. In addition, It is believed that nouns are playing more dominant role in sense identification. In cognitive linguistics, entities represented by nouns generally serve as the background, or application domain [25, p.61] for making sense of language, while events and properties, denoted by verbs and adjectives, are attached to the entity for explicit identification of senses. Furthermore, investigation on the HowNet [26][2] shows that the average sense item number for nouns is 1.083, lower than verbs, the average sense item number of which is 1.14, and adjectives, the average of sense item number of which is 1.10.

Word Status Measurement. Once the senses for the target word T are identified and represented for every sentence in a time-unit corpus, the distribution of the senses over the corpus can be collected. Thus the Word Status for T over the t time-unit corpus $\mathcal{S}_t^T$ can be represented as below:

$$\mathcal{S}_t^T = \begin{bmatrix} C_T \\ P(c) \end{bmatrix} = \begin{bmatrix} c_1, & c_2, & \ldots, & c_n \\ p(c_1), & p(c_2), & \ldots, & p(c_n) \end{bmatrix} \tag{3}$$

The senses for T is denoted with $C_T = c_1, c_2, \ldots, c_n$, the probabilities for the senses are described by $p(c_i)$.

---

[2] HowNet is an on-line common-sense knowledge base compiled by Zhendong DONG and Qian DONG, which includes as its part definitions for words in both Chinese and English. A detailed introduction can be found at
http://www.keenage.com/zhiwang/e_zhiwang.html. The average sense item numbers for nouns, verbs and adjectives are computed with Chinese words.

If the word T is regarded as a discrete source of information, the concept of Word Status, namely the number of senses and the frequency of use of the senses, can be interpreted as the uncertainty of the information source, which can be measured by the Entropy of the information source. Thus the Word Status can be summed up in Formula 4:

$$S_t^T \approx H(C_T) = E(log\frac{1}{p(c_i)}) = -\sum_{i=1}^{n}p(c_i)logp(c_i) \tag{4}$$

$$p(c_i) = \frac{count(c_i)}{count(T)} \tag{5}$$

Where $count(c_i)$ is the frequency of the sense c_i in the corpus, and $count(T)$ is the frequency of the target word T, $\sum_{i=1}^{n}p(c_i) = 1$.

Word Status fluctuates diachronically with change in the word's inner sense structure and usage. This can be easily seen in Table 1. Suppose the word *toumin* had one sense in 1951, two senses in 1959 and three senses in 2001. Their yearly distributions are indicated in the table. It can be seen that the Word Status increased sharply from 0 to 4.796, proving it to be an applaudable indicator of semantic change of the word.

Table 1. Illustration of Word Status Computation with *toumin*

Time Unit	$p(c_1)$	$p(c_2)$	$p(c_3)$	S_{toumin}
1951	1.0	0	0	0
1959	0.6	0.4	0	2.0589
2001	0.4	0.3	0.3	4.796

3.2 Word Change Pattern Detection

For the target word T, Time-Unit Based Word Status Measurement can yield a series of Word Status data $\{ = \{S_{t_1}^T, S_{t_2}^T, \ldots, S_{t_n}^T\}$ from the corpora, which is actually a time series. The task of Word Change Pattern Detection is to find a time series model to suit the data and obtain the parameters for the model as its change pattern.

To our knowledge, there is perhaps no model proposed for semantic change. But in the field of historical linguistics, one particular exponential model, namely the S-Shaped Curve, has been proposed to model language change. An early specification of "S-Shaped Curve" can be found in [27], which explicitly stipulates the model as one of principles in language change:

A given change begins quite gradually; after reaching a certain point (say, twenty per cent), it picks up momentum and proceeds at a much faster rate; and finally tails off slowly before reaching completion. The result is an s-curve: the statistical differences among isolects in the middle relative times of the change will be greater than the statistical differences among the early and late isolects [27, p.77].

The concept of "S-Shaped Curve" is also found in [28] and [29], and is testified in examination of grammatical change [30], sound change [31] and other language change researches. Semantic change taking on an S-Shaped Curve is justified by the view on semantic change as "diffusion", which regards language change as newly formed signifier-signified pair propagating through the community, and "such curves (S-Shaped Curves) are widely found in diffusions, both for cultural events and biological events"[32].

One explicit model (Formula 6) is used by [30] for the S-Shaped Curve:

$$p = \frac{e^{k+st}}{1 + e^{k+st}} \qquad (6)$$

where p is the fraction of the advancing form, t is the time variable, s and k are constants. As is discussed in [33], Formula 6 defines a set of functions which differ only in the two constants. The constant k denotes the intercept of the curve, while the constant s denotes the slope of the curve (Figure 4). Interpreted in semantic change, the constant k, the intercept of the curve, serves as the indication of the Word Status where the word starts to change. And the s indicates the slope which denotes the rate of change of Word Status. These two constants together determine the pattern of change of the time series data. The coming experiments show that the information provided by these two constants are sufficient to decide the type of semantic change for a particular word.

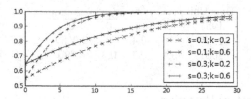

Fig. 4. Logarithmic Function with Different k and s Values

Once the time series of Word Status data is obtained for a word, and Formula 6 is chosen to model its semantic change, the two parameters can be easily obtained with curve-fitting [3]. For instance, applying curve-fitting on the Word Status series for *toumin*, we are able to have $k = -1.0319$ and $s = 0.0307$. As is seen in Figure 5, curve-fitting is able to leach away the random noise of semantic change observed in history and expose the trend of change for the word. In the figure, a violent fluctuation of change can be observed in the late 1960s and the most part of 1070s, due to external social factors in China. But curve-fitting helps to leach away its effect on the trend.

---

[3] Curve fitting is generally approached with least squares regression. To fit the function families formed with formula 4 to $S = [x_1, x_2, \ldots, x_n]$, the time series data of Word Status, least squares regression chooses the values for parameters k and s to minimize $\sum_{t=1}^{n}(x_t - m_t)^2$, where m_t is obtained with Formula 4 with certain k and s values. Please refer to [34] for more discussion. This research uses 1stopt(version 1.5, http://www.7d-soft.com/) for curve-fitting. Other tools for curve-fitting can be found in package scipy.optimize or Matlab etc.

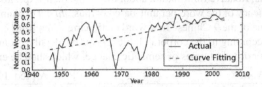

Fig. 5. Time Series Data for *toumin* and Curve-Fitting Result with $s = 0.0307$ and $k = -1.0319$

4   Experiments and Analyses

A number of 45 words are collected in the experiments, 33 from 9 Chinese New Word Dictionaries (Listed in Appendix A) which are judged to have undergone semantic change by dictionary compilers, and another 12 words not found in these dictionaries and thus considered unchanged. Features such as parts of speech and average frequency are also considered in collecting the words.

The corpora used in the research are constructed from the Chinese newspaper "People's Daily". The overall linguistic data from the newspaper are divided yearly, thus obtaining a diachronic corpora spanning from 1946 to 2004, a total of 59 years. The corpora are segmented and POS tagged with ICTCLAS[4]. The average annual token sum in the corpora is 10,886,017.

Following Figure 3, for each target word, Word Statuses are collected and formed into a time series data, and curve-fitting is then used to obtain the two constants k and s in Formula 6. Their corresponding values are given in Table 2. Examination on the value distribution of k and s in the table shows obvious regularity which can be employed to detect important semantic change distinction such as "Changed vs. Unchanged", "Broadening vs. Narrowing", and "Newly Coined, Metaphorical Change and Metonymic Change". Details are discussed below.

4.1   Changed vs. Unchanged

The gold standard used for evaluation on "Changed" and "Unchanged" categorization is defined by the *Indict* field in Table 2. If the word is included in one of the 9 Chinese new word dictionaries, it is considered to be "Changed" in semantics. Otherwise it is not. By stipulating a demarcation span of s value in the table, we can group the words into two types: "Changed" and "Unchanged". If the demarcation boundary is set to be $[-0.005 \sim 0.01]$, and stipulation is made that those words with values outside the set are considered to be "Changed", it can be seen that 32 words are correctly identified as "Changed" and 4 words are correctly identified as "Unchanged". Thus the precision for detection of "Changed Word" in the current experiment is $(32 + 4)/45 = 80\%$, the recall for the "Changed" type is $32/33 = 96.97\%$, and the recall for the "Unchanged" is $4/12 = 30\%$. The low recall rate for "Unchanged" actually indicates a problem with current approach of evaluation. The fact that a word is not found in the 9 dictionaries does not necessarily mean that it has not undergone semantic change. Based on the

---

[4] http://www.ictclas.org/, version2011

Table 2. Selected Words, Relative Information about them, and their Experiment Results. *A.Freq* stands for average frequency of the word per unit-based corpus. *InDict* explains whether the word is included in at least one of the 9 Chinese new word dictionaries. *NewWord* explains whether the word is newly coined according to the corpora (Table 3 gives the details). Four lines are drawn in the table as boundary for different types of semantic change, which shall be explained shortly.

Word	k	s	POS	A.Freq	InDict	NewWord
suoshui (shrink)	-14.09	0.248	V	6.90	Yes	Yes
fanghuoqiang (firewall)	-14.28	0.241	N	7.94	Yes	No
danchu (fade out)	-13.58	0.239	V	5.50	Yes	Yes
mohe (ink box)	-12.74	0.205	N	3.29	No	No
ruwei (be enclosed)	-10.08	0.188	V	21.30	Yes	Yes
huinuan (get warmer)	-9.31	0.144	V	3.97	Yes	Yes
chuju (be out)	-6.77	0.133	V	20.54	Yes	Yes
wangluo (net)	-5.09	0.121	N	734.67	Yes	No
digu (low valley)	-5.69	0.118	N	52.81	Yes	Yes
yongdong (surge up)	-5.42	0.112	V	45.90	Yes	Yes
ruanjian (software)	-4.84	0.108	N	537.71	Yes	Yes
chonglang (surf)	-5.92	0.102	V	7.88	Yes	Yes
lianyin (marriage)	-5.19	0.101	V	29.82	Yes	Yes
danhua (desalt)	-4.54	0.095	V	57.79	Yes	Yes
touzhi (overdraft)	-5.41	0.094	V	17.68	No	No
yanyi (deduct)	-4.59	0.093	V	28.56	Yes	No
zhandian (station)	-4.81	0.093	N	23.61	No	Yes
bankuai (plate)	-4.13	0.083	N	34.63	Yes	Yes
baitiao (IOU note)	-4.03	0.080	N	39.78	Yes	No
dan'gao (cake)	-3.01	0.065	N	30.07	No	No
daguofan (to share meal from a big cooker)	-2.74	0.063	N	102.41	Yes	No
caidan (menu)	-3.19	0.053	N	9.87	Yes	No
dayin (print)	-2.46	0.051	V	23.80	No	No
chongdian (charge)	-2.74	0.047	V	16.02	Yes	No
shangfu (float up)	-3.08	0.045	V	12.98	Yes	No
jinghua (decontaminate)	-1.82	0.039	V	89.08	Yes	No
bingdu (virus)	-1.22	0.032	N	172.16	Yes	No
touming (transparent)	-1.00	0.031	A	67.66	Yes	No
chuangkou (window)	-0.44	0.025	N	179.49	Yes	No
liushi (drain)	-1.69	0.023	V	242.18	Yes	No
tongguo (pass)	1.03	0.021	V	6522.20	No	No
laji (rubbish)	0.19	0.020	N	265.22	No	No
luse (green)	0.16	0.019	A	387.10	Yes	No
heibai (black and white)	-0.89	0.017	A	48.95	Yes	No
re (hot)	1.09	0.015	A	636.90	Yes	No
qifei (take off)	-0.55	0.012	V	104.90	Yes	No
huise (grey)	-0.33	0.010	A	42.81	Yes	No
zhengming (testify)	0.79	0.009	V	1821.03	No	No
fangwu (house)	1.07	0.004	N	427.84	No	No
zhengfa (vaporize)	-0.91	0.003	V	39.98	No	No
baozha (explode)	0.55	-0.001	N/V	370.12	Yes	No
qiche (automobile)	1.45	-0.001	N	1994.45	No	No
guanxi (relation)	1.16	-0.007	N/V	8013.55	Yes	No
diluo (low tide)	-0.77	-0.008	A	39.47	Yes	No
chazu (to lay foot on)	-0.92	-0.012	V	6.86	No	No

authors' language experience and reflection, the words as *touzhi, zhangdian, dan'gao, tongguo*, and *chazhu* have acquired new senses in the past decades. New conventionalized senses can be found for these words. But they are not included in the dictionaries.

4.2 Broadening vs. Narrowing

The distinction between word sense broadening and narrowing is associated with the change of referential range. When the relatively restricted referential range of a word looses, word sense broadening happens. Instead, when the referential range of a word's meaning gets narrow, word sense narrowing happens [35]. From their definitions, it can be further inferred that broadening leads to an increase in both the sum and types of collocating nouns with the target word, which in turn shall result in an increasing Word Status and a positive s value. However, narrowing shall reduce the number of collocating nouns and the types of collocating nouns, leading to a decreasing Word Status and a negative s value. Thus stipulation on pattern change can be made for the distinction between word sense broadening and narrowing: If $s > 0$, the word may be experiencing a process of broadening; On the contrary, if $s < 0$, the word is considered to be undergoing a narrowing semantic change.

Two words in the experiments are experiencing the typical process of sense broadening: *mohe (ink box)* and *dayin (print)*. These two words are not included in the 9 New Word Dictionaries, but both enjoy fairly high s values. This phenomenon can be explained with knowledge in computer technology. These two words were originally associated with old printing technology and were fairly limited in their usage. However, the innovation of computer technology has brought innovation in printing and has broadened the usage of the two words. Thus the referential range of these two words have been dramatically expanded to several new fields where printing technology is employed. In the experiment, three words, namely *guanxi, diluo* and *chazhu*, are found to have s values less than -0.005. In Figure 6, the Word Status data for *diluo* is given, showing a declining trend. The word originally means "low" as in "low tide". Investigation on the corpora shows that in the beginning years, the word has been used metaphorically to describe a couple of semantic domains, such as CONSUMPTION, PRODUCTIVITY, and MARKET etc. But in the ending years, only two collocation patterns are found for the word: *qingxu(emotion) diluo(low)* and *shiqi(morale) diluo(low)*.

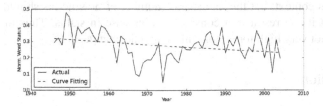

Fig. 6. Narrowing Word Semantic Change Example. Word Status data for *diluo* and its curve-fitting are shown, with $s = -0.0076$ and $k = -0.7574$.

4.3   Newly Coined Words, Metaphorical Change and Metonymic Change

Newly Coined Words are words that were not used at the beginning phase in the historical span and were coined and adopted in later stages. 13 words in Table 3 are found to be new words judged by the fact that they are not found in the first 8 years in the corpora. Examination on the k and s values of these words reveals a striking regularity: newly coined words are characterized with relatively low k values and relatively high s values. All the newly coined words in Table 2 have $k < -4.0$ and $s > 0.08$. And among the 19 words within this range, only 6 do not belong to this category. The explanation for this type is straight forward. These words were not used (thus $WordStatus = 0$), and then were propagated in the speech community (thus a sharp rise).

Table 3. New Coined Words With First Years of Occurrence

Word	First Occur.	word	First Occur.	Word	First Occur.	word	First Occur.
suoshui	1954	danhua	1959	danchu	1965	ruanjian	1977
huinuan	1957	zhandian	1959	bankuai	1973	chuju	1980
digu	1959	lianyin	1962	yongdong	1977	chonglang	1981
						ruwei	1992

Metaphorical change is one the two major mechanisms in semantic change for existing words [36, 11]. As can be seen in Table 2, this type of semantic change is faithfully reflected in the pattern of change. The examination of interval for $0.08 > s > 0.02$ and $-1.0 > k > -0.4$ in Table 2 shows that nearly all the words within the interval are involved with metaphorical change. The intuitive interpretation for lower k values is that the Chinese language, or all languages in general, prefer to choose words with less senses as candidate bearers of new senses in metaphorical change. Fairly high s values are resulted from the metaphorical transfer from one domain to another to create a new referential value.

The examination on Table 2 shows that there are 5 words with s between [0.01-0.02], and 3 of them, namely *luse*, *re* and *huise* are involved in metonymic change. By definition, metonymic change differs from metaphorical change in that the reference shift happens between two concepts which possess the contiguity relationship. Thus "metonymy operates within the same domain: it allows the transfer of referential values within a single semantic domain"[25, p.68]. Accordingly, metonymic change may result in increase of Word Status, because new usage may introduce new noun neighbors into the word's context, but the increase of number of new nouns should NOT be so significant that it can result in a conspicuous increase in status. Thus the value of s generally are not very high for metonymic semantic change.

5   Conclusions

The realm of lexical semantics, including computational lexical semantics, is under the impression that automatic semantic change computation is hard, if possible, because semantic change is "simply a chaos, a fuzzy, highly irregular procedure which is extremely difficult to predict[18, p.308]". However, this paper has demonstrated that when the the successive view of semantic change is adopted, the task of semantic change computation is feasible. The succession-based framework proposed in the paper transforms the task into pattern change analysis over time series data and employs pattern change detection techniques to uncover the regularity in the change of words' inner sense structure and outward usage. It proposes to aggregate the Word Statuses in a time unit using entropy, forms a time series from Word Statuses in different time units, and then uses curve-fitting techniques to capture the pattern of semantic change over the data. The experiments show that the change pattern, more specifically the speed of change in the pattern, is closely related to those established semantic change categories, due to the fact that speed of change is correlated with semantic structure and frequency of use. Different semantic change categories thus have different change patterns. With the framework, it is possible to determine the type of change a word is undergoing by computing its change pattern.

The framework is considered to possess several advantages over models proposed by [8] and [13]. At the foremost, the successive view of semantic change provides details of semantic change and thus enables more confidential prediction of semantic change for a given word. Secondly, Entropy based Word Status Measurement is more efficient than Latent Semantic Analysis, especially on very large corpus. The last but the most important advantage of the framework is that the sense representation of Word-Context Model makes it possible to expand automatic semantic change computation to cover most of the classic semantic change types such as "changed vs. unchanged", "broadening vs. narrowing", and "newly coined words, metaphorical change and metonymic change". With a little modification, the framework may also be able to account for "pejoration vs. amelioration".

In addition, the same approach can also be possibly applied to individual senses of a word, if the state-of-affairs of a sense within a time unit can be measured. When the trends of individual senses of a word are plotted out, together with the overall trend of the word, a full picture of semantic change of the word can be portrayed. Research on this topic is already underway.

Acknowledgments. This research is partially supported by the Chinese National Fund of Social Science (11CYY030), the Chinese National Fund of Natural Science (61272221), and Jiangshu Provincial Fund of Social Science (12YYA002). Acknowledgements should also be given to the three anonymous reviewers for their enlightening comments which help to improve the paper to a great extent.

References

1. Boussidan, A., Ploux, S.: Using topic salience and connotational drifts to detect candidates to semantic change. In: Proceedings of the 9th International Conference on Computational Semantics, pp. 315–319 (2011)
2. Cavallin, K.: Automatic extraction of potential examples of semantic change using lexical sets. In: Proceedings of the 11th Conference on Natural Language Processing, pp. 370–377 (2012)
3. Erk, K.: Unknown word sense detection as outlier detection. In: Proceedings of the Main Conference on Human Language Technology Conference of the North American Chapter of the Association of Computational Linguistics, pp. 128–135 (2006)

4. Gulordava, K., Baroni, M.: A distributional similarity approach to the detection of semantic change in the google books ngram corpus. In: Proceedings of the GEMS 2011 Workshop on GEometrical Models of Natural Language Semantics, pp. 67–71 (2011)

5. Lau, J.H., Cook, P., McCarthy, D., Newman, D., Baldwin, T.: Word sense induction for novel sense detection. In: Proceedings of the 13th Conference of the European Chapter of the Association for Computational Linguistics, pp. 591–601 (2012)

6. Hilpert, M., Gries, S.T.: Assessing frequency changes in multistage diachronic corpora: Applications for historical corpus linguistics and the study of language acquisition. Literary and Linguistic Computing 25(4), 385–401 (2009)

7. Rohrdantz, C., Hautli, A., Mayer, T., Butt, M., Keim, D.A., Plank, F.: Towards tracking semantic change by visual analytics. In: Proceedings of the 49th Annual Meeting of the Association for Computational Linguistics: Human Language Technologies, pp. 305–310 (2011)

8. Sagi, E., Kaufmann, S., Clark, B.: Semantic density analysis: comparing word meaning across time and phonetic space. In: Proceedings of the Workshop on Geometrical Models of Natural Language Semantics, pp. 104–111 (2009)

9. Sanchez-Marco, C., Evert, S.: Measuring semantic change: The case of spanish participial constructions. In: Proceedings of Quantitative Investigations in Theoretical Linguistics, vol. 4, pp. 79–83 (2011)

10. Crystal, D.: Language and the Internet, 2nd edn. Cambridge University Press, New York (2006)

11. Traugott, E.C., Dasher, R.B.: Regularity in semantic change. Cambridge University Press, Cambridge (2002)

12. Cook, P., Hirst, G.: Automatic identification of words with novel but infrequent senses. In: Proceedings of the 25th Pacific Asia Conference on Language Information and Computation, pp. 265–274 (2011)

13. Cook, P., Stevenson, S.: Automatically identifying changes in the semantic orientation of words. In: Proceedings of the 7th Conference on International Language Resources and Evaluation, pp. 28–34 (2010)

14. Cao, L.: In-depth behavior understanding and use: the behavior informatics approach. Information Sciences 180(17), 3067–3085 (2010)

15. Broad, C.D.: Examination of McTaggart's philosophy, vol. II. Cambridge Univ. Press, Cambridge (1938)

16. Andersen, H.: Understanding linguistic innovations. In: Breivik, L.E., Jahr, E.H. (eds.) Language Change: Contributions to the Study of its Causes, Mouton de Gruyter, Berlin, New York, pp. 5–27 (1989)

17. Labov, W.: Sociolinguistic Patterns. University of Pennsylvania Press, Philadelphia (1972)

18. Hock, H.H.: Principles of Historical Linguistics. 2nd rev. and updated edn. Mouton de Gruyter, Berlin (1991)

19. Turney, P.D., Pantel, P.: From frequency to meaning: vector space models of semantics. Journal of Artificial Intelligence Research 37(1), 141–188 (2010)

20. Harris, Z.S.: Distributional structure. Word 10(2-3), 146–162 (1954)

21. Firth, J.R.: A synopsis of linguistic theory, 1930-1955. In: Studies in Linguistic Analysis, pp. 1–32. Blackwell, Oxford (1957)

22. Weaver, W.: Translation. In: Locke, W., Booth, D. (eds.) Machine Translation of Languages, pp. 15–22. MIT Press, Cambridge (1955)

23. Wittgenstein, L.: Philosophical Investigations. Basil Blackwell Ltd., Oxford (1953)

24. Dunning, T.: Accurate methods for the statistics of surprise and coincidence. Computational Linguistics 19(1), 61–74 (1993)

25. Robert, S.: Words and their meanings: Principles of variation and stabilization. In: Vanhove, M. (ed.) From Polysemy to Semantic Change, pp. 55–92. John Benjamins Publishing Co., Amsterdam (2008)

26. Dong, Z.: Hownet and the Computation of Meaning. World Scientific Publishing Co., Inc., River Edge (2006)

27. Bailey, C.J.N.: Variation and Linguistic Theory. Center for Applied Linguistics, Washington, D.C. (1973)

28. Osgood, C.E., Sebeok, T.A.: Psycholinguistics: a survey of theory and research problems. The Journal of Abnormal and Social Psychology 49(4, pt. 2), 1–203 (1954)

29. Weinreich, U., Herzog, M., Labov, W.: Empirical foundations for a theory of language change. In: Lehmann, W.P. (ed.) Directions for Historical Linguistics: A Symposium, pp. 95–195. University of Texas Press, Austin (1968)

30. Kroch, A.S.: Reflexes of grammar in patterns of language change. Language Variation and Change 1, 199–244 (1989)

31. Labov, W.: Principles of Linguistic Change: Internal Factors. Language in society. Blackwell, Oxford (1994)

32. Wang, W.S.Y., Ke, J., Minett, J.W.: Computational studies of language evolution. In: Lenders, C.R.H., Lenders, W. (eds.) Computational Linguistics and Beyond: Perspectives at the Beginning of the 21st Century, pp. 65–106 (2004)

33. Zuraw, K.: Probability in language change. In: Bod, R., Hay, J., Jannedy, S. (eds.) Probabilistic Linguistics, pp. 139–176. MIT Press, Cambridge (2003)

34. Brockwell, P.J., Davis, R.A.: Introduction to Time Series and Forecasting, 2nd edn. Springer texts in statistics. Springer, New York (2002)

35. Traugott, E.C.: Semantic change: Bleaching, strengthening, narrowing, extension. In: Brown, K. (ed.) Encyclopedia of Language and Linguistics, pp. 124–131. Elsevier Science, Oxford (2006)

36. Riemer, N.: Introducing Semantics. Cambridge University Press, Cambridge (2010)

A   List of Chinese New Word Dictionaries

The 9 dictionaries are: (1)New Word Dictionary for Modern Chinese, by Wang Junxi et al, 1987, Qilu Press in Jinan; (2)Dictionary for New Words, New Expressions and New Senses in Modern Chinese, by Zhu chengliang et al, 1989, Chinese Worker Press in Beijing; (3) Dictionary for Contemporary Chinese New Words, by Wen hui et al, 1992, Dalian Press in Dalian; (4)Dictionary of New Word and New Expression, by Li Xingjian et al, 1993, Yuwen Press in Beijing; (5) Chinese New Word Dictionary, by Li Daren et al, 1993, the Commercial Press House in Beijing; (6) Dictionary for New Words and New Expressions, by Yao hanmin, 2000, Future Press in Xi'an; (7) Dictionary of New Words for Contemporary Chinese, by Wang Junxi, 2003, Chinese Dictionary Press in Shanghai; (8) Annual Anthology of Chinese New Words and New Expressions (1997-2000), by Song ziran, 2002, Sichuan People's Press in Chengdu; (9) Annual Anthology of Chinese New Words and New Expressions (2001-2003), by Song ziran, 2004, Sichuan People's Press in Chengdu.

A Connectionist Model-Based Approach to Centrality Discovery in Social Networks

Qingmai Wang, Xinghuo Yu, and Xiuzhen Zhang

RMIT University, Australia
{qingmai.wang,x.yu,xiuzhen.zhang}@rmit.edu.au

Abstract. Identifying key nodes in networks, in terms of centrality measurement, is one of the popular research topics in network analysis. Various methods have been proposed with different interpretations of centrality. This paper proposes a novel connectionist method which measures node centrality for directed and weighted networks. The method employs a spreading activation mechanism in order to measure the influence of a given node on the others, within an information diffusion circumstance. The experimental results show that, compared with other popular centrality measurement methods, the proposed method performs the best for finding the most influential nodes.

1 Introduction

Centrality measurement has long been studied to rank the importance of nodes in various network applications, e.g. measuring influence of actors in Word Of Mouth (WOM) networks, or finding out the key transfer station in logistic networks. Various methods have been proposed to study the problem. Classical methods, including degree centrality, closeness centrality, betweenness centrality and eigenvector centrality, have been reviewed in [1]. A set of recent followers have also been proposed in [2], [3] and [4]. A popular benchmark for the existing methods is their capability of detecting influential nodes in information diffusion models [5] [6]. Namely, for each measurement method, the evaluation system checks whether their high ranking nodes can influence a larger number of other nodes in the diffusion process. However, according to [7], existing methods hold different interpretations of centrality. For example, closeness centrality is interpreted as an index of expected information arrival time, where betweenness centrality measures the amount of network flow "controlled" by a given node. But none of them directly interprets the centrality as a capability of spreading the message to more nodes. As a result, there is still space for the centrality measurement to be improved for detecting influential nodes in those benchmark systems.

Probabilistic network has been widely used to model information diffusion process. Two best known models are called Linear Threshold (LT) model and Independent Cascade (IC) model [8]. In these models, an intuitive idea for measuring the influence of a given node is to sum all the other nodes' probabilities of being informed. This is quite time-consuming due to the complexity of probability propagation with large number of diverging/converging connections and the difficulty of handling such computations in loops. Connectionist method is one of the common methods that effectively simplify

L. Cao et al. (Eds.): BSIC/BSI 2013, LNAI 8178, pp. 82–94, 2013.

the probability propagation process to solve general belief propagation problems [9]. The method has been widely applied to support decision making in uncertain circumstance to replace the probabilistic network ([10], [11] and [12]). Although the connectionst method has not been formally employed to model the information diffusion in social networks, the similarity between them has been discussed in the sense that they both hold random walk structure and can explain fast and single step-based spreading process [13].

This paper proposes a novel connectionist method for measuring nodes' centralities in terms of the capability of influencing other nodes. The method arranges an activation value for every node, implying its possibility of being informed. This value is updated according to the activation value of its neighbor nodes and the weights on the links between them. To measure the centrality of a given node, assuming the node is fully activated, the system then spread the activation throughout the whole network. Finally the centrality of the given node is calculated by summing the activation values of all the nodes. The resulting value directly reflects how far the network is influenced, and can be achieved efficiently compared with other centrality measurements due to the fast single step updating of the activation value of the nodes.

Generally speaking, the motivations of applying the connectionist model in social network centrality measurement are as follows:

1. Different from the closeness, betweenness and eigenvector centralities which concentrate on the global structure of the network, the connectionist model generates the centrality index based on the local behaviors of the nodes and their interactions.
2. The connectionist model employs a spreading activation mechanism which naturally fit the information diffusion process in social networks. The informed and uninformed individuals are represented as activated and inactivated nodes respectively, and the links refer to the connection between individuals where the weights indicate the trust degree or the adoption probability.
3. The connectionist model and the information diffusion model hold similar properties, such as the random walk information flows and the information decay according to the time and flow distance.
4. The connectionist model adopts an efficient iterative distributed algorithm which consists of single-step information propagation within local neighborhoods only, regardless of the propagation path and the global network topology.

In the following discussion, we name the proposed centrality measurement as "connectionist centrality" in order for it to be differentiated from the other centrality measurements.

The rest of the paper is organized as follows: Section 2 introduces the technical details of the connectionist model; Section 3 presents the centrality calculation based on the connectionist model; Section 4 demonstrates the proposed method with a set of examples and experiments; Section 5 concludes the paper.

2   The Connectionist Model

This section introduces the details of the spreading activation mechanism in the connectionist model.

Let $G = (V, E, W)$ be a weighted and directed network with the vertex set $V(G) = v_1, v_2, ...v_n$, where each vertex v_i is attached with an activation value a_i, edge set $E(G)$, where each edge $e_{i,j} = (v_i, v_j)$ is attached with a weight $w_{i,j}$. In the diffusion models, the weight $w_{i,j}$ usually represents the probability of success for node v_i's attempt at activating v_j, which take value from 0 to 1.0. The activation value a_i also varies from 0 to 1.0, where 0 indicates the node is not activated while 1.0 indicates that the node is fully activated.

Generally speaking, spreading activation is achieved by iteratively updating the activation value of every node in the network, until the whole network reach a stable solution that represent the final activation status of the network. A nonlinear activation function, which is developed by McClelland and Rumelhart [14] for their interactive activation model, is used in this work to update the activation value. This function is sigmoid-shaped and has been frequently used in many applications, such as letter perception [14], explanation generation [10] and decision making [11]. In our study, since that all the activations and weights hold positive value, we only use the positive half of the original activation function, which is:

$$a_i(t + 1) = sat(a_i(t)decay + input_i(t)(max - a_i(t))) \tag{1}$$

where $sat()$ is a saturation function:

$$sat(x) = \begin{cases} 1, & \text{if } x \geq 1 \tag{2} \\ x, & \text{if } 0 < x < 1 \tag{3} \end{cases}$$

In the above equations, $a_i(t)$ is the current activation of node v_i, which is decayed by a *decay* factor that is smaller than 1.0. $input_i(t)$ represents the incoming activation from the neighbors of v_i at time t. max is the maximum value of activation, which is 1.0 in this case. The equation shows that the activation of v_i in the following time period $a_i(t + 1)$ is a combination of its current activation multiplied by a decay factor and the incoming activation multiplied by a scaling factor. The scaling factor indicates that the possible amount of change in activation of a node is proportional to the difference between its maximum and its current activation, resulting in an asymptotic approach to the maximum or the stabilized value. The non-linearity of the function comes from the scaling factor [15].

The incoming activation $input_i(t)$ is calculated as:

$$input_i(t) = \sum_{v_j \in N_i} w_{i,j} \cdot a_j(t) \tag{4}$$

where N_i is the set of neighbor nodes of v_i.

According to these equations, the updating process for all the nodes will finally reach a stable activation after several iterations. The resulting activation value of a node reflects its degree of being influenced by the source node. The computational complexity of a single updating calculation is proportional to the average degree of the network $\frac{E}{N}$, where N is the number of the nodes and E is the number of the edges. In addition, according to Thagard [16], although the convergence of this non-linear system has not been mathematically proved yet, large number of experiments have shown that the network will become stabilized in a bounded number of cycles k, regardless of the size of the network. As a result, the computational complexity of the spreading process is $O(\frac{E}{N} \cdot k \cdot N) = O(kE)$

3   Centrality Measurement

Based on the connectionist model discussed in Section 2, Figure 1 shows the flow chart of the connectionist centrality measurement, where c_i denotes the centrality of v_i.

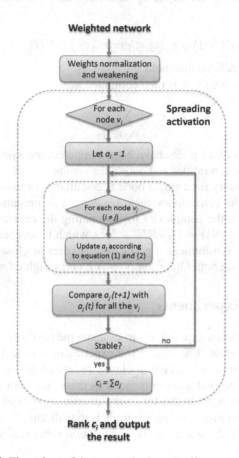

Fig. 1. Flow chart of the connectionist centrality measurement

Once a network is input, assuming that the weights on the edges represent connection strength between nodes, the first step is to normalize the weights to the range [0,1] in order to make the following calculation. In addition, as that information is easy to be diffused to all nodes in a network with high connectivity, a network with large average degree might be fully activated (all the nodes reach maximum activation) by a number of influential nodes respectively in few iterations. In this case, it is difficult to rank those nodes since that they all hold similar connectionist centralities generated by the full activation of the network. As a result, there is a need to uniformly weaken all the weights by a factor of the average degree of the network in order to avoid the full activation.

After that, the spreading activation mechanism is then employed to compute the connectionist centrality for each node in the network. For a given node v_i, assume that it is the source node that activate the network and has a constant activation value of 1.0, and all the other nodes $v_j (j \neq i)$ in the network start at an activation of 0. The system then upgrades the activation for all the v_j iteratively, until the whole network reach a stable status, namely:

$$a_j(t + 1) - a_j(t) < error \ (\forall v_j \in V(G)) \tag{5}$$

where $error$ is a predefined threshold.

c_i, which is the centrality of v_i, is then computed as:

$$c_i = \sum_{v_j \in V(G) \cap j \neq i} a_j \tag{6}$$

Once the centralities of all nodes have been computed, the system finally rank the nodes according to their centralities and output the results.

Computing the centrality for a single node is essentially a spreading activation process plus the sum of the activation values, resulting a computational complexity of $O(kE + N)$. Therefore, the complexity for computing the centralities for the whole network is $O(N \cdot (kE + N)) = O(kEN + N^2)$, which is acceptable compared with other major centrality measurement, e.g. the complexities of closeness centrality and betweenness centrality are both $O(N^2 \log N + NE)$ on weighted networks [17].

4   Example and Experiments

This section presents several experiments to evaluate the performance of the proposed method in diffusion models. The idea of the experiment is to test the nodes that are highly ranked by the proposed method in classic Independent Cascade (IC) diffusion model to check how many nodes are influenced by them, and compare the results with other centrality measurement. In the following discussion, a brief introduction of IC model is first given; a relatively simple example is then discussed showing the general experiment process; and the results of experiments on other real world networks are finally presented.

4.1   Independent Cascade Model

IC model is one of the fundamental probabilistic diffusion models that has been widely studied [8]. The general diffusion process is as follows:

1. The diffusion starts with a set of active nodes;
2. During one cycle, each active node v_i has a single chance to activate each currently inactive neighbor v_j with a probability $p_{i,j}$;

3. If v_i succeeds, then v_j becomes active and is added to the active node set in the next cycle; but whether or not v_i succeeds, it cannot make any further attempts to activate v_j;
4. Re-run step 2 and 3 until no more activations can be made;

4.2 A Simple Example

Figure 2 shows a simple network extracted from the Enron email dataset (http://www.cs.cmu.edu/enron). The network contains 13 nodes and 25 edges. Each edge is attached with a weight referring to the influence probability between the nodes. In order to test the influence of a given node, assuming that it is an active node, run the simulated diffusion process based on the above IC model, and then record the number of nodes that has been activated as the simulated result of one run. Due to the probabilistic nature of IC model, the simulated results usually have quite large variation. So the final results are generated by averaging 1000 runs in this study, as is shown in Table 1. To evaluate the centrality measurements is therefore to check how well they match the simulated results.

From Table 1, we can see that node 48 is the most influential node in the network, which averagely influence 7.774 nodes according to the simulations. The importance of node 48 is also quite obvious in the visualization of the network in Figure 2. The average number of nodes that are influenced by node 67 and node 147 are 7.362 and 7.282 respectively, which are quite similar, as that the two nodes hold quite similar connections (as shown in Figure 2). The reason why node 67 is slightly more influential than node 147 is probably that the weights on the out links of node 67 is relatively larger. Please notice that the nodes listed at the bottom of table 1 do not have any out links, so that only themselves are influenced by the end of the simulation, resulting simulated results of "1".

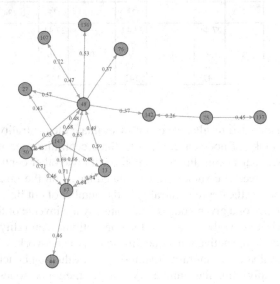

Fig. 2. Visualization of a simple example

Table 1. Simulated diffusion results on the simple network

Rank	Simulated Diffusion Result	
	Node ID	Simulated result
1	48	7.774
2	67	7.362
3	147	7.282
4	13	6.271
5	107	4.376
6	50	3.904
7	75	1.721
8	27,44,76,136, 137,142	1

Table 2. Centrality measurements on the simple network

Rank	Degree Centrality		Closeness Centrality		Connectionist Centrality	
	Node ID	Centrality Value	Node ID	Centrality Value	Node ID	Centrality Value
1	48	9	48	0.0311	48	2.332
2	67,147	5	147	0.0297	67	1.784
3			67	0.0286	147	1.687
4	13,75	2	13	0.0282	13	1.115
5			107	0.0278	107	0.629
6	50,107	1	50	0.0257	50	0.489
7			75	0.0077	75	0.284
8	27,44, 76, 136, 137, 142	0	27,44, 76, 136, 137, 142	0	27,44, 76, 136, 137, 142	0

With these simulated results, we can now evaluate the centrality measurements. Table 2 lists the ranks of nodes according to three centrality measurements, where the proposed connectionist centrality is compared with two other centrality measurements, closeness and degree. The values are calculated based on the three measurements respectively, where: 1) the degree centrality is the number of out links of the nodes; 2) the closeness centrality of a given node is calculated by the inverse of the average length of the shortest paths to the other nodes; 3) the connectionist centrality, as proposed in this paper, is the sum of the activation value throughout the network.

In order to evaluate the centrality methods, two evaluation benchmark are proposed. The first one simply sums the simulated results of the top k nodes ranked by the centrality measurements respectively, which is denoted as: $total_x^{(k)}$, where x is a certain centrality measurement. This score reflects their capabilities in detecting the most k influential nodes. In this example, the sum of top 5 nodes for each measurements are:

$$total^{(5)}_{degree} = 30.41$$
$$total^{(5)}_{closeness} = 33.065$$
$$total^{(5)}_{connectionist} = 33.065$$

where the closeness and connetionist centralities are slightly better, since both of them have correctly identified the five most influential nodes ("48, "67", "147", "13", "75") according to the simulated results.

Another evaluation benchmark used in this study is Kendall's Rank Correlation (KRC) τ [18], which measures the strength of monotonic association between two ranking vectors. τ is ranged from -1 to 1. It takes 1 if the two rankings perfectly match, and takes -1 if the two rankings are in completely reversed order. The calculation of τ is as follows:

$$\tau_x = \sum_{i<j} sign(R_x(v_j) - R_x(v_i)) \times sign(R_s(v_j) - R_s(v_i)) \tag{7}$$

where x denotes a certain centrality measurements, R_x denotes the rank of the nodes according to the centrality measurement x and R_s denotes the rank of the nodes according to the simulated results. This benchmark reflect how well a centrality measurement matches the simulated diffusion result in terms of ordering the nodes. Similar to the first benchmark, we use $\tau_x^{(k)}$ to represent the KRC for the top k nodes ranked by a given centrality measurements x, while $\tau_x^{(all)}$ denotes the KRC for all the nodes in the network. In this simple example, the KRCs for each centrality measurements are as follows:

$$\tau^{(all)}_{degree} = 0.72$$
$$\tau^{(all)}_{closeness} = 0.905$$
$$\tau^{(all)}_{connectionist} = 1$$

We can see that the perfect match between the rankings generated by connetionist centrality and simulated results leads to a KRC of 1, while the closeness centrality is slightly worse due to the misordering of nodes "147" and "67".

4.3 Experiments

The experiments are conducted on three real world networks: Karate Club network, Enron Email network and BKFRAT network, with four popular existing centrality measurements: degree, closeness, betweenness and PageRank [19] (a special case of eigenvector centrality).

Network Descriptions. The Karate Club network is a social network of friendship between 34 members of a karate club at a US university in the 1970 [20]. The network has 34 nodes and 78 edges. Since the original network is unweighted, we uniformly arrange a weight 0.5 to all the edges in the network. The network is shown in Figure 3.

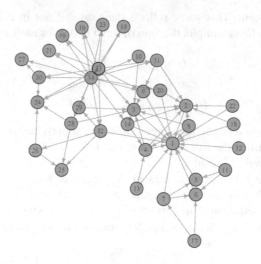

Fig. 3. Visualization of the Karate Club network

The Enron dataset used is a collection of the emails between 158 users within three years, which contains around 50k messages. Each message has 6 attributes, including message ID, sender ID, receiver ID, date, time and message length. In this experiment, a network is generated based on 10k messages, which contains 111 nodes and 536 edges. In the network, nodes represent users, while edges between nodes represent the contacts between the users. For each edge, the weight on the edge is computed according to the total length of the messages between the two vertices of the edge, which is normalized to [0,1], referring to the influence probability between the two corresponding users. The visualization of the network is shown in Figure 4.

BKFRAT is a data set about interactions among students living in a fraternity at a West Virginia College [21]. The data set is collected by an "unobtrusive" observer who walks through the college buildings and records the number of times of conversation between pairs of students. The numbers are then regarded as the weights of the connections between the students. The network constructed from the data set is quite strongly connected, which consists of 58 nodes and 1934 edges. The network is shown in Figure 5 and the results.

Experimental Results. Table 3 lists the experimental results where the five centrality measurements are compared. The highest score in each row is bolded. According to these results, the performance of the betweenness centrality is relatively poor in all the networks. The reason might be that the nodes with high betweenness centralities usually represent the key nodes that control the network flows [7], rather than the influential information sources in diffusion models. The closeness centrality performs well in Karate Network and BKFRAT network, but are relatively weak in Enron Email network, especially in detecting the few most influential node, potentially due to the weakness of closeness centrality in weakly-connected networks [1] (as its $total^{(5)}$ is poor). It is surprising that the simple degree centrality performs better than the

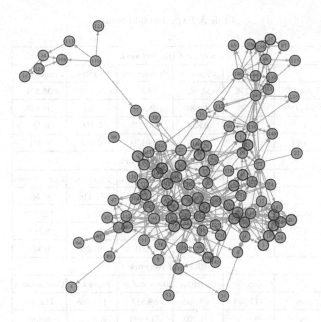

Fig. 4. Visualization of the Enron email network

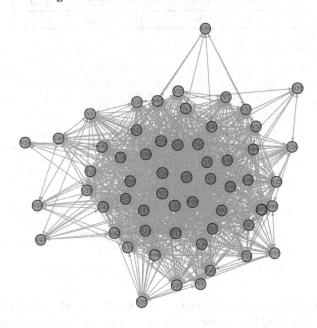

Fig. 5. Visualization of the BKFRAT network

previous two, which indicates that people with large number of contacts are indeed the influential people in most of the cases. PageRank also performs competently, especially in the strongly-connected network BKFRAT. Finally, the proposed connectionist

Table 3. Experimental results

Karate Club Network					
	Degree	Closeness	Betweenness	PageRank	Connectionist
total (5)	**35.238**	34.685	13.319	33.512	**35.238**
total (10)	48.76	**49.588**	26.476	48.647	49.538
τ (10)	0.774	**0.828**	-0.0239	0.556	0.719
τ (all)	0.809	0.852	0.0179	0.684	**0.891**
Enron Email Network					
	Degree	Closeness	Betweenness	PageRank	Connectionist
total (5)	35.91	17.522	32.92	35.416	**38.666**
total (20)	119.184	101.163	109.524	116.272	**123.579**
τ (20)	0.493	0.067	0.575	0.422	**0.689**
τ (all)	0.732	0.525	0.501	0.605	**0.949**
BKFRAT Network					
	Degree	Closeness	Betweenness	PageRank	Connectionist
total (5)	**112.968**	109.906	69.314	**112.968**	**112.968**
total (20)	398.258	371.202	318.194	400.748	**402.67**
τ (20)	0.217	0.184	0.17	0.212	**0.243**
τ (all)	0.613	0.506	0.114	**0.627**	0.622

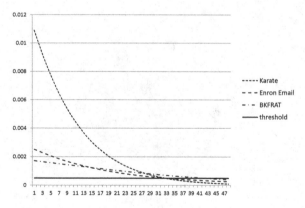

Fig. 6. Convergence of the average iterative error

centrality consistently shows good performance in all networks, which demonstrates that the proposed method is truly the most effective one in detecting the most influential nodes for information diffusion.

The convergence of the proposed method is also tested. Figure 6 illustrates the evolvement of the average iterative error generated by single spreading activation process of the node with highest connectionist centrality (the iterative error is shown in Equation (5), and the average iterative error is the average value of the iterative errors of all nodes). As previously discussed, the theoretical deduction of the converging speed of the proposed algorithm remains unsolved. However, Thagard has concluded that "empirical results for numerous connetionist models reveal that the number of cycles of activation updating required for settling does not increase as networks become larger" [16]. The results shown in Figure 6 also generally confirm this fact, where the average iterative errors of the networks all reach the predefined threshold (which is 0.0005 in this study) in similar number of cycles.

5 Conclusion

This paper has proposed a novel connectionist method to measure the nodes' centrality in terms of the influence of the nodes in the information diffusion scenario. The method employs a spreading activation mechanism which quantify how far the network is influenced by a given node through an iterative process. The resulting activation value of the network is then summed as the centrality of the given node. The algorithm takes the complexity of $O(kEN + N^2)$ which is comparatively competent among existing centrality measurements. Experiments have been conducted with a set of real world networks. The results show that the proposed method perform competently in detecting the most influential nodes in a simulated probabilistic information diffusion process based on the conventional IC model. Future works include validating the proposed method with more complex networks and with other diffusion models.

References

1. Landherr, A., Friedl, B., Heidemann, J.: A Critical Review of Centraility Measures in Social Networks. Bussiness and Information Systems Engineering 2(6), 371–385 (2010)
2. Zhang, Y., Zhang, Z., Wei, D., Deng, Y.: Centrality Measure in Weighted Networks Based on an Amoeboid Algorithm. Journal of Information and Computational Science 9(2), 369–376 (2012)
3. Yan, X., Zhai, L., Fan, W.: C-Index: A Weighted Network Node Centrality Measure for Collaboration Competence. Journal of Informetrics 7(1), 223–239 (2013)
4. Qi, X., Fuller, E., Wu, Q., Wu, Y., Zhang, C.Q.: Laplacian Centrality: A New Centrality Measure for Weighted Networks. Information Sciences 194, 240–253 (2012)
5. Kiss, C., Bichler, M.: Identification of influencers - measuring influence in customer networks. Decis. Support Syst. 46(1), 233–253 (2008)
6. Borgatti, S.P.: Identifying Sets of Key Players in A Social Network. Comput. Math. Organ. Theory 12(1), 21–34 (2006)
7. Borgatti, S.P.: Centrality and Network Flow. Social Networks 27(1), 55–71 (2005)
8. Kempe, D., Kleinberg, J., Tardos, E.: Maximizing the Spread of Influence Through a Social Network. In: Proceedings of the Ninth ACM SIGKDD International Conference on Knowledge Discovery and Data Mining, KDD 2003, pp. 137–146 (2003)
9. Mcclelland, J.L.: Connectionist Models and Bayesian Inference. Oxford University Press (1999)
10. Thagard, P., Litt, A.: Models of scientific explanation. In: The Cambridge Handbook of Computational Cognitive Modeling. Cambridge University Press (2006)

11. Glöckner, A., Betsch, T.: Modelling option and strategy choices with connectionist networks: Towards an integrative model of automatic and deliberate decision making. Judgement and Decision Making 3, 215–228 (2008)
12. Betsch, T., Glöckner, A.: Intuition in judgment and decision making: Extensive thinking without effort. Psychological Inquiry 21(4), 279–294 (2010)
13. Ratcliff, R., Zandt, T.V.: Connectionist and Diffusion Models of Reaction Time. Psychological Review 106(2), 261–300 (1999)
14. Mcclelland, J.L., Rumelhart, D.E.: An Interactive Activation Model of Context Effects in Letter Perception: I. An Account of Basic Findings. Psychological Review 88, 375–407 (1981)
15. Read, S.J., Vanman, E.J., Miller, L.: Connectionism, Parallel Constraint Satisfaction Process, and Gestalt Principles (Re) Introducing Cognitive Dynamics to Social Psychology. Personality and Social Psychology Review 1(1), 26–53 (1997)
16. Thagard, P.: Coherence as constraint satisfaction. Cognitive Science 22(1), 1–24 (1998)
17. Brandes, U.: A faster algorithm for betweenness centrality. Journal of Mathematical Sociology 25, 163–177 (2001)
18. Sheskin, D.: Handbook of Parametric and Nonparametric Statistical Procedures, 3rd edn. Taylor & Francis (2003)
19. Brin, S., Page, L.: The Anatomy of a Large-scale Hypertextual Web Search Engine. Computer Networks and ISDN Systems 30(1-7), 107–117 (1998)
20. Zachary, W.W.: An Information Flow Model for Conflict and Fission in Small Groups. Journal of Anthropological Research 33, 452–473 (1977)
21. Bernard, H.R., Killworth, P.D., Sailer, L.: Informant Accuracy in Social Network Data IV: a Comparison of Clique-level Structure in Behavioral and Cognitive Network Data. Social Networks 2(3), 191–218 (1979)

The Influence in Twitter: Are They Really Influenced?

Juyup Sung, Seunghyeon Moon, and Jae-Gil Lee[*]

Department of Knowledge Service Engineering
Korea Advanced Institute of Science and Technology
{juyup.sung,myth624,jaegil}@kaist.ac.kr

Abstract. Twitter is a popular social network service which is continuously growing. Because Twitter has become an efficient platform for advertising companies as a new vast medium, it is obvious that finding influential Twitter users and measuring their influence are important. Intuitively, users who have more followers are likely to be more influential. However, the number of followers does not necessarily mean the confidence of influence. In order to find influential users in Twitter more precisely, in this paper, we present an improvement of PageRank, which we call *InterRank* (***Inter****action **Rank***). It considers not only the follower relationship of the network but also topical similarity between users from tweet context. By using retweet information, we verify that topical similarity indeed affects the influence of a user. Then, we compare InterRank to PageRank with an assumption that influential users are more interactive with their followers. Our comparison results show that the users found by InterRank are more interactive than those by PageRank. Overall, we believe InterRank can be an attractive alternative of PageRank in finding influential users.

Keywords: Social Influence, Network Propagation, Diffusion, Topical Similarity, Social Interaction.

1 Introduction

Social influence is defined by "change in a person's cognition, attitude, or behavior, which has its origin in another person or group"[1]. This interpersonal influence process is much more important nowadays since the uprising social network is regarded as a source of information and hints on behavior and action for individuals[2]. It also means that there are more chances in online social networks to broaden the influence by connecting people all the time and making people respond quickly. As a practical example, many companies are getting more dependent on *viral marketing*, known as "company's activities to make use of customers' communication networks to promote and distribute products"[3]. Influential people can trigger larger cascades by influencing other people in the network[4]. In this regard, finding influential people is of prime importance.

Twitter is a popular social network service as well as representative micro-blogging service. It allows users to share their posts of up to 140 characters. Now that Twitter keeps growing, it has become an efficient platform for advertising companies as a

[*] Corresponding author.

L. Cao et al. (Eds.): BSIC/BSI 2013, LNAI 8178, pp. 95–105, 2013.
© Springer International Publishing Switzerland 2013

new vast medium. Under this circumstance, we choose Twitter for our study of analyzing the influence of users. Even though, intuitively, users who have more followers are likely to be more influential, it is not always true. Sometimes, the follower relationship is misleading since it is made by reciprocity[5]. Specifically in Twitter, three important factors—in-degree, retweets, and mentions—from top users are shown to have little overlap[6]. Thus, we contend that considering *only* the relationship between users (e.g., the follower relationship) may not be sufficient.

In this paper, we propose a new method of evaluating the influence of users in Twitter, which we call *InterRank* (***Inter**action **Rank***). In addition to the follower relationship widely adopted by other methods, InterRank considers *topical similarity* between users in Twitter. We empirically verify that topical similarity is strongly related to the influence of a user, as we will show in Section 5.1. In InterRank, every relationship between users is weighted based on topical similarity to reflect the degree of influence more precisely. Then, the rank of each user is calculated using the iterative or algebraic methods similar to those for PageRank.

Then, we evaluate the effectiveness of InterRank using a huge Twitter data set collected for 3.5 years. The rationale behind our evaluation is that more-influential users tend to be more interactive. This assumption is reasonable since influenced users will react to the influencers more actively, generating frequent interactions. Our comparison results between InterRank and PageRank show that the users found by InterRank are generally more interactive than those by PageRank. These preliminary results indicate that InterRank can produce more meaningful rankings for user influence.

The rest of this paper is organized as follows. Section 2 reviews related work. Section 3 explains the Twitter data set used for our analysis. Section 4 proposes our approach InterRank. Section 5 evaluates the effectiveness of InterRank. Finally, Section 6 concludes this study.

2   Related Work

Discovering influential persons in online networks is a well-known research topic. One interesting approach is "modeling the information diffusion based on the theory of the spread of infectious diseases"[7]. This model explains that particular individuals are highly effective to diffuse the "infectious" topics. There are also two popular diffusion models that detect the influence in the network, which are known as the node-specific threshold model[8] and the cascade model[9]. Both models focus on finding a set of starting nodes that maximize propagation on the network. These diffusion models, however, only contributed to represent how their words are spread out rather than specifically score influential people. Moreover, the diffusion models do not considers topical similarity that we regard as an important source.

Meanwhile, PageRank[10] has received a lot of attention as a way of measuring the importance of web pages. Although PageRank was originally designed for the Internet, it can be also used for social networks owing to the close correspondence between web pages and users as well as between hyperlinks and social relationships. However, PageRank exploits only the network topology.

There are several variations of PageRank developed for social networks, including TwitterRank[5], and TURank[11]. TwitterRank uses LDA(Latent Dirichlet Allocation) to define topics from tweets in Twitter so that it obtains topical differences between users. TwitterRank is the work closest to ours. The main difference is that InterRank is more flexible in extracting topics than TwitterRank is. In TwitterRank, the number of topics has to be designed by human in a heuristic manner, and the relative weight of each topic is not considered. On the other hand, InterRank calculates topical similarity without requiring any pre-designed topics as opposed to TwitterRank. TURank considers two types of relationships, follower relationships and retweet relationships, but does *not* take topical similarity into account.

LexPageRank[12] is a method of applying PageRank to a collection of documents, not for social networks. Here, a node is a sentence, and an edge is added if the similarity between sentences is above a certain threshold. It actually considers *only* topical similarity since the edges are created based on topical similarity.

3   Data Set

In this section, we explain the Twitter data set used in our experiments. We obtained the whole data set from MIA Lab where Korean Twitter information was crawled. This data set is mainly based on the list of user IDs from 'Korean Twitter User Self Intro' operated by @xguru(http://selfintro.xguru.net/). The data set involves 11,062 Twitter users and 5,913,885 tweets the users have produced. Also, in total, 1,830,832 links such as follower/friend relationships were obtained. We believe that this data set is *not* a biased sample because the user list above is truly a random sample of Twitter users. The tweet context in the data set was from March 3, 2007 to August 18, 2010, that is, almost 3 and half years.

When we look into the general characteristics of relationships in a social network service, it is common to discover the power-law distribution. As we expected, there are power-law distributions of user ranks with the number of followers and the number of friends. Fig. 1 (a) and (b) show that followers/friends in Twitter are not uniformly proportioned and that some heavy users exist. However, the number of tweets is exponentially distributed and is somewhat dissimilar to Fig. 1 (a) and (b). Fig. 1 (c) shows that the amount of user contribution is actually represented by the stretched exponential distribution rather than the power-law distribution as shown by Guo et al.[13]. This is possibly because any individual cannot generate a huge number of tweets in a daily basis regardless of the number of followers and friends.

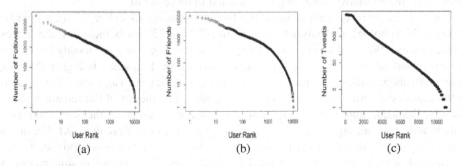

Fig. 1. Number of Followers, Friends, and Tweets according to the User Rank in Log Scale: (a) Number of Followers per User in Log-Log Scale, (b) Number of Friends per User in Log-Log Scale, (c) Number of Tweets per User in Y-Log Scale

4   Methodology

4.1   Problem Statement

First of all, we follow the definition of social influence, the real change of attitude or behavior to another person[1]. Although the number of follower relationships does not *solely* represent the influence for each user, we still need to regard this factor to be important because the information, the only means that users can be influenced, flows through the direct links (i.e., follower relationships). However, as distinct from Page-Rank, InterRank differentiates the weight by measuring the topical similarity between Twitter users.

The goal of this paper is to develop a new ranking scheme called *InterRank*. It receives the network topology (i.e., follower relationships) of Twitter users and the tweets written by the users as input. Then, for each user u_i, it produces the value of Inter-Rank(u_i) indicating the degree of u_i's influence. In calculating topical similarity, it does *not* require us to determine topics in advance unlike TwitterRank[5].

4.2   Topical Similarity

People prefer to associate and interact with similar people. This is simply defined as a *Homophily*. It limits "people's social worlds in a way that has powerful implications for the information they receive, the attitudes they form, and the interactions they experience"[14]. From this perspective, we assume that no matter how Twitter users have made follower relationships, they would react to topics that interest them. It also means that every follower relationship should not be equally treated. Therefore, it is essential to differentiate all relationships by giving different weights according to their mutual contextual information. To this end, we consider not only the real follower relationship but also its strength by measuring the *topical similarity*. To get the similarity between users in our experiment, we mainly exploit the users' tweets because they contain their topical interests.

There are many approaches to calculating similarity. In this paper, we perform three steps: (i) extraction of words, (ii) construction of term vectors, and (iii) calculation of cosine similarity. Each step is explained in more detail.

First, words are extracted from all the tweets by using KLT(Ver 2.2.0), a popular Korean Morphological Analyzer. As a result, 2,284,475 words including duplicates are extracted. We need to filter out infrequent words since they are mostly erroneous or non-standard words. For the set of keywords whose frequency is higher than 50, two students manually examine the words to check if they are valid ones. This is doable because the cardinality of the set is not so high. For the set of the remaining keywords, the same approach is infeasible since the cardinality of the set is too high (there are many infrequent words). Thus, we consult to the Korean WIKI dictionary and select the words existing in the dictionary. Finally, 42,194 words survived.

Second, a term vector is constructed for each user. The number of dimensions is 42,194. TF-IDF[15] is adopted to measure the weight of a word since it is the most widely-adopted technique in information retrieval and text mining to determine the word importance. In our environment, a document is a concatenation of all the tweets written by a specific user. These term vectors constructed are provided to the next step. One thing to note is that we disregard the users who haven't produced any tweet at all since we cannot derive their topical interests. Then, only 8,666 users were considered, and 266,049 links (i.e., follower relationships) exist among those users.

Third, cosine similarity[16] is calculated between every pair of connected users to use it as a weight of an existing link. In total, 266,049 pairs were considered for our data set. Fig. 2 shows the distribution of cosine similarity with X-axis log scale among 266,049 links. The average is 0.131, and many relationships have a low value of cosine similarity.

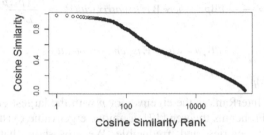

Fig. 2. Distribution of Cosine Similarity between Users

4.3   InterRank

Last, we apply the obtained weight between users to the underlying network to confirm that the weight improves the quality of rankings. Basically, the influence of a user in Twitter is similar to the importance of a web page: a user in Twitter has high influence if their followers' influence is high. Because of this correspondence, we adopt the PageRank as the baseline. PageRank is a well-known link analysis algorithm that finds the most important nodes in the network and is defined by the following formula.

$$PR(p_i) = \frac{1-d}{N} + d \sum_{p_j \in M(p_i)} \frac{PR(p_j)}{L(p_j)}$$

In the above formula, p_i represents a web page. $M(p_i)$ is the set of web pages that point to p_i. $L(p_j)$ is the number of outbound links on a web page p_j. $PR(p_i)$ and $PR(p_j)$ are the rank scores of pages p_i and p_j. d is a damping factor that is usually set to be 0.85. These variables are similarly defined for the Twitter network as follows. p_i represents a Twitter user. $M(p_i)$ is the set of followers that follow a user p_i. $L(p_j)$ is the number of the friends of a Twitter user p_j. $PR(p_i)$ and $PR(p_j)$ are the rank scores of users p_i and p_j. Because PageRank relies on only the follower relationship of the network, we modify it so that it considers topical similarity between users at the same time. The new equation is as follows.

$$InterRank(p_i) = \frac{1-d}{N} + d \sum_{p_j \in M(p_i)} CS(p_i, p_j) \frac{InterRank(p_j)}{L(p_j)}$$

In this formula, $CS(p_i, p_j)$ is the cosine similarity value between users p_i and p_j, which means topical similarity. Here, it can be considered that the credit of a Twitter user is distributed to his/her friends *in proportion to* topical similarity, whereas, in PageRank, the credit is *evenly* distributed to the neighbors. With this formula, Inter-Rank can be computed either iteratively or algebraically using the techniques used for PageRank. Theorem 1 states the existence and uniqueness of InterRank.

Theorem 1 (Existence and Uniqueness)
InterRank always has a unique solution.
Proof.
InterRank can be expressed using matrix notation as follows.

$$p = \frac{1-d}{N} + d\mathbf{B}p \quad \text{where } \mathbf{B} \text{ is a matrix with } \mathbf{B}_{ij} = \frac{CS(p_i, p_j)}{L(p_j)}$$

$$= \{\frac{1-d}{N}\mathbf{E} + d\mathbf{B}\}p \quad \text{where } \mathbf{E} \text{ is a matrix of all 1's}$$

$$= \mathbf{M}p$$

The solution of InterRank is the eigenvector p with the largest eigenvalue. According to the Perron-Frobenius theorem[17], a unique eigenvalue exists when a matrix is square with positive entries, and irreducible. We now show that $\mathbf{M}$ satisfies these properties. (i) $\mathbf{M}$ is square since both the number of rows and that of columns are the number of Twitter users (nodes) just like the adjacency matrix $\mathbf{B}$. (ii) $\mathbf{M}$ has positive entries because d has a value between 0 and 1, and so does cosine similarity. (iii) $\mathbf{M}$ is irreducible. By definition, if a graph is strongly connected, its adjacency matrix is irreducible. Since we are using one large Twitter network where all pairs of nodes are connected, $\mathbf{B}$ (i.e., $\mathbf{M}$) is irreducible. Therefore, the eigenvector in the above formula always exists and is unique. □

5   Evaluation

5.1   Effect of Topical Similarity

Before we evaluate the effectiveness of InterRank, it is necessary to know if a user has a greater tendency to be influenced by another user with a relation of high topical similarity. However, verifying this in a quantitative way is not trivial because there is no absolute information we can use for estimating the amount of influence. In Twitter, fortunately, *retweet* is a promising way because it reflects the usefulness of information: users will retweet a friend's tweet when they think it is valuable by mentioning the name of the friend whom they follow.

For our test based on retweet, we obtain a user set that includes the users who have been retweeted by someone else at least once. Only 2,705 users out of 8,666 are extracted. When we calculate the average of cosine similarity by counting *only the relationships where retweet occurred*, it was **0.206**, which is higher than the average (0.131) of all the relationships. Furthermore, we examine each of 2,705 users to identify whether he/she has a higher value of topical similarity (i.e., cosine similarity) with his/her followers than the overall average. Table 1 shows that about 80 percent of such users have a higher value than the average.

Table 1. Ratio of Users Comparing Two CS Types

Attribute	User	Ratio
Total	2705	1
RTed AVG > Total AVG	2172	0.803
RTed AVG < Total AVG	533	0.197

Overall, this simple test shows that retweet, which is a good indication of influence, is more likely to occur when topical similarity is higher between a user and his/her followers, leading to our expectation that topical similarity is one of important factors in estimating the degree of influence between users.

5.2 Comparison between InterRank and PageRank

Please remind that InterRank considers both the number of followers and closeness between a user and followers. Thus, we would like to first show that InterRank and PageRank produce somewhat similar rankings because both consider the number of followers and then show that InterRank performs better than PageRank owing to our additional feature of considering closeness between the user and followers.

First, we measure the correlation between the rank lists of InterRank and PageRank by using Kendall's r and Spearman's r. As shown in Table 2 and in Fig. 3, it turns out that both InterRank and PageRank look similar but not perfectly identical. A high correlation implies that InterRank also considers the number of followers, as Page-Rank does. On top of this, InterRank improves the rankings by applying topical similarity that potentially leads to a better result.

Table 2. Correlation between InterRank and PageRank

	Kendall's tau_b	Spearman's rho
InterRank vs. PageRank	0.782**	0.936**

**. Correlation is significant at the 0.01 level (2-tailed).

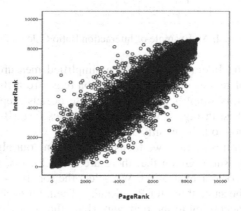

Fig. 3. Correlation between InterRank and PageRank

We are about to discuss the advantage of InterRank over PageRank. Since there is no absolute measure of estimating the amount of influence, we design our own approach for this comparison. The rationale behind our approach is as follows. If a person is more influential than others, his/her followers will be more responsive to him/her. That is, the followers will react to the influential person to ask about, object to, or appreciate information, thereby generating more interactions between them. Thus, it is reasonable to measure the frequency of interactions by means of *reply* in Twitter, and we define the *Interaction Ratio* in Definition 1.

Definition 1 (Interaction Ratio)

If a user A has replied to another specific user B more than to others, the user B can be considered as an influential person to the user A. With this assumption, we calculate the *Interaction Ratio* as follows.

$$InteractionRatio(u_i) = \frac{\sum_{follower \in Follower_i} ReplyCount(follower)}{\sum_{follower \in Follower_i} TweetCount(follower)}$$

Follower_i is the set of users who follow u_i. Whenever *Follower_i* replies to u_i, *ReplyCount* increases. *TweetCount* counts all the tweets that *Follower_i* has produced in the test period. As an example, suppose there are three users A, B, and C. Users B and C are following User A and have produced tweets as represented in Fig. 4. In this case, the Interaction Ratio of User A is described as 25%.

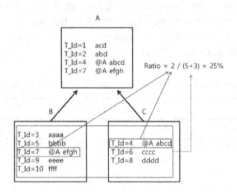

Fig. 4. An Example of Interaction Ratio Calculation

Please note that the Interaction Ratio is a simplified measure in the sense that it counts the number of replies only in one direction (e.g., from B or C to A in Fig. 4). However, we think this simplification makes sense because replies usually occur in *both* directions. That is, in Fig. 4, writing many replies from B to A implicitly indicates that A has replied to B frequently as well.

In the remaining of this section, we focus on comparing our algorithm to PageRank using the Interaction Ratio. Given that there are 11,062 users, we decide to choose representative users for our evaluation. We select the top 100 users according to InterRank and repeat the same thing for PageRank. Then, for each set of top-100 users, we choose 10 users according to the rank gap. Here, the *rank gap* of a user is defined as the difference of two rankings (the ranking of the user by PageRank – that of the user by InterRank). For the first set of top-100 users, the 10 users whose rank-gaps are the largest are chosen. We call them *positive users*. For the second set, 10 users whose rank-gap is the smallest (i.e., negative with the largest absolute value) are chosen. We call these *negative users*. Table 3 shows 20 users and their rank gaps.

Table 3. 20 Users Who Have Highest Rank Gap between InterRank and PageRank

Positive User				Negative User			
ID	InterRank	PageRank	Rank Gap	ID	InterRank	PageRank	Rank Gap
72170166	89	1296	1207	57259766	1296	26	-1270
94230388	52	490	438	46276391	955	63	-892
44795514	98	514	416	96002694	679	44	-635
91945707	11	360	349	56948026	712	87	-625
99715643	93	402	309	69884118	609	98	-511
17575820	68	364	296	47009269	555	76	-479
98819844	56	339	283	96251026	504	30	-474
49476941	53	279	226	48349182	430	93	-337
43854726	100	322	222	58708612	368	51	-317
70078285	92	281	189	70878532	359	59	-300

We then calculate the Interaction Ratio for those 20 users. Table 4 shows the results with absolute reply and tweet counts. The average Interaction Ratio, when considering the whole set of users, is 0.071%. The average Interaction Ratio value is used as a baseline in Fig. 5.

Table 4. The Result of Interaction Ratio and Their Absolute Values

	ID	Tweet Count	Reply Count	Interaction Ratio
Positive Rank Gap	72170166	52649	79	0.15%
	94230388	91678	181	0.20%
	44795514	108799	382	0.35%
	91945707	62191	138	0.22%
	99715643	128017	290	0.23%
	17575820	141286	256	0.18%
	98819844	78082	141	0.18%
	49476941	135004	260	0.19%
	43854726	261399	133	0.05%
	70078285	230017	317	0.14%
Negative Rank Gap	57259766	1270183	441	0.03%
	46276391	571644	547	0.10%
	96002694	918010	86	0.01%
	56948026	461435	1226	0.27%
	69884118	298414	1873	0.63%
	47009269	388406	237	0.06%
	96251026	1163426	20	0.00%
	48349182	381302	158	0.04%
	58708612	828204	645	0.08%
	70878532	813436	434	0.05%

In Fig. 5, it is quite clear that those positive users who have high scores in Inter-Rank are more interactive than those on the baseline. Moreover, the users selected by PageRank do not frequently interact with their followers except for a few users (e.g., user IDs 56948026 and 69884118). The average Interaction Ratio of positive users is 0.17% while that of negative users is 0.08%. Among ten positive users, nine of ten have an Interaction Ratio value higher than the average; however, among ten negative users, only four have an Interaction value higher than the average.

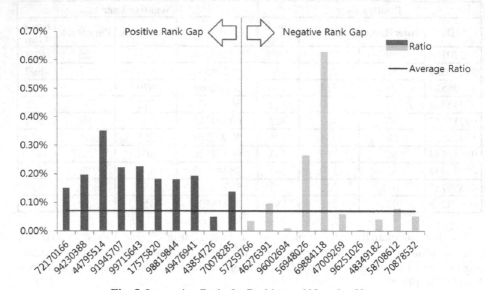

Fig. 5. Interaction Ratio for Positive and Negative Users

In general, the users selected by InterRank show higher Interaction Ratio values than those selected by PageRank, implying that InterRank finds more influential users by our criterion. These preliminary results indicate that considering both types of information—network topology and topical similarity—can produce more meaningful rankings for user influence.

6   Conclusions

Our study discusses who the most influential persons are in Twitter. *InterRank* is designed to consider the follower relationship as well as topical similarity. Based on our experiences, we confirmed that topical similarity is related to the diffusion of influence: there is a tendency that people retweet more in a relationship with higher similarity. Influence is not only a matter of the number of followers, but also a matter of actual interactions between users. Hence, we evaluated the effectiveness of our approach in a quantitative way by using the Interaction Ratio. When we looked into the tweet status of a user who is very highly ranked in InterRank, the user tends to interact more frequently with his/her followers than the average users or even the top-rankers in PageRank. Finally, we conclude that InterRank has potential to become an attractive alternative for measuring the influence of users.

Acknowledgement. This research was supported by Basic Science Research Program through the National Research Foundation of Korea (NRF) funded by the Ministry of Education, Science and Technology (2012012954) and by the National Research Foundation of Korea (NRF) grant funded by the Korea government (MEST) (No. 2011-0029185).

References

1. Raven, B.H.: Social influence and power. DTIC Document (1964)
2. Wellman, B., et al.: Computer networks as social networks: Collaborative work, telework, and virtual community. Annual Review of Sociology, 213–238 (1996)
3. Helm, S.: Viral marketing-establishing customer relationships by 'word-of-mouse'. Electronic Markets 10(3), 158–161 (2000)
4. Watts, D.J., Dodds, P.S.: Influentials, networks, and public opinion formation. Journal of Consumer Research 34(4), 441–458 (2007)
5. Weng, J., et al.: Twitterrank: finding topic-sensitive influential twitterers. ACM (2010)
6. Cha, M., et al.: Measuring user influence in twitter: The million follower fallacy (2010)
7. Gruhl, D., et al.: Information diffusion through blogspace. ACM (2004)
8. Granovetter, M.: Threshold models of collective behavior. American Journal of Sociology, 1420–1443 (1978)
9. Goldenberg, J., Libai, B., Muller, E.: Talk of the network: A complex systems look at the underlying process of word-of-mouth. Marketing Letters 12(3), 211–223 (2001)
10. Page, L., et al.: The PageRank citation ranking: Bringing order to the web (1999)
11. Yamaguchi, Y., Takahashi, T., Amagasa, T., Kitagawa, H.: TURank: Twitter user ranking based on user-tweet graph analysis. In: Chen, L., Triantafillou, P., Suel, T. (eds.) WISE 2010. LNCS, vol. 6488, pp. 240–253. Springer, Heidelberg (2010)
12. Erkan, G., Radev, D.R.: Lexpagerank: Prestige in multi-document text summarization (2004)
13. Guo, L., et al.: Analyzing patterns of user content generation in online social networks. ACM (2009)
14. McPherson, M., Smith-Lovin, L., Cook, J.M.: Birds of a feather: Homophily in social networks. Annual Review of Sociology, 415–444 (2001)
15. Salton, G., Buckley, C.: Term-weighting approaches in automatic text retrieval. Information Processing & Management 24(5), 513–523 (1988)
16. Salton, G., McGill, M.J.: Introduction to modern information retrieval (1986)
17. Zhang, D., Dong, Y.: An efficient algorithm to rank web resources. Computer Networks 33(1), 449–455 (2000)

Micro-blog Post Topic Drift Detection
Based on LDA Model

Quanchao Liu, Heyan Huang, and Chong Feng

Department of Computer Science and Technology,
Beijing Institute of Technology
Beijing, China
{liuquanchao,hhy63,fengchong}@bit.edu.cn

Abstract. Micro-blog posts imply a large number of topics, which contain a lot of useful information as well as a lot of junk information making the micro-blog post topic a characteristic of high drift. The changes of micro-blog post topic over time and noises introduced with the increase of the number of micro-blog posts are two main aspects of micro-blog post topic drift. We propose a method of topic drift detection based on LDA model, using Gibbs sampling algorithm to obtain the probability distribution of micro-blog post words based on words correlation, identifying the topic boundary in dynamic constant method, extracting topic words by computing lexical information entropy in the topic field, and detecting the topic drift by topic words sequence alignment based on discrete-time model. According to the experiment on topic drift detection based on LDA model, we find our method very effective in micro-blog post topic drift detection.

Keywords: Topic drift, LDA model, Micro-blog post, Topic drift detection, Evolutionary analysis.

1   Introduction

Internet new media makes it possible for Internet users to edit the web instead of simply read it. As a result, the Internet contains huge amount of user generated content (UGC), especially in micro-blog posts. Even though more and more people are enjoying the convenience of publication of micro-blog posts, such as timeliness, diversity and arbitrariness [1,2], it has a great challenge for topic identification and extraction as high-quality topics are often mixed with junk information.

Topic drift is the main interference of topic detection and tracking validation. There are two main reasons for topic drift: Firstly, the concern of topic is transferring over time, which is unable to avoid; Secondly, text features are growing with the increase of topic related text, which makes it hard for topic detection and tracking technology based on text clustering and classification. In other words, as the result of the information redundancy and topic divergence of micro-blog post, the micro-blog post topic is very likely to drift.

Topic tracking technology based on the traditional clustering techniques is unable to solve the problem for massive micro-blog posts. It is an urgent need to detect micro-blog post topic drift in new methods, including micro-blog post topic recognition, micro-blog post topic relationship mining, topic boundary identification, and topic

L. Cao et al. (Eds.): BSIC/BSI 2013, LNAI 8178, pp. 106–118, 2013.

tracking. We propose a method of micro-blog post topic drift detection in this paper and it will be essentially helpful for information extraction, text classification, topic tracking and other fields.

The remainder of this paper is structured as follows. In Section 2, we briefly summarize related work. Section 3 gives an overview of micro-blog post topic drift model, including data description and topic drift model. LDA model used in micro-blog post is described in Section 4, including Gibbs sampling algorithm. In Section 5, we introduce several methods to measure the coherence of topic content and identify the boundary of the topic. Using information entropy to extract topic words is described in Section 6. Experiments and results are reported in Section 7 and Section 8 concludes our work.

2   Related Work

The present text topic recognition technologies are: text topic recognition based on lexical aggregation, linguistic features and statistical probability, as well as other text topic identification methods. Lexical aggregation based text topic recognition [3] assumed that the similar or related words tend to occur in the same topic. They believed that, the organic organization of the text is an important feature of the text, while an arbitrary sentence set is not. They thus defined five kinds of lexical aggregation form in two situations: one is the word repetition or covert duplication; the other is the term systematic or non-systematic semantic relation, such as TF·IDF, lexical chain and dotplotting lexical aggregation method. In addition, according to weights based on word frequency and the distance between the words, Richmond calculated similarity of text in adjacent regions, and used the similarity for topic identification [4].

Topic drift is often accompanied with a number of linguistic features of the text. Nakhimovsky [5] proposed four situations of the topic drift: (1) topic change; (2) time and space transform; (3) the character and the scene change; (4) perspective of discusses change. Grimes [6] also presented four indicative boundary features of topic drift: (1) scene; (2) participants; (3) chronology; (4) topic of conversation. He thought the change of the action scenes, characters, time or dialogue topic means the beginning of a new topic. Researchers also put forward some other language features, such as Youmans [7] puts forward the concept of first uses, that first used words within a document are usually accompanied with document topic shift.

Beeferman, Berger and Lafferty et al. identified text topic through the probability statistical model [8]. They proposed an exponential model and adopted it on the training corpus in which the topic boundary has been labeled to extract some features indicating the boundary: topicality features and cue-word features.

Choi [9] introduced the latent semantic analysis model (LSA). LSA builds matrix of sentences and words with the word frequency, using the singular value decomposition (SVD) on matrix reduction to obtain various parameters through the training corpus. The experiment result shows that, LSA is more accurate than the cosine similarity in the measure of sentence similarity. As a variant of LSA, probabilistic latent semantic analysis (PLSA) has a solid mathematical foundation and it is easy to generate the model. PLSA has been shown to provide a better lexical matching for information extraction. However, the disadvantage of the model is that the document probability relates to the specific document, making the lack of processing a new document. At the same time, the model is prone to over fitting, as the numbers of parameters to be estimated increase linearly with the growth of documents [10].

Compared with PLSA, the Latent Dirichlet Allocation (LDA) model [11] is considered to be a fully generative model. The LDA model transfers the topic mixture weights to the K dimension parameters of the underlying random variables, rather than directly links to the individual parameters collection with the training data. The parameters of LDA are estimated by Laplace Approximation, Variation Approximation, Markov Chain Monte Carlo or Expectation-Propagation method, which overcomes the deficiency of PLSA.

In this paper, a micro-blog post corpus provided by NLPIR[1] is used as data set, and the topic drift detection method is designed and implemented based on a LDA model for micro-blog post topic. Concrete steps are as follows:

(1) The LDA generation model for micro-blog post topic is trained by Gibbs sampling on the micro-blog post training set, taking each micro-blog post text as a text unit;

(2) Probability distribution $\phi^{(z)}$ and $\psi^{(d)}$ are calculated by Gibbs sampling;

(3) The probability distribution $P(w \mid d)$ for micro-blog post word W in micro-blogpost text d is calculated based on probability distribution $\phi^{(z)}$ and $\psi^{(d)}$;

(4) Based on $P(w \mid d)$, the correlation between micro-blog post texts is calculated using micro-blog post correlation algorithm;

(5) Topic field boundaries are identified using the boundary recognition strategy;

(6) Based on the topic words obtained with the information entropy theory in topic field, the micro-blog post topic evolution and drift are showed in the discrete time model.

3   Micro-blog Post Topic Drift Model

3.1   Data Description

Micro-blog users have been more than 300 million in China[2], and most of them are users of Sinaweibo or Tencentweibo. Micro-blog is "A 140-character Twitter with Facebook look-and-feel, in a country with very few high-quality traditional media". Common micro-blog posts on the Web display as shown in Figure 1. "##" indicates the micro-blog topic, "//" indicates forwarding relation, "@" indicates the user, namely to @ user for forwarding, commenting and other operations. From Figure 1, Li Kaifu forwarded and commented on Yingyonghui's original post, and then Toby_Bit forwarded and commented on Li Kaifu's post. The appearance of pictures and emotional symbols indicates that the expression of micro-blog content is varied.

---

[1] http://www.nlpir.org/download/weibo_content_corpus.rar
[2] The Eleventh China Network Media Forum.

Fig. 1. Micro-blog post example

3.2   Topic Drift Model

We use the topic words' probability density to express a topic, as shown in Figure 2. Topic drift refers to the changes of topic words' probability distribution over time, and it is indicated by the changes of the key words' probability. We define an undirected graph $G = \{V, E\}$ to describe the micro-blog topic propagation model, where V represents a topic node set, which consists of micro-blog posts on the topic at current state. E is composed of all the edges connecting the nodes of V, representing the propagation path between topics, including forwarding and comments of the micro-blog posts.

Topic	Information Entropy
郎朗	16.2
钢琴	13.8
指挥	8.07
音乐	7.80
演出	7.10
艺术	4.09

Fig. 2. Topic Representation about Langlang

The concerns of micro-blog users on a topic are changing over time and it is important to discover the law of these changes. In the discrete time model, t_0 indicates the initial moment, and $t_1, t_2, \cdots, t_n, \cdots$ indicate the time after $1, 2, \cdots, N, \cdots$ units from the beginning. $N_{topic}(t_n)$ is the topic at t_n, and the transmission rate $R^E_{topic}(t_n)$ represents a set of micro-blog in $(t_{n-1}, t_n]$, in which every two of the micro-blog posts have a relation of E. Topic drift model is constructed as follows:

$$N_{topic}(t_n) = N_{topic}(t_{n-1}) + R^E_{topic}(t_n) \tag{1}$$

This model shows that the topic drift depends on the changes of the micro-blog posts over time as well as the influence of the previous topic at t_{n-1} for the same topic at t_n. Propagation rate $R^E_{topic}(t_n)$ indicates the degree of the change of the topic over time.

4   LDA Model

4.1   Model Description

Latent Dirichlet Allocation (LDA) submitted in 2002[11] is a probabilistic generative model, and is used to solve the latent semantic analysis. The fundamental assumption is: a text contains a number of topics, and the specific word in the text can reflect the specific topic. Thus, each text is seen as a probability distribution of certain topics, and each topic is considered as a probability distribution of all the words.

We have a collection of texts with M texts, K topics, and W words, and the text is an orderly sequence of the W words. In a given text D, the probability of w_i can be expressed as follow:

$$P(w_i) = \sum_{j=1}^{K} P(w_i \mid z_i = j) P(z_i = j) \tag{2}$$

z_i is a latent variable, indicating the w_i is included in the topic; $P(z_i = j)$ represents the probability of the topic j appeared in current text; and $P(w_i \mid z_i = j)$ is the probability of the word w_i appeared in the topic j. Therefore, the purpose of the LDA model is to infer two important probability distributions: one is the multinomial distribution $\phi^{(z=j)} = P(w \mid z = j)$ of a word W in topic j; the other is the multinomial distribution $\phi^{(d)}_{z=j} = P(z = j)$ of the topic j in text d. Then, the probability of the word W in the text d can be expressed as:

$$P(w \mid d) = \phi^{(z=j)}_w \cdot \psi^{(d)}_{z=j} \tag{3}$$

In order to handle new texts beyond the training corpus and simplify the inference of model parameters, LDA model uses prior probability hypothesis $Dirichlet(\alpha)$ and $Dirichlet(\beta)$ respectively in $\phi^{(z)}$ and $\psi^{(d)}$ [12]:

$$w_i \mid z_i, \phi^{(z_i)} \sim Dirichlet(\phi^{(z_i)}), \phi^{(z_i)} \sim Dirichlet(\beta) \qquad (4)$$

$$z_i \mid \psi^{(d_i)} \sim Dirichlet(\psi^{(d_i)}), \psi^{(d_i)} \sim Dirichlet(\alpha) \qquad (5)$$

As a result, the key of the LDA model is the inference of two important Dirichlet distributions, one is the distribution $\psi^{(d)}$ of the texts and topics, and the other is the distribution $\phi^{(z)}$ of the topics and words. We adopt the Gibbs sampling algorithm to obtain $\phi^{(z)}$ and $\psi^{(d)}$ indirectly.

4.2   Parameter Estimation and Gibbs Sampling

Gibbs sampling is a simple implementation of Markov-Chain Monte Carlo (MCMC). The purpose of Gibbs sampling is to construct a Markov chain converging to the target probability distribution in the high dimensional model (such as LDA), and extract sample distribution closest to the target probability distribution from Markov chain. In the LDA model, $\phi^{(z)}$ and $\psi^{(d)}$ can be represented through the joint statistics between the word w_i and the potential topic z_i, so it would work only sampling on z_i. The posterior probability $P(z_i = j \mid z_{-i}, w_i)$ is derived through the Gibbs sampling algorithm, and the calculation formula is as follows:

$$P(z_i = j \mid z_{-i}, w_i) = \frac{\dfrac{n_{-i,j}^{(w_i)} + \beta}{n_{-i,j}^{(.)} + K\beta} \cdot \dfrac{n_{-i,j}^{(d_i)} + \alpha}{n_{-i,.}^{(.)} + K\alpha}}{\displaystyle\sum_{j=1}^{K} \dfrac{n_{-i,j}^{(w_i)} + \beta}{n_{-i,j}^{(.)} + K\beta} \cdot \dfrac{n_{-i,j}^{(d_i)} + \alpha}{n_{-i,.}^{(.)} + K\alpha}} \qquad (6)$$

$z_i = j$ means w_i in the vocabulary sequences is assigned to the topic j; z_{-i} represents all distributions $z_k (k \neq i)$. $n_{-i,j}^{(w_i)}$ is the times of w_i assigned to the topic j; $n_{-i,j}^{(d_i)}$ is the number of all words assigned to the topic j in the text d_i; $n_{-i}^{(d_i)}$ is the number of all topics assigned to d_i. The distribution $z_i = j$ is not included in all the above number of the words.

Gibbs sampling [13] is described as follows:

(1) z_i is initialized to a random integer between 1 to K. i loops from 1 to N

(N is the number of words appeared in the corpus). It is the initial state of the Markov chain.

(2) i loops from 1 to N. According to the formula (6), the word was assigned to the topic, which is the next state of the Markov chain.

(3) After enough times iteration of the subsection (2), the Markov link is seen as the target distribution. The current value of z_i (i loops from 1 to N) is recorded as the sample. In order to get a smaller autocorrelation, other samples are recorded after a certain number of iterations. For each sample, $\phi^{(z)}$ and $\psi^{(d)}$ can be calculated as follows:

$$\tilde{\phi}_w^{(z=j)} = \frac{n_j^{(w)} + \beta}{n_j^{(\cdot)} + W\beta} \tag{7}$$

$$\tilde{\psi}_{z=j}^{(d)} = \frac{n_j^{(d)} + \alpha}{n_{\cdot}^{(d)} + K\alpha} \tag{8}$$

$n_j^{(w)}$ represents the times of word W assigned to the topic j; $n_j^{(\cdot)}$ represents the number of all words assigned to the topic j; $n_j^{(z)}$ is the number of words assigned to the topic j in the text d; $n_j^{(d)}$ represents the number of all words assigned to a topic in the document d.

5   Topic Boundary Identification

5.1   Micro-blog Post Similarity

The goal of the similarity measure of Micro-blog is to maximum topic correlations within the topic fields, and minimal topic correlations between the different topic fields. We take each micro-blog post as the basic processing unit, LDA model is adopted for topic analysis on each micro-blog post. Probability distribution $\phi^{(z)}$ and $\psi^{(d)}$ are calculated by Gibbs sampling, and $P(w|d)$ is inferred. [14] and [15] provided 5 methods to measure similarity:

(1) Cosine Similarity

$$Sim_{cos} = \frac{\sum_{w \in W} P(w|d_i)P(w|d_{i+1})}{\sqrt{\sum_{w \in W} P(w|d_i)^2}\sqrt{\sum_{w \in W} P(w|d_{i+1})^2}} \tag{9}$$

(2) L1 Distance

$$Sim_{L1} = 1 - \frac{\sum_{w \in W} |P(w|d_i) - P(w|d_{i+1})|}{2} \tag{10}$$

(3) Hellinger Distance

$$Sim_{Hel} = \sum_{w \in W} \sqrt{P(w \mid d_i)P(w \mid d_{i+1})} \tag{11}$$

(4) Clarity Similarity

$$Sim_{Clr} = -KL(P(w \mid d_i) \parallel P(w \mid d_{i+1})) + KL(P(w \mid d_i) \parallel GC)$$
$$- KL(P(w \mid d_{i+1}) \parallel P(w \mid d_i)) + KL(P(w \mid d_{i+1}) \parallel GC) \tag{12}$$

GC stands for $f(w)$, the frequency of word w in the training corpus. $KL(\cdot \parallel \cdot)$ is known as relative entropy:

$$KL(P(w \mid d_i) \parallel P(w \mid d_{i+1})) = \sum_{w \in W} P(w \mid d_i) \log_2 \frac{P(w \mid d_i)}{P(w \mid d_{i+1})} \tag{13}$$

(5) Jensen–Shannon divergence

$$Sim_{JS} = -KL(P(w \mid d_i) \parallel \frac{P(w \mid d_i) + P(w \mid d_{i+1})}{2})$$
$$- KL(P(w \mid d_{i+1}) \parallel \frac{P(w \mid d_i) + P(w \mid d_{i+1})}{2}) \tag{14}$$

5.2   Topic Boundary Identification

The micro-blog similarity is used to determine the topic boundary between topic fields. The basic idea is: when the similarity between micro-blog posts is large enough, the two micro-blog posts are combined into one field; otherwise, a topic boundary is built to identify the micro-blog post topic drift. We used dynamic constant method [15] to achieve topic boundary identification, assuming there are n micro-blog posts, the similarity between adjacent micro-blog posts are Similarity=$\{Sim_1, Sim_2, \cdots, Sim_{n-1}\}$, where $Sim_i = Sim(d_i, d_{i+1})$, $1 \le i \le n-1$. The average similarity of the n micro-blog posts is as follows:

$$Sim_{avg} = \frac{(Sim_1 + Sim_2 + \cdots + Sim_{n-1})}{n-1} \tag{15}$$

Where $Sim_{avgm} = \frac{((Sim_2 - Sim_1) + (Sim_3 - Sim_2) + \cdots + (Sim_{n-1} - Sim_{n-2}))}{n-2} \tag{16}$

if $Sim_{avgm} \le Sim_i \le Sim_{avg}$, micro-blog posts belong to different topic fields.

6   Topics' Extraction and Evolution

The micro-blog posts are divided into several topic fields TF_1, TF_2,..., TF_m, and topic words are extracted by calculating the Shannon information of the words in topic field.

First, each topic within the field TF_i ($1 \leq i \leq$ m) is seen as a processing unit, and the probability distribution of the word w given topic field TF_i is calculated according to the formula $P(w \mid TF_i) = \sum_{j=1}^{m} \phi_w^{(z=j)} \cdot \psi_{z=j}^{(TF_i)}$. Shannon information can be calculated using the probability distribution of word w given TF_i as follows [16]:

$$I(w) = -N(w) \ln P(w \mid TF_i) \qquad 1 \leq i \leq m \qquad (17)$$

$N(w)$ is the frequency of the word w in the topic field TF_i. The larger Shannon information is, the larger the word's representation is in this topic field. As a result, the topic filed is represented by a topic word sequence including words with larger Shannon information. From the equation above, the Shannon information not only represents the knowledge for the corpus, but also reflects the information of topic fields, which is helpful to improve the accuracy of the topic word extraction.

7   Experiments and Result

The open source software jGibbLDA[3], an implement of LDA model with Gibbs sampling, is used in our experience. [14] and [15] have proved that the combination of L1 distance and dynamic constant method is satisfactory for identifying topic field. We take the micro-blog corpus provided by NLPIR as data set, and extract 230 thousands micro-blog posts from 2011 Sinaweibo. The file size is 117M in XML format. We convert XML into text format, and divide them into 12 folders by month, representing 12 discrete time series. Comparing with topic words in the discrete time model, we can find the problem of micro-blog topic drift. The training procedure is as follows:

Step 1: Use the Chinese word segmentation tool ICTCLAS[4] for word segmentation of training text set, and remove stop words;

Step 2: Put all preprocessed texts into a model training document (.dat). The first row of the document represents the number of texts in training set, and each of the other rows represents a text, each columns of the row is one word in the text (excluding stop words). The numbers of columns in different rows are different.

---

[3] http://jgibblda.sourceforge.net/
[4] http://www.nlpir.org/?action-category-catid-23

Step 3: Set parameters of the jGibbLDA. The LDA model file is generated by jGibbLDA training module based on training texts.

After training, the steps of topic analysis using LDA model are as follows:

Step 1: Use the Chinese word segmentation tool ICTCLAS for word segmentation of the micro-blog set to be predicted, and remove stop words;

Step 2: Write all preprocessed texts into a model prediction document(.dat). Similar to the training, the first row of the document represents the number of texts in training set, and each of the other rows represents a text, each columns of the row is one word in the text;

Step 3: Set parameters of the jGibbLDA. The model predicts based on the model prediction document and generates the LDA prediction file;

Step 4: Calculate micro-blog probability distribution of words $P(w \mid d)$ based on the value of the probability distribution $\phi^{(z)}$ and $\psi^{(d)}$ in the prediction file;

Step 5: Calculate the similarities of the micro-blog posts using the L1 distance metric method based on $P(w \mid d)$. The similarity table is

$$\text{Similarity} = \{\text{Sim}_1, \text{Sim}_2, \cdots, \text{Sim}_{n-1}\};$$

Step 6: Identify the boundary of topic fields, using the dynamic constant method described in the above;

Step 7: Calculate Shannon information value of all words in each topic fields and select 10 words with the largest Shannon information value to form topic words sequences, on behalf of the topic fields.

Parameter settings: set topic number K=200, iterative parameters niters=1000, hyper parameters α and β with default values.

Topics 1, 3, 5, 7, 9 are chosen as an example, as shown in Figure 3. Each topic is represented by 10 words with the largest Shannon information value. The topic probability distributions are constantly changing and the topic words in December 2011 is shown in Figure 3 as an example. We can get the change trends of topics' strength from the line chart of Figure 3, and know some words representing the topics are overlapped from the table in the Figure 3. Topic strength S (topic) is defined as follows:

$$S(topic) = \frac{1}{N} \sum_{i=1}^{N} I(w_i) \qquad (8)$$

The topic strength is measured by the average of N largest Shannon information value. Five Topics with the highest strength are shown in the line chart of Figure 3, and topic 5 with higher strength is different from other four topics. Because of some topic words sequence are overlapped, the strengths of topic 1, 3, 7, 9 are similar with each other, but the strength of topic 3,7,9 are increasing while the topic 1 is coming down.

We Detecting Topic drift on topic 1, as shown in Figure 4, the column represents the strength distance of topic 1 in the adjacent time; the length of a column chart represents topic strength in a certain period of time, namely the degree of change of

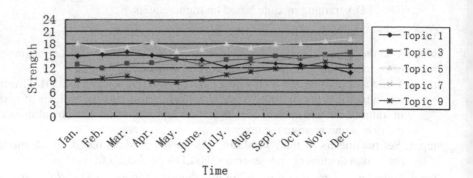

Topic 1	Topic 3	Topic 5	Topic 7	Topic 9
中国	出版	中国	经济学家	稳定
教师	工作	昆曲	投资	社会
全球	美国	融合	全球	政治
收入	大学	剧种	体制	中国
老师	经营	科班	管理	谈话
垫底	编辑	演出	收入	矛盾
灰色	存货	京剧	配置	融合
这样	成本	演员	持续性	收入
理由	册	戏校	垫底	工作
大学	定价	传统	潜力	灰色

Fig. 3. The Change Trends of Topics' Strength and Topic Words in December

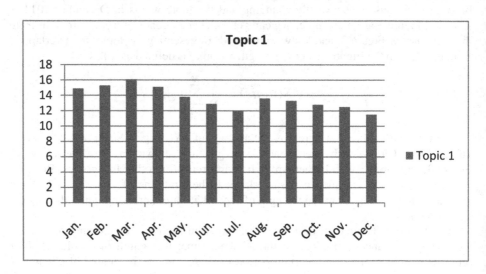

Jan.	Feb.	Mar.	Apr.	May.	Jun.	Jul.	Aug.	Sep.	Oct.	Nov.	Dec.
学校	专业	教育部	途径	社会	道德	费用	原因	大学	年青人	**收入**	**中国**
素质	人才	教学	人们	自己	公平	压力	思考	学生	费用	中国	教师
氛围	国家	关注	体制	道德	素质	什么	物质	讲师	项目	红包	全球
可持续	文明	素质	环境	精神	评论	提高	生活	大	讲师	幼儿园	收入
途径	开展	投入	发扬	体制	行为	专心	钱	基本	大学	老师	老师
就业	学生	GDP	教育者	人们	暴力	公平	学校	外快	灰色	钱	垫底
国人	质量	财政	技术	灰色	招收	道德	工资	教学	基本	送礼	灰色
环境	人们	老师	成人	教育	孩子	越	高兴	时间	幼儿园	垫底	这样
老师	问题	学生	身心	某些	家庭	没有	低	博导	家长	排位	理由
小学生	多	国际	学制	原因	教育	精力	办法	钱	豪车	羡慕	大学

Fig. 4. Evolution Trend of Topic 1 in 2011

topic 1 over time. The drift of topic 1 can be observed through mutations of the column chart. For example, the distance of topic strength increases rapidly from July to August, indicating that there is a significant change of topic 1 during this period of time. Through observing the topic words sequence and comparing the topic words between July and August, we find that the Shannon information of the topic words relating to the teacher's salary is generally increasing, and this trend is still increasing after July, these indicate that the content of topic 1, the quality problem of education in China, is gradually evolved into the income problem of Chinese teacher.

8   Conclusions and Future Work

Micro-blog post in China is loved by more and more people. However, Micro-blog posts contain a lot of useful information as well as a lot of junk information making the topic of micro-blog post a characteristic of high drift, and there is a lack of an effective method for micro-blog topic drift detection. In this paper, according to the characteristics of transmission of micro-blog posts in the discrete time model, we propose a method based on LDA model for micro-blog topic drift detection, and other aspects on micro-blog topic drift detection including topic boundary identification and topic words extraction. The experimental results show that our method based on LDA model for micro-blog topic drift detection is efficient and feasible, and it depicts the change of micro-blog post topic. The next step of this paper will focus on the method of online micro-blog topic evolution analysis based on LDA model, and the establishment and realization of online LDA model.

Acknowledgments. This paper is financially supported by Key Project of Chinese National Programs for Fundamental Research and Development (973 Program, No. 2013CB329605). We would like to thank the anonymous reviewers for many valuable comments and helpful suggestions.

References

1. Kang, J.H., Lerman, K., Plangprasopchok, A.: Analyzing Microblogs with affinity propagation. In: Proceedings of the 1st KDD Workshop on Social Media Analytic, pp. 67–70. ACM, New York (2010)
2. Zhang, C., Sun, J., Ding, Y.: Topic Mining for Microblog Based on MB-LDA Model. Journal of Computer Research and Development 48(10), 1795–1802 (2011)
3. Halliday, M., Hasan, R.: Cohesion in English. Longman Group, New York (1976)
4. Richmond, K., Smith, A., Amitay, E.: Detecting Subject Boundaries within Text: A Language Independent Statistical Approach. In: Proceedings of the Second Conference on Empirical Methods in Natural Language Processing (EMNLP 1997), pp. 47–54 (1997)
5. Nakhimovsky, A.: Aspect, assectual class, and the temporal structure of narrative. Computational Linguistics 14(2), 29–43 (1998)
6. Grimes, J.E.: The Thread of Discourse. Mouton, The Hague (1975)
7. Youmans, G.: Measuring lexical style and competence: The type token vocabulary curve. Style 24, 584–599 (1990)
8. Beeferman, D., Berger, A., Lafferty, J.: Statistical Models for Text Segmentation. Machine Learning 34, 177–210 (1999)
9. Choi, F.Y.Y., Wiemar-Hastings, P., Moore, J.: Latent Semantic Analysis for Text Segmentation. In: Proceedings of the 6th Conference on Empirical Methods in Natural Language Processing, pp. 109–117 (2001)
10. Shi, J., Li, W.: Research on comparison of three topic segmentation approaches. Computer Engineering and Applications 45(18), 135–138 (2009)
11. Blei, D.M., Ng, A.Y., Jordan, M.I.: Latent dirichlet allocation. Journal of Machine Learning Research 3, 993–1022 (2003)
12. Griffiths, T.L., Steyvers, M.: Finding scientific topics. Proceedings of the National Academy of Sciences, 5228–5235 (2004)
13. Heinrich, G.: Parameter Estimation for Text Analysis. Technical Report, University of Leipzig, Germany (2008)
14. Brants, T., Chen, F., Tsochantaridis, I.: Topic-Based Document Segmentation with Probabilistic Latent Semantic Analysis. In: Proceedings of the Eleventh International Conference on Information and Knowledge Management, pp. 211–218 (2002)
15. Shi, J., Hu, M., Shi, X., Dai, G.: Text Segmentation Based on Model LDA. Chinese Journal of Computers 31(10), 1865–1873 (2008)
16. Li, H., Yamanishi, K.: Topic analysis using a finite mixture model. Information Processing and Management 39(4), 521–541 (2003)

A Network-Based Approach
for Collaborative Filtering Recommendation*

Xuefeng Ma, Bo Li, and Qi An

School of Computer Science and Engineering, Beihang University, Beijing, China
{maxf,libo,anqi}@act.buaa.edu.cn
http://scse.buaa.edu.cn

Abstract. Collaborative filtering used in recommender systems produces predictions about the interests of a user by collecting preferences or taste information from many users. A substantial part of collaborative filtering centers on similarity computation. The most popular similarity metrics are Pearson correlation, cosine constrained Pearson's correlation, Spearman rank correlation and mean squared difference. In this paper, we propose a new metric to compute the similarity between two users, based on Jaccard similarity, $inter_1$-link similarity and $inter_0$-link similarity. Extensive experimental results and comparisons with other existing recommendation methods based on MovieLens dataset show our proposed recommender system is more effective than traditional collaborative filtering algorithms in terms of accuracy.

Keywords: recommender systems, collaborative filtering, similarity, Jaccard.

1 Introduction

Recommender system is a class of applications dealing with information overload, which helps solve this problem by recommending items to users based on their previous preferences. Many applications have used recommender systems, especially in the e-commerce domains. However, the current generation of recommender systems still requires further improvements to make recommendation methods more effective and applicable to an even broader range of real-life applications.

The basic principle of recommender system is to predict the rating of an active user on an un-rated item or recommend some items for the active user based on the existing ratings. Techniques in recommender systems [1] can be divided into three categories: content-based, collaborative filtering and hybrid approaches. In content-based systems, items that are similar to the ones that the user liked

* We acknowledge Jianxin Li for his contributions to the algorithm of this work. We also thank the anonymous reviewers for their valuable comments and help in improving this paper. This work is supported by National Nature Science Foundation of China under Grant No.61202424, and by the National Key Technology R&D Program under Grant No.2012BAH46B04.

L. Cao et al. (Eds.): BSIC/BSI 2013, LNAI 8178, pp. 119–128, 2013.

in the past are recommended. Collaborative filtering recommend items based on aggregated user preferences of those items, which does not depend on the availability of item descriptions. In collaborative filtering, preference information from a set of users is utilised to make predictions about the interests of the active user by assuming that user preferences hold over time. Hybrid approaches make recommendations by combining collaborative filtering and content-based recommendation.

Collaborative filtering systems are divided into two categories, i.e. memory-based and model-based. Memory-based approaches [10,12,14,15,16] use heuristics to make rating predictions by identifying the neighborhood of the active user to whom the recommendations will be made, based on the agreement of user's past ratings. Then we predict a missing rate by aggregating the ratings of the nearest neighbours of the user we want to recommend to. Model-based approaches [1,2,6,9,11,15] use the collection of ratings to learn a model, which is then used to make rating predictions. Generally, commercial recommender systems use memory-based approaches, while model-based approaches are usually associated with research recommender systems.

There has been much work done both in the industry and academia on developing new approaches to recommender systems. The interest in this area still remains high because it constitutes a problem-rich research area and because of the abundance of practical applications that help users to deal with information overload and provide personalized recommendations, content and services to them. These improvements of recommender systems include better methods for representing user behavior [5] and the information about the items to be recommended, more advanced recommendation modeling methods, incorporation of various contextual information into the recommendation process, utilization of multi-criteria ratings, development of less intrusive and more flexible recommendation methods that also on the measures that more effectively determine performance of recommender systems.

The organization of the paper is as follows. In Section 2, we construct the item network and use network, describe three different similarity weight between two users and establish the mathematical formulation of the new similarity metric. In Section 3, some numerical and simulation results are demonstrated through efficient implementations of the network-based recommender system. In Section 4, we conclude this paper and describes our future work.

2   Design of Network-Based Approach

2.1   The Item Network and the User Network

We construct an item network by linking all items i, j that are co-rated in any one user and assigning link weights $w(i, j)$ as follows

$$w(i, j) = \frac{|U_i \cap U_j|}{|U_i| + |U_j|}. \tag{1}$$

Using this to construct the item network results in extremely dense connectivity, so we prune all links with weight below threshold $w_{min} = 0.01$ to eliminate links between items where one is very common and one is relatively rare as such connections contribute only limited information. More formally, we get a network of items $G = (I, E)$, where I is the set of items and E a set of links. We denote each link by $(i, j) \in E$ meaning there exists a link from an item i to an item j. Namely, $w(i, j) > 0.01$.

Each user u can be represented as a graph $u = \{I_u, E_u\}$, where $E_u = \{(i, j)|(i, j) \in E$ and $i, j \in I_u\}$. In order to characterize the relation between two users, we classify the a pair of items from the two users into four categories: the same items, similar items, relevant items and unrelated items. Given two users a and u, if $i \in I_a$, $j \in I_u$ and $i, j \in I_a \cap I_u$, then we call i, j as the same items; If $i \in I_a \backslash I_u$, $j \in I_u \backslash I_a$ and $(i, j) \in E$, then we call i, j as similar items and (i, j) as an inter$_1$-link between users a and u; If $(i, j) \notin E$ and $w(i, j) > \theta$, we call i, j as relevant items and (i, j) as an inter$_0$-link between users a and u, where

$$\theta = \frac{1}{2}[\sum_{(k,l)\in N(I_u)} \frac{w(k,l)}{|N(I_u)|} + \sum_{(k,l)\in N(I_a)} \frac{w(k,l)}{|N(I_a)|}] \qquad (2)$$

and $N(I_u) = \{(k, l)|w(k, l) \le 0.01, k, l \in I_u\}$. The rest item pairs between users a and u are called as unrelated items.

Note that Inter$_1$-links connect a pair of items from different users which have direct interactions (links). This means that these item pairs are co-rated by a number of users. Inter$_0$-links connect a pair of items from different users which do not have direct interactions but are co-rated by some similar users, which implies that the number of these similar users is not large enough to make the item pairs have an inter$_1$-link. Fig. 1 depicts 6 users $u_1, \cdots, u_6$ and the item network inside these users where the nodes are items and there are two different types of links, i.e. inter$_1$-links and inter$_0$-links.

In traditional collaborative filtering approach, we would simply consider the k nearest neighbors to make a prediction for an active user on some un-rated item

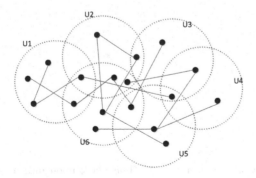

Fig. 1. The item network

i. However, due to the sparsity of the data the amount of information provided by each neighbor may be limited, i.e. the probability of a neighbor having rated item i is low. Moreover, some users only have a relatively small number of neighbors and hence increasing k is ineffective. In Fig. 2, only two neighbors have rated item i for the active user indicted by the black node, providing little confidence in the prediction.

To overcome this limitation, we construct a user network by finding the k nearest neighbors of each active user and connecting them via directed links. When predicting the rating on item i for an active user, if an immediate neighbor does not have rated item i, we recursively query this nearest neighbor network with depth-first search up to depth l. Fig. 2 illustrates this process for the same example as before, but this time using the network with search depth $l = 2$. Four different users with i now contribute to the final rating, increasing our confidence in the prediction. A neighbor makes a contribution to the final rating proportional to its similarity if he has rated the item i, and none otherwise.

2.2   Formalization of the New Similarity Metric in the User Network

Note that different recommender systems may take different approaches in order to implement the user similarity calculations and rating estimations as efficiently as possible. Recall that some items are co-rated by multiple users and they are thus located in the intersections of these users. If there are many common items in two separate users, then these two users are probably similar. A straightforward measure of the similarity between two users a and u could then be defined as the number of items they have in common

$$sim_0(a, u) = |I_a \cap I_u|. \tag{3}$$

This problem with this definition is that some users have one hundred or more items that have been rated and are therefore similar to most other users. To counter the effect we can use a quantity known as Jaccard similarity to

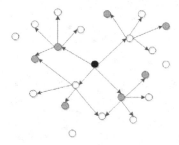

Fig. 2. The user network ($k = 4, l = 2$). The black node indicates the active user, nearest neighbors are connected via direct links. Neighbors who have rated item i are shaded, those who do not are transparent.

compute similarity normalized by the total number of items two users share,

$$sim_1(a, u) = \frac{|I_a \cap I_u|}{|I_a \cup I_u|}. \tag{4}$$

Another problem is that co-rated items between two users are rare and it is not adequate to only compute the Jaccard similarity between two users by equation (13). In an attempt to correct this limitation, we consider the relationship between two items from different users after removing the co-rated items. If there are a lot of $inter_1$-links from two users, then the two users are highly likely to be similar. Hence we propose the $inter_1$-link similarity between two users as follows

$$sim_2(a, u)$$
$$= \frac{|\{(i, j)|(i, j) \in E, i \in I_a \backslash I_u, j \in I_u \backslash I_a\}|}{|I_a \backslash I_u| \times |I_u \backslash I_a|}$$
$$= \frac{|\{inter_1 - links\ between\ users\ a\ and\ u\}|}{|I_a \backslash I_u| \times |I_u \backslash I_a|}. \tag{5}$$

If users have not too much $inter_1$-links, then we consider that the $inter_0$-links from different users and give the $inter_0$-link similarity between two users as follows

$$sim_3(a, u)$$

$$= \frac{|\{(i, j)|w(i, j) > \theta, w(i, j) \notin E, i \in I_a \backslash I_u, j \in I_u \backslash I_a\}|}{|I_a \backslash I_u| \times |I_u \backslash I_a|}$$
$$= \frac{|\{inter_0 - links\ between\ users\ a\ and\ u\}|}{|I_a \backslash I_u| \times |I_u \backslash I_a|}. \tag{6}$$

In this paper, we present a network-based collaborative filtering recommendation which combines three similarity weights based on Jaccard, $inter_1$-links and $inter_0$-links and make new prediction for the active user on an item in the user network. Through the combination processing, we use the weighted sum in place of $sim(a, u)$ in equation (2). More specifically,

$$sim(a, u) = \alpha sim_1(a, u) + \beta sim_2(a, u) + \gamma sim_3(a, u), \tag{7}$$

where $\alpha + \beta + \gamma = 1$ and α, β, γ are parameters to adjust the weighs for the importance of $sim_1(a, u), sim_2(a, u)$ and $sim_3(a, u)$. The traditional collaborative filtering method described is going to be used as the baseline system in our study.

3   Experiments and Evaluation

3.1   Experimental Data

In this section we present experiments we have conducted for evaluating the performance of our proposed recommender system. In order to discover the behavior of the network-based appraoch proposed, we use the "MovieLens" database (http://www.movielens.org) as the data source for our experiment.

The database contains 943 users, 1682 items and 100000 ratings, with every user having at least 20 ratings. The items represent films and the rating ranges vary from 1 to 5 stars. From the MovieLens dataset, we randomly extract 80% of each user's ratings to form a training set. The remaining part is a test set for measuring quality and performance of the proposed recommendation algorithm.

3.2   Experimental Method

For the purpose of measuring the effectiveness of a strategy we choose the widely used metric mean absolute error (MAE) which measures the average absolute deviation between a predicted rating and the user's actual rating. MAE has been used to evaluate recommender systems in several cases [2,3,8,12]. Formally, MAE is defined as follows:

$$\bar{E} = \frac{\sum_{i,j} |p_{i,j} - r_{i,j}|}{n}$$

where n is the number of ratings over all the test cases, $p_{i,j}$ is the prediction rating of user i on item j and $r_{i,j}$ is the actual rating. MAE is the difference between the actual rating and predicted rating. The smaller MAE is, the better the recommendation method is.

3.3   Experimental Results and Performance Evaluation

To evaluate the performance of the proposed recommender system, it is compared to the conventional collaborative filtering system. The performance of the proposed and conventional collaborative filtering systems is represented in MAE. The recommender system is 'good' (i.e., prediction is accurate) as the resulting value MAE is close to 0.

Next, we describe the experimental setting. For each item predicted, the user's k nearest neighbors that have rated the item in question are used to compute a prediction. Note that this means that a user may have a different set of k nearest neighbors for each item. All users in the database are examined as the potential k nearest neighbors for a user-no sampling is performed. The quality of a given prediction algorithm can be measured by comparing the predicted ratings to the actual ratings. In the experiment, we select a different number of nearest neighbors and calculate several times. The previous process was carried out for each of the different values of k, from 10 to 100 with a step of 10. In our experiments, we set the number of nearest neighbor set as 50 (Fig. 3).

Note that the need to compute pair-wise similarities between two users is too time-consuming for large networks. To improve the efficiency of our technique, we only select these user pairs which are potentially similar to compute their similarities. In our proposed recommendation algorithm, for each active user, we will find the candidate nearest neighbor set where the items rated by the active user have been also frequently rated by the each user in the candidate nearest neighbor set. In our experiments, the number of candidate nearest neighbor set is set as 150, but we have also tested the sensitivity how the size of candidate nearest neighbor set affects our proposed recommender system in Fig 4.

Let us now present the experiments. Fig. 3 shows the MAE error obtained in MovieLens by applying different similarity settings. The network-based approach achieves significant fewer errors in practically all the experiments carried out (by varying the number of k nearest neighbors) than Pearson correlation and cosine similarity. Compared with only using Jaccard similarity, $inter_1$-link similarity as well as $inter_0$-link similarity, the network-based approach also generated better results, illustrating that integrating the Jaccard similarity, $inter_1$-link similarity as well as $inter_0$-link similarity improves the performance and the quality of the recommendation. The results of Jaccard similarity and $inter_0$-link similarity are better than $inter_1$-link similarity in terms of MAE error. In comparison, by weighting and combining different similarity measures, we observe that the new metric is much more meaningful than Jaccard similarity, $inter_1$-link similarity as well as $inter_0$-link similarity.

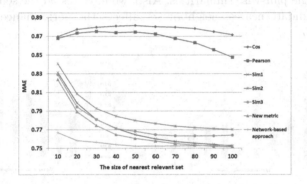

Fig. 3. Performance comparison of different similarity measures with different size of nearest neighbor set

The performance curve of the network-based approach goes down as the number of nearest neighbor set increases until the number of the nearest neighbor set gets up to 50. As for the new metric, the performance curve of the new metric has always been on the decline as the number of the nearest neighbor set increases. The performance curve of the network-based approach and the performance curve of the new metric coincide when the number of the nearest neighbor set gets up to 80. In addition, the new metric produces a better result than the network-based approach when the number of the nearest neighbor set is greater than 80. This is because when the number of the nearest neighbor set is too large, the active user and its neighbors with depth-first search up are not the most similar in the user network. In this case the new metric turns out a better result than the network-based approach. Hence, the network-based approach achieves the best result when the number of the nearest neighbor set is less than 80 and the new metric obtains the best result when the number of the nearest neighbor set is greater than 80. According to the number of the nearest neighbor set, we can choose to use the network-based approach and the new metric to make the predictions. As for the new metric, we set the number of the nearest neighbor set as 100 from the results of Fig. 3.

Given an active user, we want to find its candidate nearest neighbor set, which consists of potential nearest neighbors. Fig. 4 shows that the performance of our proposed recommender system with different sizes of candidate nearest neighbor set, from 1 to 10 with a step of 1. The value of MAE decreases as the size of candidate nearest neighbor set increases from 1 to 7, but it increases when the size of candidate nearest neighbor set goes beyond 8. Fig. 4 indicates that after the size of the candidate nearest neighbor set has increased to a certain degree-in this case, 8-more computation is no longer useful for improving the performance of the network-based approach as it only increases the computational time without increasing the quality of the recommendation. It also shows that our candidate nearest neighbor set has effectively captured the more related nearest neighbors so that it can save a large amount of computational time, as compared with computing all the pair-wise similarities. Also, we have tested the sensitivity how the size of candidate nearest neighbor set affects the performance of the new metric in Fig. 5.

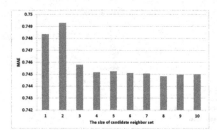

Fig. 4. Performance of the network-based approach with different candidate neighbor set

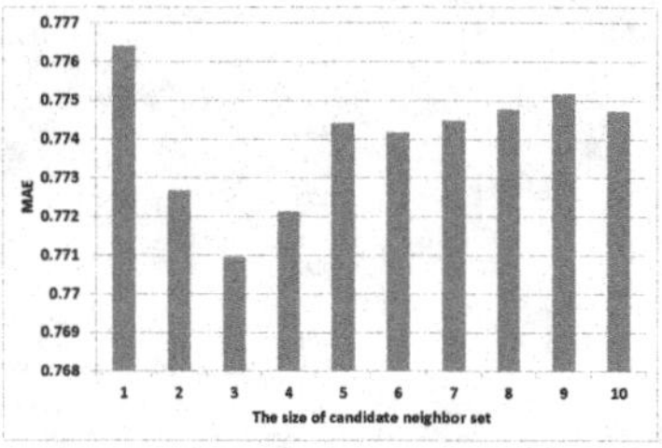

Fig. 5. Performance of the new metric with different candidate neighbor set

4   Conclusion

In this paper, we have proposed a network-based approach to collaborative filtering recommendation technique. Unlike conventional collaborative filtering approaches, our proposed recommender system makes use of the weighted sum based on the Jaccard similarity, $inter_1$-link similarity and $inter_0$-link similarity between two users. After all, the traditional collaborative filtering algorithms can be used to efficiently generate the recommendations. We present our experiments with the MovieLens dataset. Comparisons with traditional collaborative filtering algorithms show that our proposed recommender system can get a better recommendation results.

In our future work, we also would like to perform the evaluation on item-based recommender systems based on networks: constructing the user network by linking all users a, u that co-rate one item and assigning link weights

$$w(i,j) = \frac{I_u \cap I_a}{I_a + I_u}. \tag{8}$$

Further, we get a user network by finding the k nearest neighbors of each active item and using the depth-first search. Then we present a new similarity metric which combines three similarity weights based on Jaccard, $inter_1$-links and $inter_0$-links in the item network instead of the user network. Moreover, we plan to generalize our current approach to apply social networks and trust networks. We will leave this as our future work.

References

1. Adomavicius, G., Tuzhilin, A.: Toward the next generation of recommender systems: A survey of the state-of-the-art and possible extensions. IEEE Transactions on Knowledge and Data Engineering 17(6), 734–749 (2005)
2. Bobadilla, J., Serradilla, F., Bernal, J.: A new collaborative filtering metric that improves the behavior of recommender systems. Knowledge Based Systems 23(6), 520–528 (2010)
3. Bobadilla, J., Ortega, F., Hernando, A., Bernal, J.: Generalization of recommender systems: Collaborative filtering extended to groups of users and restricted to groups of items. Expert Systems with Applications 39, 172–186 (2012)
4. Burke, R.: Hybrid recommender systems: Survey and experiments. User Modeling and User-Adapted Interaction 12(4), 331–370 (2002)
5. Cao, L.: In-depth Behavior Understanding and Use: the Behavior Informatics Approach. Information Science 180(17), 3067–3085 (2010)
6. Park, M.-H., Hong, J.-H., Cho, S.-B.: Location-based recommendation system using bayesian user's preference model in mobile devices. In: Indulska, J., Ma, J., Yang, L.T., Ungerer, T., Cao, J. (eds.) UIC 2007. LNCS, vol. 4611, pp. 1130–1139. Springer, Heidelberg (2007)
7. Gao, L.Q., Li, C.: Hybrid personalizad recommended model based on genetic algorithm. In: International Conference on Wireless Communication Networks and Mobile Computing, pp. 9215–9218 (2008)
8. Herlocker, J.L., Konstan, J.A., Borchers, A., Riedl, J.: An algorithmic framework for performing collaborative filtering. In: SIGIR 1999: Proceedings of the 22nd Annual International ACM SIGIR Conference on Research and Development in Information Retrieval, New York, USA, pp. 230–237 (1999)
9. Ingoo, H., Kyong, J.O., Tae, H.R.: The collaborative filtering recommendation based on SOM cluster-indexing CBR. Expert Systems with Applications 25, 413–423 (2003)
10. Kong, F., Sun, X., Ye, S.: A comparison of several algorithms for collaborative filtering in startup stage. In: Proceedings of the IEEE Networking, Sensing and Control, pp. 25–28 (2005)
11. Li, X.-L., Tan, A., Yu, P.S., Ng, S.-K.: ECODE: Event-Based Community Detection from Social Networks. In: Yu, J.X., Kim, M.H., Unland, R. (eds.) DASFAA 2011, Part I. LNCS, vol. 6587, pp. 22–37. Springer, Heidelberg (2011)

12. Sanchez, J.L., Serradilla, F., Martinez, E., Bobadilla, J.: Choice of metrics used in collaborative filtering and their impact on recommender systems. In: Proceedings of the IEEE International Conference on Digital Ecosystems and Technologies DEST, pp. 432–436 (2008)
13. Steinhaeuser, K., Chawla, N.V.: A network-based approach to understanding and predicting diseases. In: Social Computing and Behavioral Modeling (2009)
14. Symeonidis, P., Nanopoulos, A., Manolopoulos, Y.: Providing justifications in recommender systems. IEEE Transactions on Systems, Man and Cybernetics, Part A 38(6), 1262–1272 (2008)
15. Yager, R.R.: Fuzzy logic methods in recommender systems. Fuzzy Sets and Systems 136(2), 133–149 (2003)
16. Yang, J.M., Li, K.F.: Recommendation based on rational inferences in collaborative filtering. Knowledge-Based Systems 22(1), 105–114 (2009)

A Novel Framework for Improving Recommender Diversity

Jinpeng Chen[1], Yu Liu[1], Jun Hu[1], Wei He[1], and Deyi Li[2]

[1] State Key Laboratory of Software Development Environment,
BeiHang University
chenjinpeng@nlsde.buaa.edu.cn,
liuyu@buaa.edu.cn, junhu@cse.buaa.edu.cn, informan@163.com
[2] Institute of Electronic System Engineering
deyi_li@nlsde.buaa.edu.cn

Abstract. Recommender systems are being used to assist users in finding relevant items from a large set of alternatives in many online applications. However, while most research up to this point has focused on improving the accuracy of recommender systems, other important aspects of recommendation quality, such as the diversity of recommendations, have often been overlooked. In this paper, we present a novel recommendation framework, designed to balance and diversify personalized top-N recommendation lists in order to capture the user's complete spectrum of interests. Systematic experiments on the real-world rating data set have demonstrated the effectiveness of our proposed framework in learning both accuracy and diversity of recommendations.

Keywords: Collaborative filtering, diversity, accuracy, recommender systems, metrics.

1 Introduction

Recommender system is one of the most effective tools to deal with information overload, which has been used in a lot of websites to recommend products (books, movies, music etc.) that a customer may be most likely to purchase [1, 2, 23, 24]. Most research and development efforts in the Recommender Systems field have been focused on accuracy in predicting and matching user interests. There have been many studies on developing new algorithms that can improve the accuracy of recommendations. In contrast, in recent years, several researchers have indicated that recommender systems with high accuracy do not always satisfy users [3, 4, 5, 22, 25]. They say that it is not sufficient to have accuracy as the sole criteria in measuring recommendation quality, and we should consider other important dimensions, such as diversity, novelty, serendipity, confidence, trust, to generate recommendations that are not only accurate but also useful to users.

Suppose that Tom likes "The Princess Diaries I". To recommend "The Princess Diaries II" or "The Princess Diaries III" to him is monotone and not surprising. Although, from the view point of accuracy, this recommendation is good, it is hard to say that the recommendation satisfies him. Recommender systems should satisfy users by providing them with diversification and useful items.

L. Cao et al. (Eds.): BSIC/BSI 2013, LNAI 8178, pp. 129–138, 2013.

Diversity as a relevant dimension of retrieval quality is receiving great attention in the Information Retrieval (*IR*) and Recommender Systems (*RS*) fields. We focus on diversity, which is one of the measures beyond accuracy. Although the definition of diversity has not yet been fixed, Drosou et al. [6] define diversity as a measure of the degree to which recommendations are both attractive and surprising to users.

In this paper, we present a novel recommendation framework, designed to balance and diversify personalized recommendation lists in order to better capture the user's range of tastes, and empirically demonstrate how this new framework can overcome the accuracy-diversity tradeoff.

The rest of the paper is organized as follows. Section 2 presents the related work. Section 3 shows our evaluation metrics for top-N recommendation. Section 4 describes our recommendation algorithm in detail. Section 5 provides experimental evaluation of the various parameters of the proposed algorithm and compares it against the state-of-the-art algorithms. Finally, we make some conclusions in Section 6.

2   Related Work

There are many important previous works done in the problem of enhancing the recommendation diversity. Bradley et al. [7] proposed the bounded greedy algorithm, which is the first attempt to explicitly enhance the diversity of a recommendation list without significantly compromising their query similarity characteristics in case-based recommender systems. Most diversity-enhancing methods follow this fundamental re-ordering strategy [9, 11]. Adomavicius and Kwon [8] addressed diversity as the ability of a system to recommend as many different items as possible over the whole population – a form of aggregate diversity, defined as the union of sets of recommended items to all users in the system. Raman et al. [10] proposed an online learning model and algorithms for learning diversified recommendations and retrieval functions from implicit feedback.

Some authors consider the diversity problem from the perspective of clustering. Kummamuru et al. [12] presented their clustering scheme that groups search results into clusters of related topics. Hofmann [13] put forward model-based recommendation algorithms using *k*-means and *PLSA* clustering to improve system accuracy. To better acquire the user's range of tastes, Zhang at al. [14] suggested partitioning the user profile into clusters of similar items and composing the recommendation list of items that match well with each cluster, rather than with the entire user profile. Our work is motivated by researchers such as [15] who extend the traditional CF algorithms by utilizing the sub-groups information for improving their top-N recommendation performance, while our algorithm based on the state-of-the-art collaborative filtering algorithms is to solve a top-N recommendation problem via self-adaption cluster analysis.

3   Evaluation Metrics

Evaluation metrics are essential in order to judge the quality and performance of recommender systems. In this paper, we evaluate our algorithm using accuracy metrics and diversity metrics. This section gives an outline of popular metrics.

3.1   Accuracy Metrics

Mean Absolute Error (MAE)

MAE [16] is a measure of the deviation of predicted recommendations from their true user-specific values. The MAE is computed by first summing those absolute errors between predicted and true value of the N corresponding ratings-prediction pairs and then computing the average. Formally,

$$MAE = \frac{\sum_{i=1}^{N} |pre\_Score_i - score_i|}{N}$$

where pre_Score_i and $score_i$ denote the predicted and true value, respectively. The lower the MAE, the more accurate the recommendation engine predicts user ratings.

3.2   Diversity Metrics

Intra-List Similarity

The diversity of a set of recommendations in a typical recommender system is defined based on their intra-list similarity ($Intra$-S). Here, diversity may refer to all kinds of features, e.g., genre, author, and other discerning characteristics. This approach is shown in [18]:

$$Intra - S = \frac{2}{K(K-1)} \sum_{i=1}^{K} \sum_{j>i}^{K} d(i_i, i_j)$$

where K is the recommendations number and $d(.,..)$ is a distance metric.

Inter-List Diversity

Inter Diversity [17] ($Inter$-D) measures the differences of different users' recommendation lists. Denote $list_i$ and $list_j$ as the recommendation list of user u_i and u_j respectively, then

$$Inter - D = \frac{2}{n(n-2)} \sum_{i \neq j} 1 - \frac{|list_i \cap list_j|}{N}$$

where N is the length of recommendation list.

4   Recommendation Diversity Algorithm

We first introduce two basic concepts: Cloud Model [19] and Gaussian Cloud Transformation ahead of introducing our recommendation algorithm.

4.1   Notations Definitions

Given: a set of users $U = \{u_1, u_2, \ldots, u_n\}$, a set of items(or products) $I = \{i_1, i_2, \ldots, i_m\}$, and partial rating functions $score_i$. We estimate a predicted rating, denoted as $pre\_Score(i)$. Here, $P = |U|$ is the total population of system users and

$Q = |I|$ is the total number of items (or products). Negative values $score_i$ denote utter dilike, while positive values express u_i's liking of item(or product) i_j.

4.2   Cloud Model

Cloud Model is an uncertainty transforming model between qualitative concept and quantitative numerical values. The cloud model integrates the two uncertainties and forms the mapping from qualitative to quantitative. Forward Cloud Generator transforms a qualitative concept to its quantitative description and Reverse Cloud Generator vice verse.

Definition 1(Cloud) Cloud is defined as follows. Let V be a universal set described by precise number, and C be the qualitative related to V. If there is a number $x \in V$, which randomly realizes the concept C, and the certainty degree x for C, i.e., $\mu(x) \in [0,1]$, is a random value with stable tendency.

$$\mu : U \rightarrow [0,1] \quad \forall x \in U, x \rightarrow \mu(x)$$

Then the distribution of x on V is defined as a cloud $C(x)$, and x is defined as a cloud drop. The certainty degree μ also refers as membership grade.

Cloud Model uses expectation Ex, entropy En and hyper entropy He to describe a specific concept. Ex expresses the point which is the most suitable to represent the domain of the concept and it is the most typical sample while quantifying the concept. En represents a granularity of a concept which could be measured (the larger of En, the larger of the granularity, the concept is more macro). It reflects the range of domain space which could be accepted by the specific concept and can be used to express the relationship between randomness and fuzziness. He describes the uncertain measurement of entropy. Vector $v = (Ex, En, He)$ is the eigenvector of a cloud.

4.3   Gaussian Cloud Transformation

Gaussian Cloud Transformation (*GCT*) is proposed based on Cloud Model [19] and Gaussian Transformation [20], which transforms data distribution of the problem domain into data clustering based on conception. *GCT*, without assigning the number of concept, can adaptively generate multiple granularity concepts, which accord with human cognition. *GCT* is minutely depicted in Algorithm 1. Note that, in Algorithm 1 we use the basic algorithm *B-GCT*. *B-GCT* is described as follows.

Basic Gaussian Cloud Transformation (*B-GCT*), utilizing prior-knowledge (input the number of conception), invokes Gaussian Transformation and generates expectation (*Ex*), variance, amplitude of M Gaussian distributions, respectively. Note that, the expectation of M Gaussian distributions is the same as M Clouds. And then, on the basis of the overlap degree among Gaussian distributions, we acquire entropy (*En*), hyper entropy (*He*) of each Cloud. Thus, we transform the quantitative data frequency distribution into a number of qualitative cognitive concepts using Gaussian Cloud Transformation.

Algorithm 1. *GCT*

X: Data set $\{x_i | i = 1,2 \dots, N\}$

β: The overlap degree of concepts   //β is an empirical value. Here, we let $\beta = 0.0663$.

mGC: *M* Clouds $(C(Ex_k, En_k, He_k) | k = 1,2, \dots, M)$

1.   define *A-GCT(X, β)*
2.   begin
3. $p(x_i) \leftarrow$ Statistical frequency distribution of *X*
4. $m \leftarrow$ The crest number
5. $mGC \leftarrow$ m Gaussian Clouds of *X* using *B-GCT*
6.   Sort β_k and compute β for each Cloud
7.   if $\beta_k = \frac{He_k}{En_k}$ is more than β
8. $m \leftarrow m - 1$
9.   end if
10.   while β_k is more than β
11.   goto *Line 5*
12.   end while
13.   return *mGC*
14. end

4.4   Recommendation Diversity Algorithm

Recommendation Diversity Algorithm (*RDA*) is presented based on traditional *CF* recommendation algorithm and *GCT*. *RDA* is fully depicted in Algorithm 2. A brief textual sketch is given in Figure 1.

Algorithm 2. *RDA*

s: The user rating scale

list: Top-N list

1.   define *RDA(s)*
2.   begin
3.   *queue* $\leftarrow$ Discover *K* nearest neighbors according to Pearson correlation or cosine distance
4.   Case 1: for $u_i \in U$ do
5. $pre\_Score(i_i) \leftarrow \overline{score_{u_j}} + \dfrac{\Sigma_{u_j \in queue(u_i)} s(u_i, u_j) \times (score(i_i) - \overline{score_{u_i}})}{\Sigma_{u_j \in queue(u_i)} s(u_i, u_j))}$
6.   end for
7. $List_{score} \leftarrow$ Get the recommended item list in the term of $pre\_Score(i)$
8. $List_{score-rel} \leftarrow$ Obtain the related recommended list leveraging the relevance threshold θ
9.   *list* $\leftarrow$ Generate top-N recommendation list using *GCT* based on $List_{score-rel}$
10.   return *list*
11. end

Based on *RDA*, our proposed recommendation framework is shown in Figure 1.

1. Generate the candidate list $List_{score}$ using the traditional *CF* technology. Here, the neighborhood number is a significant input parameter, which can achieve optimal value by executing multiple experiments (*Line 1-7* in Algorithm 2).
2. Generate the related recommended list $List_{score-rel}$ by considering the relevance threshold θ, which can sift through the candidate list $List_{score}$. Here, θ controls accuracy-diversity trade-off. θ changes over different recommendation system, e.g. $\theta = 3.5$ in the movielens data set (*Line 8* in Algorithm 2).
3. Get top-N recommendation list via making *GCT* cluster analysis for the data of $List_{score-rel}$. Subsequently, *M* clusters are produced, that is, *TYPE(i):{i = 1,2...M}*. Next, according to rating, genre et al. of items, we make statistic analysis leveraging voting method and get the number of item in each *TYPE(i)*, *vote(TYPE(i))*. The proportion of each *TYPE(i)* is also calculated, *percent(TYPE(i))*. Eventually, top-N recommendation list is produced (*Line 9-10* in Algorithm 2).

Fig. 1. The Framework of *RDA*

In the next section, we will estimate the validity of the *RDA* framework.

5   Data Design and Empirical Analysis

5.1   Data Design

Our experiments are performed on the real data set [21]: the Book Crossing (*BX*). This dataset is from the Book-Crossing community. It contains 278,858 users (anonymized but with demographic information) providing 1,149,780 ratings (explicit/implicit) about 271,379 books. Then we reduced the candidate set of books and users by restricting that each book has been rated by more than 30 users and each user has rated more than 30 books. So we get a subset of 2,134 users and 4,259 books.

5.2   Empirical Analysis

For the computation of the mentioned metrics in section 3, the data are split into training and test sets. In *BX* data set we use the 80-20% rating splits provided in the data set distribution, providing for 5-fold cross-validation.

We use the popular collaborative filtering techniques (*user-based*) and binary solution (*BS*) [5], which is based on the dissimilarity between the individual items considered, as baselines, and top-N ($N = 5, 10, 20, 30, 40, 50$) items are recommended for each user. We set predicted relevant threshold as $\theta = 3.5$ (out of 5) to ensure that only relevant items are recommended to users. The performance of each approach was measured in terms of accuracy in top-N list and diversity in top-N list ($N = 5, 10, 20, 30, 40, 50$), and, for comparison purposes, its accuracy loss with respect to the baseline approaches was calculated. Here, Accuracy Loss = [Accuracy-in-top-N of proposed *RDA*] – [Accuracy-in-top-N of standard *CF* approach (or *BS*)].

Figure 2 plots the *MAE, Intra-S*, and *Inter-D* against *N*. It can be seen that the proposed diversification methods work properly. The explanation for this is that *RDA* without requiring semantic information and considering prior-knowledge, solves the top-N recommendation problem via self-adaption cluster analysis. From Figure 2(a), with the number of *N* increasing, *MAE* of three algorithms has maintained themselves in a steady state. However, the average accuracy loss of the proposed algorithm is only 0.0014 and 0.0011, comparing with *user-based* and *BS* respectively. We think our proposed algorithm has same accuracy with the typical *user-based* algorithm and *BS*. Figure 2(b) presents three algorithms show the same types of sensitivity. That is, with the increase of the recommendations number, *Intra-S* of two algorithms is trending downward. But *Intra-S* of the proposed algorithm improves by 24.7 times and 33.7 percent, comparing with *user-based* and *BS* respectively. From Figure 2(c), we can see that *RDA* can already increase *Inter-D* by one time and 20.6 percent, comparing with *user-based* and *BS* respectively.□

Figure 3 plots the *MAE, Intra-S*, and *Inter-D* against the neighbor number *K* with *K* varied in the range [10, 60]. We can observe that the proposed algorithms obviously outperform the standard *CF* approach and *BS* in all of three metrics. The possible reason for this is similar to the explanation for Figure 2. From Figure 3(a), with the number of neighbor increasing, *MAE* of three algorithms has maintained themselves in a steady state. However, the average accuracy loss of the proposed algorithm is only 0.023 comparing with *user-based* and is nearly the same as *BS*. Figure 3(b) presents three algorithms show the same types of sensitivity. That is, with the increase of the neighbor number, *Intra-S* of three algorithms is trending downward. But *Intra-S* of the proposed algorithm improves by 34 times and 31.9 percent, comparing with *user-based* and *BS* respectively. From Figure 3(c), we can see that, along with the neighbor number increasing, *Inter-D* of the typical *user-based* algorithm has a downward trend, and *Inter-D* of the proposed algorithm and *BS* shows a rising trend. The proposed algorithm does not outperform the typical *user-based* algorithm and *BS* until the number of neighbor reaches 50. So we take the number of the neighbor (*K* = *50*) as an optimal value in the TOP-N recommendation.

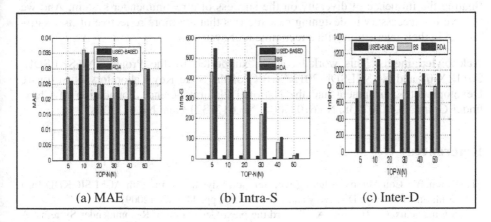

(a) MAE   (b) Intra-S   (c) Inter-D

Fig. 2. Results of the proposed metrics with the state-of-art recommender algorithms and *RDA* (*BX* dataset, 50 neighbors, θ = 5)

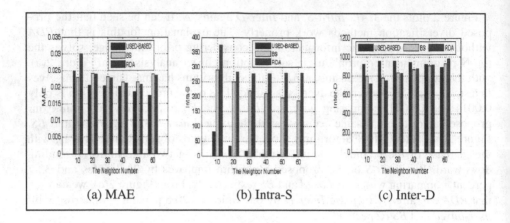

(a) MAE   (b) Intra-S   (c) Inter-D

Fig. 3. *MAE* and diversity of the recommended set of size *N* = *30*, plotted against the number of neighbors (*BX* dataset, θ = *3.5*)

6   Conclusions and Future Work

We believe that the diversity of recommendations should be given more weight in evaluating the recommendation quality, and more research is needed to further explore the tradeoff between accuracy and diversity in recommender systems. In this work, we present a novel recommendation framework that aims to improve the diversity of recommender systems. Our experimental results demonstrate that our proposed recommendation framework improves performance in the terms of some metrics discussed in section 3. Moreover; our proposed framework efficiently generates recommendations, which achieve a good balance between accuracy and diversity. Our future work includes validating our findings in other items domains, comprehensively investigating the influence of diversity on the success of a recommender system. And we believe it is necessary in designing new metrics that are more reflective of user satisfaction in their interaction with a recommender system.

Acknowledgments. This work has been supported by the Project (No.SKLSDE-2011ZX-08 and No.SKLSDE-2012ZX-0X) of the State Key Laboratory of Software Development Environment and the National Natural Science Foundation of China under Grant No.61202238, No.61035004, No.61273213 and No.61170087.

References

1. Koren, Y.: Collaborative filtering with temporal dynamics. In: 15th ACM SIGKDD Int'l Conf. on Knowledge Discovery and Data Mining, pp. 447–456 (2009)
2. Adomavicius, G., Tuzhilin, A.: Toward the Next Generation of Recommender Systems: A Survey of the State-of-the-Art and Possible Extensions. IEEE Trans. on Knowledge and Data Engineering 17(6), 734–749 (2005)

3. Herlocker, J.L., Konstan, J.A., Terveen, L.G., Riedl, J.T.: Evaluating collaborative filtering recommender systems. ACM Transactions on Information Systems 22(1), 5–53 (2004)
4. Hijikata, Y., Shimizu, T., Nishida, S.: Discovery-oriented collaborative filtering for improving user satisfaction. In: 13th International Conference on Intelligent User Interfaces, pp. 67–76 (2009)
5. Zhang, M., Hurley, N.: Avoiding Monotony: Improving the Diversity of Recommendation Lists. In: 2008 ACM Conference on Recommender Systems, Lausanne, Switzerland, pp. 123–130 (2008)
6. Drosou, M., Pitoura, E.: Search result diversification. SIGMOD Record (2010)
7. Bradley, K., Barry, S.: Improving Recommendation Diversity. In: Twelfth Irish Conference on Artificial Intelligence and Cognitive Science, Maynooth, Ireland, pp. 85–94 (2001)
8. Adomavicius, G., Kwon, Y.: Overcoming Accuracy-Diversity Tradeoff in Recommender Systems: A Variance-Based Approach. In: 18th Workshop on Information Technology and Systems (2008)
9. McSherry, D.: Diversity-Conscious Retrieval. In: Craw, S., Preece, A.D. (eds.) ECCBR 2002. LNCS (LNAI), vol. 2416, pp. 219–233. Springer, Heidelberg (2002)
10. Raman, K., Shivaswamy, P., Joachims, T.: Online learning to diversify from implicit feedback. In: KDD 2012, Beijing, China, pp. 705–713 (2012)
11. Shimazu, H.: ExpertClerk: navigating shoppers' buying process with the combination of asking and proposing. In: 17th International Joint Conference on Artificial Intelligence, vol. 2, pp. 1443–1448. Morgan Kaufmann Publishers Inc., Seattle (2001)
12. Kummamuru, K., Lotlikar, R., Roy, S., Singal, K., Krishnapuram, R.: A hierarchical monothetic document clustering algorithm for summarization and browsing search results. In: Thirteenth International Conference on World Wide Web, pp. 658–665. ACM Press (2004)
13. Hofmann, T.: Collaborative filtering via gaussian probabilistic latent semantic analysis. In: SIGIR 2003: the 26th Annual International ACM SIGIR Conference on Research and Development in Information Retrieval, pp. 259–266. ACM (2003)
14. Zhang, M., Hurley, N.: Novel item recommendation by user profile partitioning. In: 2009 IEEE/WIC/ACM International Conferences on Web Intelligence, pp. 508–515 (2009)
15. Xu, B., Bu, J., Chen, C., Cai, D.: An Exploration of Improving Collaborative Recommender Systems via User-Item Subgroups. In: WWW 2012: 21st International Conference on World Wide Web, pp. 21–30 (2012)
16. Sarwar, B., Karypis, G., Konstan, J., Reidl, J.: Item-based collaborative filtering recommendation algorithms. In: 10th International Conference on World Wide Web, pp. 285–295 (2001)
17. Zhou, T., Kuscsik, Z., Liu, J.G., Medo, M., Wakeling, J.R., Zhang, Y.C.: Solving the apparent diversity-accuracy dilemma of recommender systems. National Academy of Sciences 107(10), 4511–4515 (2010)
18. Ziegler, C.N., McNee, S.M., Konstan, J.A., Lausen, G.: Improving Recommendation Lists through Topic Diversification. In: 14th International World Wide Web Conference, pp. 22–32 (2005)
19. Li, D.: Artificial Intelligence with Uncertainty, pp. 171–177. National Defense Industry Press, Beijing (2005)
20. Reynolds, D.A.: Gaussian Mixture Models. Encyclopedia of Biometric Recognition. Springer, Journal Article (2008)
21. Grouplens, http://www.grouplens.org/
22. Mcnee, S.M., Riedl, J., Konstan, J.A.: Being accurate is not enough: how accuracy metrics have hurt recommender systems. In: CHI 2006 Extended Abstracts on Human Factors in Computing, pp. 1097–1101 (2006)

23. Resnick, P., Iakovou, N., Sushak, M., Bergstrom, P., Riedl, J.: GroupLens: An Open Architecture for Collaborative Filtering of Netnews. In: 1994 Computer Supported Cooperative Work Conf. (1994)
24. Billsus, D., Pazzani, M.: Learning Collaborative Information Filters. In: Int'l Conf. Machine Learning (1998)
25. Zhang, Y.C., Séaghdha, D.Ó., Quercia, D., Jambor, T.: Auralist: introducing serendipity into music recommendation. In: Fifth ACM International Conference on Web Search and Data Mining, pp. 13–22. ACM (2012)

RNRank: Network-Based Ranking on Relational Tuples

Peng Li[1], Ling Chen[2], Xue Li[2], and Junhao Wen[1]

[1] College of Computer Science and Technology,
Chongqing University, Chongqing, China 400030
[2] School of Information Technology and Electrical Engineering,
The University of Queensland, Brisbane QLD 4072, Australia
{pengli,jhwen}@cqu.edu.cn, ling.chen@uqconnect.edu.au,
xueli@itee.uq.edu.au

Abstract. Conventional relational top-k queries ignore the inherent referential relationships existing between tuples that can effectively link all tuples of a database together. A relational database can be viewed as a network of tuples connected via foreign keys. With respect to the semantics defined over the foreign keys, the most referenced tuples, therefore, can be regarded as either the most influential, relevant, popular, or authoritative objects stored in a relational database according to its domain semantics. In this paper we propose a novel network-based ranking approach to discover those tuples that are mostly referenced in a relational database as top-k query results. Compared with the conventional relational top-k query processing, our approach can provide information about network structured relational tuples and expand top-k query results as recommendations to users using linkage information in databases. Our experiments on sample relational databases demonstrate the effectiveness and efficiency of our proposed RNRank (Relational Network-based Rank) approach.

Keywords: Relational tuples, Network-based ranking, Information network.

1 Introduction

In application domains, end-users may be more interested in the *"mosts"* — the most important, relevant, popular, or authoritative answers – than the conventional search-condition matched results. This is especially true when the search space is huge, for example, the whole WWW for Web page search. This type of queries is often referred as the "top-k" queries. One common way to identify the top-k data objects is to rank them based on some ranking function that scores an object according to its attributes or the aggregation over partial order of multiple objects.

A relational tuple is characterized by that: (1) it represents a fact or a data object that is unique within the entire database; (2) its uniqueness is defined by a primary key and the primary key can be referred to by foreign keys from other tuples. A tuple may include a foreign key that refers to the primary key of another tuple; (3) all tuples are referred to each other via foreign key linkages [1]. Ranking functions discussed in the relational databases can be classified into three categories [2], namely monotone ranking function, generic ranking function and none-ranking function. Monotone ranking functions involve linear combinations of multiple scoring predicates or maximum/minimum

L. Cao et al. (Eds.): BSIC/BSI 2013, LNAI 8178, pp. 139–150, 2013.

functions, examples can be seen in TA [3] and UPPER [4]. The generic approach models top-k query as an optimization problem, as the pruning of unqualified objects at an early stage is not straightforward in the monotone approach. For example, the optimization goal function in [5] consists of a Boolean expression to filter tuples based on query predicates and a ranking function to score the tuples. The none-ranking function especially refers to the strategy of skyline queries. A skyline query returns a set of "interesting" objects that are not dominated by any other objects based on a set of dimensions/predicates [6].

To our knowledge, none of the above-mentioned ranking functions considers the connectivity among data objects or treats the relational tuples as network-connected objects; rather, they are all value-based, i.e., scoring objects based on some aggregation and sometimes constraints over attribute values. This is not surprising, as the history of database development suggests that when the Network Data Model proposed by the Conference on Data Systems Languages (CODASYL) was replaced by the Relational Model in 1970, the network linkage information was "hidden" by the foreign key linkages ever since.

Algorithms that endeavour to take advantages of linkage information and rank objects on a graph structure are often called link-analysis ranking algorithms [7]. They are first known as the PageRank [8] and HITS [9] algorithms for Web search. The success of the Google search engine suggests that the link-analysis ranking algorithms are good at finding the "*mosts*", e.g., the most important or relevant Web pages on WWW. The network-based ranking approaches have also been successfully extended to the computer science literature by ranking-based clustering methods such as RankClus [10] and NetClus [11].

In this paper, we approach the traditional database top-k query problem from a new direction. We look into the intrinsic relationships/linkages amongst data objects in relational databases. We propose a top-k query framework RNRank that clusters and ranks objects based on the relational tuples extracted as a relational network. Our experiments show that the proposed RNRank algorithm is effective. Compared with the conventional value-based top-k query processing, this research opens a new dimension for the top-k query processing in relational database. The overall framework can be found in Fig.1.

The rest of paper is organized as follows. Section 2 discusses the related work. In Section 3, we define the related concepts. In Section 4, we propose the RNRank algorithm. Section 5 describes the experiment and evaluation. Section 6 gives our conclusions.

2   Related Work

Recently, there is a trend of ranking relational data in terms of probability theory. In [12], Ben Taskar *et al.* provided a Probabilistic Relational Models for relational data clustering and classification which considers probabilistic dependencies between related instances and ranks instances based on the Bayesian network probabilistic distribution. In [13], Bo Long *et al.* proposed a probabilistic model for relational clustering.

With the development of data mining, Link Mining as another related research area has drawn many research interests [14] [15] [16]. Link mining is associated with link

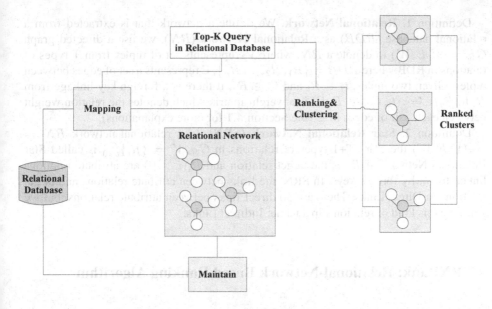

Fig. 1. Framework of Top-K query processing

analysis, hypertext, web mining, relational learning, inductive logic programming, and graph mining. Jiawei Han *et al.* [14] provoked a new research trend that treats database as information network and performs network related data mining and knowledge discovery.

In information network research, it considers relationships or links in information network as important factors on network ranking and clustering. Among those researches, RankClus [10] and NetClus [11] are the two mostly well-known approaches and applied on concurrent clustering and ranking of network-structured objects.

RankClus proposes an interlaced clustering-rank method for processing objects in information network which fits for bi-network. NetClus is extended from RankClus in order to fit for more than two types of objects in heterogeneous information networks. Both RankClus and NetClus are based on clustering while ranking. These algorithms perform clustering and ranking contemporaneously.

Some researches on database transformation and extraction, such as Rania Soussi *et al.* [17], proposed an extraction method of database to social network using a graph model. Balmin *et al.* [18] introduced a *PageRank*-like algorithm called *ObejctRank* for keyword search in databases based on a database graph. However, none of the above-mentioned work is considered with relational databases as an extension to traditional top-k queries. To the best of our knowledge, there is no direct research on top-k queries in relational database based on network linkage analysis.

3   Problem Definition

In this section, we define the problem of top-k query in relational databases with respect to network rankings.

Definition 1. **Relational Network.** We define a network that is extracted from a relational database (RDB) as a Relational Network (RN), we use a directed graph $G_R = (V, E, W)$ to denote a RN, where V represents set of tuples from T types of relations in RDB where $RDB = \{R_1, R_2, ..., R_n\}$, E represents a set of edges between tuples. Given two tuples, $t_i \in R_i$ and $t_j \in R_j$, if there is a foreign key linkage from R_i to R_j, $e = < t_i, t_j > \in E$. W is a weight matrix which denotes the relation weight between each pair of edges in E (see Section 4.1 for more explanations).

Definition 2. **Star Relational Network (SRN).** In a relational network $RN = G_R(V, E, W)$ there are T+1 types of relations in G_R, $V = \{R_t\}_{t=0}^T$ is called Star Relational Network, if R_0 is the target relation and $R_i(i > 0)$ are attribute relations linked to R_0 by foreign keys. In SRN, the links between attribute relations and target relation are Direct Links. There are no direct links between attribute relations, but we still give this kind of relationship a name: Indirect Links.

4   RNRank: Relational-Network Based Ranking Algorithm

In this section, we introduce our network-based relational rank algorithm RNRank on relational database. We treat a relational database as a network of relational tuples. The main idea of ranking algorithm is ranking while clustering on network-connected relational tuples. The algorithm is modified from $NetClus$ [11] with our proposed probabilistic model on relational databases. The key difference lies in the $DirectLink$ $RankingFunction$ (Eq. 2) proposed below. In $NetClus$, global ranking is used instead.

4.1   Probabilistic Ranking Model

In an extracted relational network SRN, the occurrence of one target tuple is the concurrent of all its linked attribute tuples. In order to give a linkage considered distribution for a SRN we use probabilistic statistics to define our ranking model.

Suppose we have a network SRN from a RDB which meets $SRN = (V, E, W)$ where $V = R_0 \cup R_1 ... \cup R_n$ where R_0 is the tuples set in target relation and $R_i(0 < i \le n)$ are tuples set in attributes relations, t_i is a target tuple from SRN where $t_i \in R_0$ the probability of t_i can be expressed by the occurrence probabilities of all the attribute objects $\{t_1, t_2, ..., t_n\}$ linked to t_i:

$$P(t_i|SRN) = \prod_{t_x \in L(t_i)} (\lambda_D F_{DL}(t_x) + (1 - \lambda_D)(F_{IL}(t_x)P(R_{t_x})))^{W_{i,x}} \quad (1)$$

In Eq.(1), $P(t_i|SRN)$ is the probabilistic distribution of t_i in SRN, $L(t_i)$ is the linked tuples of t_i, $F_{IL}(t_x)$ is the ranking distribution of attribute tuple t_x based on the indirect link ranking function as we introduced in last section, R_{t_x} is the relation of t_x, $F_{DL}(t_x)$ is the Direct Link Ranking of t_x and $F_{IL}(t_x)$ is the Indirect Link Ranking of

t_x, λ_D is the weight parameter of ranking functions, $W_{i,x}$ is the link weight between t_i and t_x, the definition of two kinds of ranking functions are shown as follows:

Direct Link Ranking Function. For each attribute tuple $t_i \in R_i$, the direct link ranking distribution is defined as Eq.(2)

$$F_{DL}(t_i) = \frac{\sum_{t_0 \in R_0} W(t_i, t_0)}{\sum_{t_j \in R_i} \sum_{t'_0 \in R_0} W(t_j, t'_0)} \tag{2}$$

The ranking score of each attribute relation is the links counting with target relation, W is the weight of SRN edges, when a tuple $t \in R_i$ has a link with target relation, $W(t, 0) = 1$, otherwise $W(t, 0) = 0$.

Indirect Link Ranking Function. Suppose in a star relational network $SRN = G_R(V, E, W)$, any two types of attribute relations R_A and R_B, the indirect link ranking function through target relation R_C is defined as Eq.(3):

$$\begin{aligned} F_{IL}(R_A) &= W_{AC} W_{CB} F_{IL}(R_B) \\ F_{IL}(R_B) &= W_{BC} W_{CA} F_{IL}(R_A) \end{aligned} \tag{3}$$

W_{AC} is the weight matrix of relation R_A and R_C, W_{CB} is the weight matrix between R_C and R_B in W_{AC}. The ranking of tuples in R_A and R_B is an iteration computing process.

4.2 Posterior Probabilistic Model

In the initial process of clustering we partition the whole network to M tuple clusters, for each tuple cluster ω_i, based on the Probabilistic Ranking Model(Eq.(1)), we obtain the probability model for target objects $P(t_i|\omega_i)$. After probability model is derived, for improving the ranking results, we calculate the posterior probabilistic distribution by the Bayesian rule. The probability for each target object can be expressed as:

$$P(\omega_i|t) = \frac{P(t|\omega_i) \times P(\omega_i)}{P(t)} \tag{4}$$

$P(t|\omega_1)$ is the probability that tuple object t belongs to tuple cluster ω_i, $P(\omega_i)$ is the relative size of cluster ω_i overall.

4.3 Ranking and Clustering on Target Relation

We use a $k - means$ approach to cluster tuples $\omega_1, \omega_2, ..., \omega_M$. We denote a target object as an M dimensional vector $s(t) = (P(\omega_1|t), P(\omega_2|t), ..., P(\omega_M|t))$. The center for each cluster is also an M dimensional vector, the distance computing between every tuple vector to mean vector is according to Cosine similarity:

$$CosDis(\Omega, \Phi) = 1 - \frac{(\Omega.\Phi)}{(||\Omega||.||\Phi||)} \tag{5}$$

Where Ω and Φ are the vectors which denote the tuple vector and mean vector in M dimensions.

The details of our algorithm on target objects are given in Algorithm 1. From Algorithm 1 we get the ranked clusters of target tuples.

4.4   Ranking and Clustering on Attribute Relations

In a relational database the target relation is linked together with its attribute relations with foreign keys. After we calculated the clustered ranking scores of target tuples we get the probabilities for attribute tuple objects as follows:

$$P(t|\omega_i) = \sum_{t_0 \in L(t)} P(t_0|\omega_i) \tag{6}$$

Where $L(t)$ is the target tuples linked to attribute tuples in cluster ω_i. From the equation we can find the probability of an attribute tuple that is calculated based on the probability of its target probability. The higher probability that the target tuple belongs to the cluster, the higher probability the attribute tuple has.

5   Experiment and Evaluation

In this section we show the effectiveness and efficiency of our network based ranking method with two real-world relational databases.

5.1   Datasets

The datasets we used in our experiments are sub-sets of real data extracted from the IMDB website (http://www.imdb.com/) and UCI Machine Learning Repository. In our experiment, we use two databases: (1) Sub-database from IMDB which considers "romance" and "action" movies between years of 1985 and 2011. In romance-action IMDB database, there are 3,327 movies, 2,717 directors, and 7,212 stars; (2) The second database is Credit database which is obtained from the German credit card dataset provided by UCI Machine Learning Repository [19]. In the Credit database there are 1,000 credit records. There are 20 attributes (with 7 numerical and 13 categorical).

5.2   Result Analysis

In the first experiment, we choose the romance-action dataset. We have firstly extracted the IMDB relational network from IMDB relational database (costed 1800 microseconds on a normal setting PC machine). Three types of tuple objects are in the network, namely Movie, Director and Star. The tuples transferred from database are mapped to objects in network and links between them are extracted from the foreign keys between the relational tables in IMDB database.

We set the cluster number to 2 (ω_1, ω_2) in order to cluster the IMDB network to romance and action clusters. After clustering, we choose top-5 ranked items which are shown as Tables 1 and 2.

It can be seen that the tuples from IMDB database are ranked and clustered into two clusters labelled as "Romance" and "Action". The movies, directors and stars tuples in the same cluster have more links with each other and in the different tuples have less links with each other. In the "Romance" cluster, movies, directors and stars are ranked by our RNRank method that considers the relational links between different types of tuples.

Algorithm 1. Ranking and Clustering for Target Tuples

Input: $G_R(V, E, W)$, relational network ; M,cluster number
Output: M ranked tuple clusters $\omega_1, \omega_2, ..., \omega_M$
//Step 1:Clustering partition
$\{\omega_m^0\}_{m=1}^M = RandomPartition(1, M)$;
$Centers = newClustercenters(M)$;
//Repeat Steps 2 to 4 until $\varepsilon < minchange$ or $iteration > max$
for $d = 0$ **to** $itermax$ and $epsi > \varepsilon$ **do**
    //Step 2: Ranking for each cluster
    for $i = 0$ **to** M **do**
        for $j = 0$ **to** $\omega_i.len$ **do**
            $P(t_j|\omega_i) = \prod_{t_x \in L(t_j)}(\lambda_D F_{DL}(t_x) + (1 - \lambda_D)(F_{IL}(t_x)P(R_{t_x})))^{W_{j,x}}$;
        end
    end
    for $i = 0$ **to** M **do**
        for $j = 0$ **to** $\omega_i.len$ **do**
            $P(\omega_i|t_j) = \dfrac{P(t_j|\omega_i) \times P(\omega_i)}{P(t_j)}$;
        end
    end
    //Step 3: Get the new center for each cluster
    for $m = 1$ **to** M **do**
        s_m = re-calcute centers ;
        $Centers.add(s_m)$;
    end
    //Step 4: Clusters Adjusting
    for $n = 1$ **to** $V.len$ **do**
        $t = V[n]$;
        for $m = 1$ **to** M **do**
            $CosDis(t, Centers(m))$;
        end
        $m_0 = minCosDis(t, Centers(m))$;
        $V(C_{m_0}).add(t)$;
    end
    return ranked tuple clusters $\omega_1, \omega_2, ..., \omega_M$;
end

Table 1. Top-5 ranking results of romance cluster

Order	Movie	Director	Star
1	Husbands and Wives	Woody Allen	Woody Allen
2	Everyone Says I Love You	Garry Marshall	Mia Farrow
3	Anything Else	Amy Heckerling	Julia Roberts
4	Deconstructing Harry	Steven Soderbergh	Alec Baldwin
5	New York Stories	Charles Shyer	Kirstie Alley

In the second experiment, the German credit dataset is used which is a representative case for credit card risk analysis. In order to analyse the risk status of credit cards, we classify the credit cards as "good" or "bad" ones. The traditional researches on credit

Table 2. Top-5 ranking results of action cluster

Order	Movie	Director	Star
1	Spy Kids	Robert Rodriguez	Antonio Banderas
2	Once Upon a Time in Mexico	Martin Campbell	Alexa Vega
3	Grindhouse	Gore Verbinski	Daryl Sabara
4	Planet Terror	Tony Scott	Johnny Depp
5	The Adventures of Sharkboy and Lavagirl	Garry Marshall	Rose McGowan

card risk analysis are based mainly on classification algorithms (e.g. support vector machine (SVM), logistic regression (LR), decision tree (C4.5), or neural networks (NN) [20]). However, a classification algorithm can only divide credit cards into either good and bad categories. In this case, within a category of either good or bad, different credit cards may be of different extent of good or bad. In our work we use a network-based ranking approach to cluster as well as rank the credit cards for their risk analysis that can differentiate the seriousness (i.e., ranks) of risks of credit cards.

In our experiment, cluster number is set as 2 for good or bad credit. In practical application, we usually pay more attention to the rank of credit card records. Therefore, in our research we only consider the top-k query results of the center type "Credit". The clustering result of credit tuples based on RNRank method is shown as Table 3.

Table 3. Credit prediction result

Order	Good Cluster ID(Attributes)	Bad Cluster ID(Attributes)
1	162(A14,A34,A61)	653(A11,A33,A61)
2	644(A14,A34,A61)	553(A11,A33,A61)
3	961(A14,A34,A61)	875(A11,A33,A61)
4	325(A14,A34,A61)	841(A11,A33,A61)
5	518(A14,A34,A61)	928(A11,A33,A61)
6	37(A14,A34,A61)	262(A11,A33,A61)
7	985(A14,A34,A61)	641(A11,A33,A61)
8	86(A14,A34,A61)	144(A11,A33,A61)
9	367(A14,A34,A61)	656(A11,A33,A61)
10	235(A14,A34,A61)	752(A11,A33,A61)

From Table 3 we can see that credit records in two clusters have two kinds of attribute features, the "good" cluster contains records mostly have $A14$, $A34$ and $A61$ which mean "no checking account", "other credits existing" and "save less than 100 DM" values for $check\_statues$, $credit\_history$ and $save\_account$ attributions. In the "bad" cluster, the records are mainly with attributes of $A11$, $A33$ and $A61$ for three attribute types which mean "less than 0 DM", "delay in paying off in the past" and "save less than 100 DM". According to the different attributes, credit records are clustered to two clusters which tagged as "good" or "bad".

5.3   Clustering Evaluation

In this experiment, we use Precision/Recall and F-Measure to evaluate the performance of the clustering process in our method. We choose the real categories (e.g. in IMDB movies tagged as "Romance" or "Action", Credit records tagged as "good" or "bad") in database as our ground true values to compare with the clustering results.

The computing functions used for Precision/Recall are defined as:

$$Precision = \sum_{i=0}^{M} \frac{|\omega_i|}{N} \frac{Correct(\omega_i)}{Correct(\omega_i) + Error(\omega_i)} \tag{7}$$

$$Recall = \sum_{i=0}^{M} \frac{|\omega_i|}{N} \frac{Correct(\omega_i)}{Correct(\omega_i) + MissCorrect(\omega_i)} \tag{8}$$

Where M is the clusters number, $|\omega_i|$ is the tuples number in cluster ω_i, N is the total tuples number in all the clustering result on some relation from database, $Correct(\omega_i)$ is the tuples number which correctly clustered to ω_i, $Error(\omega_i)$ is the tuples number which clustered to ω_i incorrectly, $MissCorrect(\omega_i)$ is the tuples number which should be clustered to ω_i but missed.

The F-Measure equation is defined as:

$$F = \frac{2 \times Precision \times Recall}{Precision + Recall} \tag{9}$$

Where F is the similarity of clustering result compared with the real category value in database, $Precision / Recall$ are the clustering precision and recall rates.

After defining the clustering evaluation functions, we design two groups of experiments: one group is compared with NetClus method using the small IMDB database ("Romance" and "Action") and the other is compared with four classification methods using Credit database.

In the first group of comparison, for our RNRank method, we run our network-based method on IMDB database. To compare with NetClus method, we use the same dataset extracted from our IMDB databse to run NetClus algorithm. The comparisons on clustering with Precision/Recall and F-Measure are shown in Fig.2(a). In comparison with NetClus, it can be seen that the Precision/Recall and F-Measure values of our method are all relatively higher.

In the second experiment, we use Credit database to compare with other methods. To predict risks of credit cards, many classification methods are used such as SVM, LR, C4.5, and NN. In our experiment, we run the dataset of the Credit database on four classification methods and then they are compared with our method on Precision/Recall and F-Measure. The experiment platform for four classification methods is based on Weka (http://www.cs.waikato.ac.nz/ ml/weka/) which is an open source Java-based machine learning and data mining software. The compared results are shown in Fig.2(b).

From the results we can see that compared with other four classification methods our method has the highest Precision/Recall and F-Measure values. So, our network-based ranking and clustering method on relational databases has advantage over classical classifications, with respect to the credit card risk analysis.

5.4   Parameters Study

In our RNRank ranking model, there is a parameter λ_D which denotes the percentage of ranking from direct link ranking score. In order to get the most suitable λ_D from

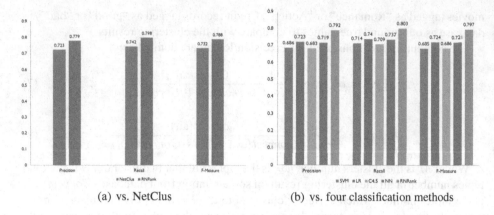

(a) vs. NetClus   (b) vs. four classification methods

Fig. 2. Clustering comparisons

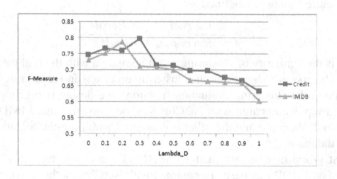

Fig. 3. Accuracy and λ_D

ranking, we design an experiment to test it. In the experiment, we select different λ_D from $[0.0, 1.0]$, to run RNRank on romance-action IMDB database and Credit database, the F-Measure similarity for clustering results on different λ_D is shown in Fig.3. It can be seen that the most suitable λ_D is 0.2 for IMDB database and 0.3 for Credit database.

6   Conclusions

In this paper we propose a new dimension of top-k query processing in relational databases based on network ranking and clustering. In our approach, we firstly extract network from a relational database, then the tuples of the relational network are ranked and clustered. The ranked tuples in clusters are returned as the top-k query result. Compared with the conventional top-k query processing in relational databases, our work gives a new network-based method to extend the capacity of top-k queries of relational databases. The experiments on IMDB and Credit databases have shown the effectiveness and efficiency of our approach. The further implementation of SQL extension should be straightforward.

In our approach, we regard the foreign-key linkages between relations are important factors in top-k queries within relational databases, because the highly referenced relational tuples should be searchable and made available to database users. Our proposed approach has satisfied this requirement. The current experiments are based on star-schema relational databases. In future, we will consider top-k query processing on more complicated relational-to-CODASYL database schemas that are referred to as the relationally-stored networks. The dynamic extraction and maintenance of relational networks with vary large volume of tuples will also be considered.

Acknowledgement. This work is supported by China Natural Science Foundation Project No. 61075053 and No. 71102065, supported by Natural Science Foundation Project of CQ CSTC2010BB2244 and the Fundamental Research Funds for the Central Universities Project No. CDJZR10090001. The research project is performed with the first author visiting at the University of Queensland, Australia.

References

1. Date, C.J.: An Introduction to Database Systems, 8th edn. Pearson/Addison Wesley, Boston (2004)
2. Ilyas, I.F., Beskales, G., Soliman, M.A.: A survey of top-k query processing techniques in relational database systems. ACM Comput. Surv. 40(4), 1–58 (2008)
3. Fagin, R., Lotem, A., Naor, M.: Optimal aggregation algorithms for middleware. In: PODS 2001, pp. 102–113 (2001)
4. Bruno, N., Chaudhuri, S., Gravano, L.: Top-k selection queries over relational databases: Mapping strategies and performance evaluation. ACM Trans. Database Syst., 153–187 (2002)
5. Zhang, Z., won Hwang, S., Chang, K.C.C., Wang, M., Lang, C.A., Chang, Y.C.: Boolean + ranking: querying a database by k-constrained optimization. In: SIGMOD Conference 2006, pp. 359–370 (2006)
6. Brzsnyi, S., Kossmann, D., Stocker, K.: The skyline operator. In: ICDE 2001, pp. 421–430 (2001)
7. Borodin, A., Roberts, G.O., Rosenthal, J.S., Tsaparas, P.: Link analysis ranking: algorithms, theory, and experiments. ACM Trans. Internet Techn., 231–297 (2005)
8. Page, L., Brin, S., Motwani, R., Winograd, T.: The pagerank citation ranking: Bringing order to the web. Technical Report 1999-66, Stanford InfoLab (November 1999)
9. Kleinberg, J.M.: Authoritative sources in a hyperlinked environment. J. ACM, 604–632 (1999)
10. Sun, Y., Han, J., Zhao, P., Yin, Z., Cheng, H., Wu, T.: Rankclus: integrating clustering with ranking for heterogeneous information network analysis. In: EDBT 2009, pp. 565–576 (2009)
11. Sun, Y., Yu, Y., Han, J.: Ranking-based clustering of heterogeneous information networks with star network schema. In: KDD 2009, pp. 797–806 (2009)
12. Taskar, B., Segal, E., Koller, D.: Probabilistic classification and clustering in relational data. In: IJCAI 2001, pp. 870–878 (2001)
13. Long, B., Zhang, Z.M., Yu, P.S.: A probabilistic framework for relational clustering. In: KDD 2007, pp. 470–479 (2007)
14. Han, J., Sun, Y., Yan, X., Yu, P.S.: Mining knowledge from databases: an information network analysis approach. In: SIGMOD Conference 2010, pp. 1251–1252 (2010)

15. Senator, T.E.: Link mining applications: progress and challenges. SIGKDD Expl., 76–83 (2005)
16. Yin, X., Han, J., Yu, P.S.: Linkclus: Efficient clustering via heterogeneous semantic links. In: VLDB 2006, pp. 427–438 (2006)
17. Soussi, R., Aufaure, M.A., Zghal, H.B.: Towards social network extraction using a graph database. In: DBKDA 2010, pp. 28–34 (2010)
18. Balmin, A., Hristidis, V., Papakonstantinou, Y.: Objectrank: Authority-based keyword search in databases. In: Proceedings of the Thirtieth International Conference on Very Large Data Bases, vol. 30, pp. 564–575. VLDB Endowment (2004)
19. Frank, A., Asuncion, A.: UCI machine learning repository (2010)
20. Yu, H., Huang, X., Hu, X., Cai, H.: A comparative study on data mining algorithms for individual credit risk evaluation. In: ICMeCG 2010, pp. 35 –38 (2010)

Interaction-Based Social Relationship
Type Identification in Microblog

Qiao Deng[1], Zhoujun Li[1], Xiaoming Zhang[1], and Jiali Xia[2]

[1] State Key Laboratory of Software Development Environment,
Beihang University, Beijing, China
[2] School of Software and Communication Engineering,
Jiangxi University of Finance and Economics, Nanchang, China
doris_789@126.com, {lizj,yolixs}@buaa.edu.cn, xiajl65824@263.net

Abstract. Relationships in Microblogging services are lack of explicit meaningful labels, such as "colleagues", "family members", etc. The state-of-the-arts
mainly work on mining only one particular relationship type such as advisor-
advisee relationship for specific social networks. Moreover, few work focuses
on relationship identification in Microblog based on link analysis. In Micro-
blog, words in interactive tweets between users may provide clues for relationship type identification. In this study, we propose a two-step framework to
infer the different social relationship types between users in Microblog. Firstly,
a generative model UIRCT (User Interaction-based Relationship-related Community Topic) is proposed to discover relationship-related communities based
on interactive content between users. We then profile the discovered communities with different relationship type labels by utilizing external resource.
Experiment results on Sina Weibo dataset demonstrate that our proposed
framework can identify different meaningful relationship types effectively.

Keywords: Relationship type identification, community discovery, generative
models, interactive tweets.

1   Introduction

Microblog becomes a popular web service in the Web 2.0 era and plays an important
role in our social life. In China, the most well-known microblog site is Sina Weibo,
which has more than 500 million registered users by the end of 2012, posting 100
million tweets every day. Users in Microblog are talking about their daily life and
following their interested people.

Microblog has been extensively studied [1, 2]. However, most studies treat the
connections in social networks homogeneous, and ignore the fact that our physical
social network is colorful where people connect to each other by various relationship
types, e.g., family members, colleagues, or friends with similar interests. It is obvious
that the different types of social relationships have essentially different influence on
people. Thus for online services, such as recommendation [3], relationship type could
be significant, so social network applications may benefit from encouraging users to

L. Cao et al. (Eds.): BSIC/BSI 2013, LNAI 8178, pp. 151–164, 2013.
© Springer International Publishing Switzerland 2013

specify relationship types. Although users are encouraged to label their followers into different groups, they often skip this step. Recently, some efforts have been made on relationship identification. For example, Diehl et al. [4] try to mine manager subordinate relationships by learning a ranking function. Wang et al. [5] focus on identifying advisor-advisee relationship in publication network. However, they focus on specific relationship type in a particualr domain such as email and publication network, while Microblog is an open environment where various relationship types exist. Therefore, new approaches for identifying relationship types in Microblog are needed.

Our aim here is to identify various relationship types in Microblog. Since the interactive content between users can reflect the types of their relationship to some extent, users' interactive content is used as an information resourse to infer the relationship types among users. In another word, given the interactive tweets between two users, we estimate how likely they have a specific relationship type. Here we focus on identifying four relationship types: Family Member, Colleague, Schoolmate and Interests-oriented Friend. To accomplish this, an interaction based relationship learning framework is proposed to classify the relatonship types. Our framework consists of two components: discovering relationship-related communities and labeling those communities with external resources.

The main contributions of our study can be summarized as follows:

- A generative model is proposed for relationship-related community discovery based on Microblog conversations.
- A relationship learning framework is introduced to profile the detected communities with the relationship's distributions over words.
- The efficacy of our proposed framework is evaluated on a real world Microblog dataset collected from Sina Weibo. Experimental results show that our framework can discover meaningful relationship types between users.

The rest of the paper is organized as follows. Section 2 introduces the details of our proposed framework. We explain the community discovery model and community profiling procedure in Section 3 and 4 respectively. Section 5 gives experimental results. We discuss related work in Section 6 and conclude the paper in Section 7.

2 Overview of the Framework

In this section, we first define the terminologies related to relationship identification in Microblog. Then the proposed framework is presented in detail.

2.1 Terminology Definition

Definition 1. Interactive Social Network

An interactive social network can be denoted by a graph $G = (V, E, l)$, where V is the users set in the network, and E is the set of links among users. Each edge $e(u,v) \in E$ denotes that some interactive activities exist between u and v. l is an edge labeling function $l : E \rightarrow L$, where L is a set of labels $L = \{l_0, l_1, ..., l_k\}$. Here we define L as a relationship labels set, i.e., {Family Member, Colleague, Schoolmate, Interests-oriented Friend}. For $e \in E$, $l(e) \in L$ is called the relationship label of e.

Definition 2. Relationship-related Community

A relationship-related community is a group of users who share the same relationship label among each other. We use $G(V')$ to denote the subgraph induced by a subset of vertices $V' \subseteq V$. Given a user $v \in V$, $N(v)$ denotes the set of neighbors, and the subgraph $G(N(v))$ means a set of disjoint "communities" formed by v. Users having the same relationship with v tend to belong to a same community in $G(N(v))$.

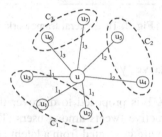

Fig. 1. An interactive social network of user u

Fig. 1 illustrates the interactive social network of user u who is located at the center. All other nodes are his/her friends, i.e., $N(u) = \{u_1, u_2, ..., u_7\}$. $l(e(u, u_1)) = l_1$ means that user u_1 has a relationship label l_1 with u. $N(v)$ can be divided into three communities: $C_1 = \{u_1, u_2, u_3\}$, $C_2 = \{u_4, u_5\}$ and $C_3 = \{u_6, u_7\}$, according to the edge labels.

Definition 3. Relationship Identification

Given an unlabeled social network graph $G = (V, E)$ and the set of relationship labels L, relationship identification is to assign each link $e \in E$ a label from L. In other words, the objective is to turn the unlabeled social network $G = (V, E)$ into an interactive social network $G = (V, E, l)$.

2.2 Overall Solution Framework

Fig. 2 shows the overall framework of the proposed approach. The input is an interactive tweet corpus, an unlabeled network, and external resources. The output is the relationship-related communities with the corresponding labels.

The framework consists of two components, i.e., community discovery, and community profiling. In the community discovery component, an interaction based generative model, called UIRCT (User Interaction-based Relationship-related Community Topic), is proposed to discover the relationship related communities. In the community profiling component, Wikipedia is used to construct the relationship ontology, and then the discovered communities are profiled with the relationship's distributions over words. In the following sections, these two components will be discussed in detail.

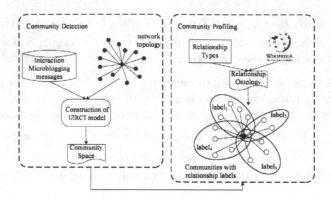

Fig. 2. The general framework

3   Community Discovery

The generative model UIRCT is proposed to discover the relationship-related communities based on the interactive tweets among users. The basic assumption is that the involved users of a tweet are generated from a latent community and they have the same relationship with the author.

3.1   The Generative Model UIRCT

Fig. 3 presents the hierarchy of the Bayesian network of UIRCT, and the variable descriptions are shown in Table 1.

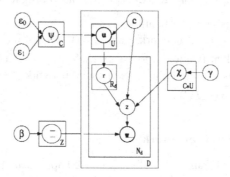

Fig. 3. Probabilistic graphic representation of UIRCT

The distributions among variables are defined as follows:

- Each topic is associated with a multinomial distribution over words, represented by ϕ, which has a symmetric Dirichlet prior with hyperparameter β:

$$\varphi_z \sim Dirich(\beta), \quad z = 1, 2, ..., Z \qquad (1)$$

- Each community is associated with a multinomial distribution over users, represented by ψ, and $\psi_{c,u}$ means user u's activeness in community c, which has a Beta distribution with hyperparameters $\varepsilon_0, \varepsilon_1$:

$$\psi_{c,u} \sim Beta(\varepsilon_0, \varepsilon_1), c = 1,2,...,C; u = 1,2,...,U \qquad (2)$$

- Each <community, user> pair is associated with a multinomial distribution over topics, represented by χ, which has a Dirichlet prior with hyperparameter γ:

$$\chi_{c,u} = Dirich(\gamma), \quad c = 1,2,...,C; u = 1,2,...,U \qquad (3)$$

Table 1. Variable descriptions

Symbols	Description
β	Dirichlet distribution parameter
γ	Dirichlet distribution parameter
ε_0	Beta distribution parameter
ε_1	Beta distribution parameter
Z	The number of topics
C	The number of communities
ψ_c	User distribution over community c
φ_z	Word distribution over topic z
$\chi_{c,u}$	Topic distribution over community-user pair<c, u>

Typically, a tweet d is generated by three steps:

1. A community c_d is chosen by maximizing the likelihood of community membership: users, topics and words:

$$c_d = \arg\max_c \log(L(d,c))$$
$$= \arg\max_c \{\log(L(d,c,R_d,a_d)) + \log(L(d,c,z_d) + \log(L(d,c,W_d)))\} \qquad (4)$$

2. We assume that the author and the recipient set of tweet d are a_d and R_d respectively. For each participant slot $i, 1 \le i \le |\{a_d, R_d\}|$, a participant p is chosen by running a Bernoulli trial according to p's activeness in c_d:

$$y_{d,p} | \psi_{c_d} \sim Bernoulli(\psi_{c_d,p}), 1 \le p \le U \qquad (5)$$

3. For each word slot j, $1 \le j \le |W_d|$:

   (a) A participant $p_{d,j}$ is chosen from the participants set $\{a_d, R_d\}$ uniformly;

   (b) Choose a topic assignment based on the community c_d and user $p_{d,j}$:

$$z_{d,j} \mid \chi, c_d, p_{d,j} \sim Multi(\chi_{c,p_{d,j}}) \qquad (6)$$

(c) Choose a word $w_{d,j}$ from the $z_{d,j}$-th topic-word distribution:

$$w_{d,n} \mid \varphi, z_{d,n} \sim Multi(\varphi_{z_{(d,i)}}) \qquad (7)$$

3.2   Parameter Estimation

Given an interactive tweet corpus with a user set, UIRCT model enables the discovery of relationship-related communities and the latent topics of interaction in each community. From a Bayesian network perspective, given the observable variables a_d, R_d and W_d, i.e., the author, recipient set and word set of tweet d, our goal can be carried out by doing inference over latent variables.

Our goal is to compute the posterior probability $p(c_d, p_d, z_d \mid W_d, R_d, a_d)$ for a tweet d. Posterior probability can be computed theoretically by the joint distribution. Considering the joint distribution of all variables as follows:

$$
\begin{aligned}
& p(c_d, R_d, a_d, p_d, z_d, W_d \mid \alpha, \beta, \gamma, \varepsilon) \\
& = p(W_d \mid z_d) p(z_d \mid c_d, p_d) p(p_d \mid R_d, a_d) p(R_d, a_d \mid c) p(c_d) \\
& \propto p(c_d) \prod_{r \in \{R_d, a_d\}} p(r \mid c_d) \prod_{n=1}^{N_d} p(z_{(d,n)} \mid c_d, p_{d,n}) p(w_{(d,n)} \mid z_{(d,n)})
\end{aligned}
\qquad (8)
$$

Gibbs Sampling

Due to the coupling between hidden variables, the posterior distributions cannot be exactly inferred. Various algorithms have been used to solve the problem, such as variational approximation [6] and Gibbs sampling [7]. Here Gibbs Sampling is used to train the model, whose process is illustrated as follow:

```
for each tweet d in D do
    assign d to random community
    assign each w_d in d to random user and topic
/*Markov Chain Convergence*/
for i=1:1000 iterations do
  for each tweet d do
    draw c_d by maximizing likelihood of community
membership according to Eq.(9)
    for each word W_(d,n) in tweet d do
        draw p_(d,n) and z_(d,n) by using Eq.(13)
```

Gibbs sampling is carried out by starting with a random assignment to all latent variables. Then a Markov chain is constructed to converge to the target distribution. In each simulation trail, Gibbs Sampling updates by two steps:

Step 1: Update latent community c_d conditioned on other variables by maximizing the likelihood of community membership, including users, topics and words:

$$c_d = \arg\max_c \log(L(d,c))$$
$$= \arg\max_c \{\log(L(d,c,R_d,a_d)) + \log(L(d,c,z_d)) + \log(L(d,c,W_d)))\} \tag{9}$$

- The log-likelihood function of community membership for users:

$$\log(L(d,c,R_d,a_d)) = \log p(c,\varepsilon_0,\varepsilon_1) = \log \int p(\vec{\psi_c};\varepsilon_0,\varepsilon_1) p(c\,|\,\vec{\psi_c}) d\vec{\psi_c}$$
$$= \log \int \left(\prod_{u=1}^{|(a_d,R_d)|} \frac{1}{B(\varepsilon_0,\varepsilon_1)} \psi_{c,u}^{\varepsilon_0-1}(1-\psi_{c,u})^{\varepsilon_1-1} \right) \times \prod_{u=1}^{|(a_d,R_d)|} \prod_d^{D_c} \psi_{c,u}^{y_{d,u}}(1-\psi_{c,u})^{1-y_{d,u}} d\vec{\psi_c} \tag{10}$$
$$= \sum_{u=1}^{|(a_d,R_d)|} \log \frac{B(\varepsilon_0 + \sum_d^{D_c} y_{d,u}, \varepsilon_1 + D_c - \sum_d^{D_c} y_{d,u})}{B(\varepsilon_0,\varepsilon_1)}$$

where D_c is the number of tweets assigned to community c; $y_{d,u}=1$ indicates that user u is a participant of tweet d, else $y_{d,u}=0$; $B(\varepsilon_0,\varepsilon_1)$ indicates the Beta distribution with $B(\varepsilon_0,\varepsilon_1) = \Gamma(\varepsilon_0)\Gamma(\varepsilon_1)/\Gamma(\varepsilon_0+\varepsilon_1)$.

- The log-likelihood function of community membership for topics:

$$\log(L(d,c,z_d))$$
$$= \sum_{p\in\{a_d,R_d\}} \left[\sum_{z=1}^{Z} \log\Gamma\left(D_{d,pz} + n_{(c,p)}^{(z)} + \gamma\right) - \log\Gamma\left(\sum_{z=1}^{Z}(D_{d,pz} + n_{(c,p)}^{(z)} + \gamma)\right) \right] \tag{11}$$

where $D_{d,pz}$ is the number of times z was generated from participant p in tweet d; $n_{(c,p)}^{(z)}$ is the number of times z was generated from community-user pair $<c,p>$.

- The log-likelihood function of community membership for words:

$$\log(L(d,c,W_d)) = \sum_{z=1}^{|Z_d|} \left[\sum_{w=1}^{|W_{d,z}|} \sum_{j=1}^{n_{z,d}^w} \log(\beta + n_z^w - j) - \sum_{j=1}^{n_d^z} \log(Z \cdot \beta + n_z - j) \right] \tag{12}$$

where $|Z_d|$ is the number of topics assigned in d; $|W_{d,z}|$ is the number of words assigned to topic z in d; $n_{z,d}^w$ is the number of times word w was assigned to topic z in d; n_d^z is the number of times topic z was assigned in d.

Step 2: For each word $w_{(d,n)}$ in tweet d, updating participant topic pair $< p_{(d,n)}, z_{(d,n)} >$ conditioned on other variables.

$$p(p_{(d,n)} = u, z_{(d,n)} = k \mid c_d, R_d, a_d, w_{(d,n)} = w, \neg d, \neg(d,n))$$

$$= \frac{n_{k,-(d,n)}^w + \beta}{\sum_{w=1}^V n_{k,-(d,n)}^w + V\beta} \times \frac{n_{(c_d,u),-(d,n)}^k + \gamma}{\sum_z n_{(c_d,u),-(d,n)}^z + Z\gamma} \tag{13}$$

where $n_{k,-(d,n)}^w$ is the number of times word w being generated from topic k other than the nth word in d; $n_{(c,u),-(d,n)}^k$ is the number of times topic k being generated by community-user pair $< c_d, u >$ other than the nth word in tweet d.

After the estimation process, each parameter is estimated from the ending state:

$$\psi_{c,u} = \frac{n_c^{(u)} + \varepsilon_0}{D_c + \varepsilon_0 + \varepsilon_1} \tag{14}$$

$$\chi_{(c,u),z} = \frac{n_{(c,u)}^{(z)} + \gamma}{\sum_{z=1}^Z n_{(c,u)}^{(z)} + Z \times \gamma} \tag{15}$$

$$\varphi_{z,w} = \frac{n_z^w + \beta}{\sum_{w=1}^V n_z^w + V \times \beta} \tag{16}$$

3.3   User-Community Assignment

After the training process, users' active distribution among communities is as follows:

$$p(u \mid c) = \frac{n_c^{(u)} + \varepsilon_0}{D_c + \varepsilon_0 + \varepsilon_1} \tag{17}$$

Given community c, users whose activeness in it is higher than a certain threshold can be regarded as a member of c, i.e., $U_c = \{u \in U \mid p(u \mid c) > threshold\}$. Therefore, we classify user and his/her friends into various communities, and then we can obtain the community-word distribution for each community based on $\chi_{(c,u),z}$ and $\varphi_{z,w}$.

4   Community Profiling

In this section, we present how to utilize UIRCT model parameters and external resource to infer relationship. The assumption is that each relationship type has its associated keywords that can provide clues to infer it. For example, if two users have the colleague relationship, many of their interactive tweets may contain keywords such as boss, work, or salary. Thus, the relationship type can be identified by the relationship-word distribution. In this study, we mainly identify four relationship types, i.e., **Family Member, Colleague, Schoolmate**, and **Interests-oriented Friend**. As for the fourth type, it means close friend or friends with similar interests, including Sports, Politics, Technology and Entertainment.

Based on the structure of articles, the relationship-related words are extracted from Wikipedia text. Firstly, the tf-idf model is used to measure the relevance of words to each category. Then we manually assign each category to only one relationship type. Thus we get the distribution for each relationship: $Relation_r\{(w_1, weight_1),...,(w_n, weight_n)\}$

By computing the similarity between community-word distributions and relationship-word distributions, communities can be profiled with relationship labels.

5   Experiment

To validate the performance of our approach, a set of experiments are conducted on a real world dataset, collected from Sina Weibo. To illustrate the benefit of UIRCT model, CUT [8] and CART [9] models were adopted as the benchmark methods. In the following subsections, a qualitative evaluation of the discovered communities is presented first. Then some evaluation metrics are adopted to evaluate our method.

5.1   Datasets

Datasets in experiments are collected from Sina Weibo and Wikipedia respectively.

- **Sina Weibo:** The tweets dataset is collected from Sina Weibo. Our aim is to identify user's relationships with his/her friends. Thus we manually select 9 users from Sina Weibo, including 6 celebrities (Yao Chen, Kaifu Lee, Pan Shiyi, Jiang Tao, Ma Yili, Ma Shaoping) and 3 common users. To study their tweets exchange with other Weibo users, we crawl all their interactive tweets and the interactive friends, which resulted in a total of 5,500 users and 52,000 interactive tweets. In the experiments, the bi-direction interactions are considered..
- **Wikipedia:** The latest chinese Wiki XML corpus is downloaded to train the relationship-word distributions. After data processing, we get 137,332 articles and their corresponding categories. The details are displayed in Table 2.

Table 2. The article numbers of different categories

Entertainment	17,103	Education	16,710
Business	17,981	Sports	16,832
Science&Tech	19,196	Politics	17,219
Music	16,386	Life	15,905

5.2   Result Analysis

Qualitative Analysis
Here we show the discovered communities by modeling Yao Chen's interactive tweets with 15 topics and 4 communities in Fig. 4. Yao Chen is a famous Chinese actress who has more than 40 million followers in Sina Weibo up to now. The top ranked topics, users which are presented as "@*chinese screenname* (translated

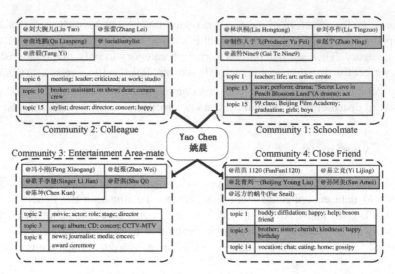

Fig. 4. Yao Chen relationship-related communities

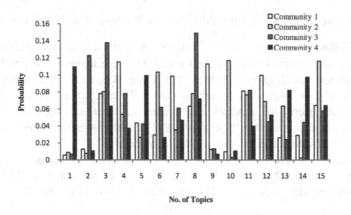

Fig. 5. Topic profiles for discovered communities

name)", as well as the relationship label are presented to visualize each community. And each topic is represented by the top 5 words (translated from chinese). It is shown that her communities can be roughly represented as: Close Friend, Colleague, Entertainment Area-mate, and Schoolmate.

Fig. 5 presents the plot of topic probabilities over communities. Taking Community 1 as example, it shows that topic 4, 9 and 12 are very prominent in C1 (short for Community 1), which typically consists of words about school life, like teacher, student and art. By utilizing external relationship-word distributions, C1 is labeled with "Schoolmates" group which means users in C1 are likely to be the school friends of Yao Chen. For example, user Lin Hongtong (translated), a professor of Beijing Film Academy, is classified into C1 since he was Yao Chen's teacher in Film Academy.

It can be concluded that our proposed framework can discover users' relationship-related communities effectively and label concrete relationship type.

Community Analysis
Next, we evaluate the quality of communities discovered by UIRCT models against two baseline methods: i.e., CUT and CART models. Newman [10] proposed the concept of modularity, which has been shown to be an effective quantity to measure community structure [11, 12]. It assumes that a good division of a network is that the number of edges between groups is smaller than expected. A larger modularity indicates denser within-group interaction. However the discovered communities of our model is a fuzzy community structure, where each node belongs to a certain community with a certain probability. Thus we adopt a variant of modularity, i.e., fuzzy modularity Q_f [13] to quantify the quality of a probabilistic partition. It is defined as:

$$Q_f = (probabilistic \; number \; of \; edges \; within \; communities)$$
$$- (expected \; probabilistic \; number \; of \; such \; edges)$$

Fig. 6 compares the average fuzzy modularity of our model with the baseline models (CUT and CART model). The number of topics was set to 20 for these experiments as we vary the number of communities.

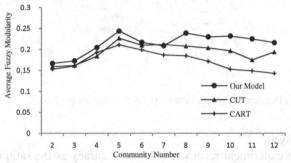

Fig. 6. Comparison of average fuzzy modularity

It is observed that our proposed model outperforms other methods which discover community purely based on interest, such as CUT model. In addition, although CART model also extracts topically meaningful communities using interactive content, it is less suitable for sparse datasets like Microblog. This is shown by much weaker values for CART model in Fig. 6. The high modularity values support our assumption that the inter-connected people who share the same relationships often form communities.

Perplexity Analysis
Perplexity is a common metric to evaluate language models [14], which measures the log-likelihood of generating latent data from known data. A smaller value of perplexity means a stronger generative power of the model. the perplexity is computed as:

$$perplexity(W_d) = \exp \left\{ - \frac{\sum n_d^w p(C, R_d, Z, w, a_d)}{N_d} \right\} \quad (18)$$

where W_d is the word sequence, and N_d is the length.

Fig. 7 show a simple comparison of perplexity for different parameters sets. We can see that our UIRCT model performs better than CUT and CART for having lower perplexity. Moreover, the optimal parameter settings can be obtained by analyzing how the perplexity is affected by the parameters. Fig. 7(a) plot the perplexities against the number of topics, in which the number of communities was set to 4. It shows that the perplexities have the minimum values at around 10-15 topics. Fig. 7(b) plots the perplexities against the number of communities, where the number of topics was set to 15. It shows that the perplexities have the minimum values at around 3-5 communities. Based on these experiments, the optimal parameter settings can be obtained.

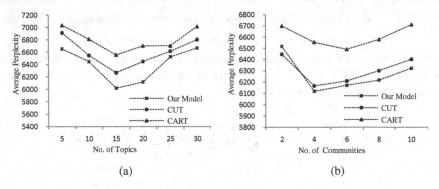

(a)   (b)

Fig. 7. Perplexity comparison vs (a) No. of topics (b) No. of communities

Accuracy Analysis

Throughout the experiment results, we define accuracy as the ratio of the number of links which are labeled correctly by our method to the total number of links. A manual labeling method is adopted to generate the real relationship type between users in our dataset. 4 volunteers are divided into 2 teams to label the relationship independently and when two teams label a different relationship type for a particular user pair, we will ask them to re-label this relationship type.

Table 3. Accuracies on different relationship types

Relationship Type	Accuracy
Family Members	46.7%
Colleagues	73.3%
Schoolmates	51.3%
Interests-oriented Friends	73.5%
Average	**61.2%**

Table 3 shows the accuracy for each relationship types. Here the optimal parameter settings are adopted to conduct the experiment. It is observed that most of the relationship types achieve accuracy score higher than 0.5, and the best accuracy score is up to 0.735 (Interests-oriented Friends).

6   Related Work

Relationship mining is an important research direction in social network analysis. As a research branch, some recent efforts had been made on predicting unknown links in social networks. These link prediction methods can be generally classified into two categories: one is using topology to capture the link structure of the social network, for example, Liben-Nowell and Kleinberg [15] study the unsupervised methods for link prediction based on the meatures for analyzing the "proximity" of nodes in social network, and the other is combining attribute similarity features with topology, for example Taskar et al. [16] define a joint probabilistic model over entity attributes and links for link prediction. Another related research direction has focused on estimating the strength of social links. Xiang et al. [17] develop a latent variable model to estimate relationship strength from interaction activity and user similarity.

However, those works assume the relationship type between every people is the same. Recently, there are several works on mining the meanings of social relationships. Wang et al. [5] propose an unsupervised model to identify the advisor-advisee relationships in publication network. Tang [18] propose a semi-supervised framework for learning to infer the type of social ties. However, these algorithms mainly focus on a specific domain, such as email or publication works, and ignore the information contained in texts. Moreover, most methods is semi-supervised learning, which needs partially labeled data. Another research is relational learning [19,20], which refers to the classification when entities are presented in multiple relation network. It is different from the our study since we explore the relationship types mining in Microblog.

7   Conclusion and Future Work

In this paper, we focus on the problem of identifying relationship types between users in Microblog. To solve this problem, we propose a relationship identification framework which contains two components: community discovery and community profiling. In community discovery component, a model UIRCT (User Interaction-based Relationship-related Community Topic) is proposed to discover the relationship-related communities. The external resource, Wikipedia, is then used to build relationship ontology to profile the discovered communities. Experimental results on Sina Weibo dataset validate the feasibility and effectiveness of our proposed framework.

Identifying the meaningful relationship types makes online social network closer to the physical network, and also can be applied to many other applications, such as link prediction and personalized recommendation, etc. In our future work, we will study other approaches to build relationship ontology to improve the accuracy.

Acknowledgements. This work was supported by the National Natural Science Foundation of China [grant number 61170189,61202239], the Fundamental Research Funds for the Central Universities, the Research Fund for the Doctoral Program of Higher Education [grant number20111102130003] and the Fund of the State Key Laboratory of Software Development Environment [grant number KLSDE-2013ZX-19].

References

1. Li, J., Chen, Z., Huang, J.W.: Micro-blog Impact Evaluation Study. Netinfo Security (2012)
2. Gaonkar, S., Li, J., Choudhury, R.R., et al.: Micro-blog: Sharing and Querying Content Through Mobile Phones and Social Participation. In: Proceedings of the 6th International Conference on Mobile Systems, Applications, and Services, pp. 174–186. ACM (2008)
3. Chen, K., Chen, T., Zheng, G., et al.: Collaborative Personalized Tweet Recommendation. In: Proceedings of the 35th International ACM SIGIR Conference on Research and Development in Information Retrieval, pp. 661–670. ACM (2012)
4. Diehl, C.P., Namata, G., Getoor, L.: Relationship Identification for Social Network Discovery. In: Proceedings of the National Conference on Artificial Intelligence, vol. 22(1), p. 546. AAAI Press, MIT Press, Menlo Park, Cambridge (1999)
5. Wang, C., Han, J., Jia, Y., et al.: Mining Advisor-advisee Relationships From Research Publication Networks. In: Proceedings of the 16th ACM SIGKDD International Conference on Knowledge Discovery and Data Mining, pp. 203–212. ACM (2010)
6. Blei, D.M., Ng, A.Y., Jordan, M.I.: Latent Dirichlet Allocation. Machine Learning Res. 3, 993–1022 (2003)
7. Griffiths, T.L., Steyvers, M.: Finding Scientific Topics. Proceedings of the National academy of Sciences of the United States of America 101(suppl. 1), 5228–5235 (2004)
8. Zhou, D., Manavoglu, E., Li, J., et al.: Probabilistic Models for Discovering E-communities. In: Proceedings of the 15th International Conference on World Wide Web, pp. 173–182 (2006)
9. Pathak, N., DeLong, C., Banerjee, A., et al.: Social Topic Models for Community Extraction. In: The 2nd SNA-KDD Workshop, vol. 8 (2008)
10. Newman, M.E.J.: Modularity and Community Structure in Networks. Proceedings of the National Academy of Sciences 103(23), 8577–8582 (2006)
11. Danon, L., Diaz-Guilera, A., Duch, J., et al.: Comparing Community Structure Identification. Journal of Statistical Mechanics: Theory and Experiment 2005(09), P09008(2005)
12. Fortunato, S.: Community Detection in Graphs. Physics Reports 486(3), 75–174 (2010)
13. Liu, J.: Fuzzy Modularity and Fuzzy Community Structure in Networks. The European Physical Journal B 77(4), 547–557 (2010)
14. Chen, S.F., Beeferman, D., Rosenfield, R.: Evaluation Metrics for Language Models (1998)
15. Liben-Nowell, D., Kleinberg, J.: The Link-prediction Problem for Social Networks. Journal of the American Society for Information Science and Technology, 1019–1031 (2007)
16. Taskar, B., Wong, M.F., Abbeel, P., Koller, D.: Link Prediction in Relational Data. In: Neural Information Processing Systems, vol. 15 (2003)
17. Xiang, R., Neville, J., Rogati, M.: Modeling Relationship Strength in Online Social Networks. In: Proceedings of the 19th International Conference on World Wide Web, pp. 981–990 (2010)
18. Tang, J., Lou, T., Kleinberg, J.: Inferring Social Ties Across Heterogenous Networks. In: Proceedings of the Fifth International Conference on Web Search and Data Mining (2012)
19. Mooney, R.: Relational learning of pattern-match rules for information extraction. In: Proceedings of the Sixteenth National Conference on Artificial Intelligence, pp. 328–334 (1999)
20. Getoor, L.: Introduction to Statistical Relational Learning. The MIT Press (2007)

Personalized Recommendation Based on Behavior Sequence Similarity Measures

Yuqi Zhang and Jian Cao[*]

Shanghai Jiaotong University, China
Zyuqi7@gmail.com, cao-jian@cs.sjtu.edu.cn

Abstract. Personalized recommendation is attracting more and more attentions nowadays. There are many kinds of algorithms for making predictions for the target users, and among them Collaborative Filtering (CF) is widely adopted. In some domains, a user's behavior sequences reflect his/her preferences over items so that users who have similar behavior sequences may indicate they have similar preference models. Based on this fact, we discuss how to improve the collaborative filtering algorithm by using user behavior sequence similarity. We proposed a new Behavior Sequence Similarity Measurement (BSSM) approach. Then, different ways to combine BSSM with CF algorithm are presented. Experiments on two real test data sets prove that more precise and stable recommendation performances can be achieved.

1 Introduction

With the development of technology, the Internet has penetrated into people's lives in all areas of study and work to develop the largest information database in today's world. Faced with such a large amount of information, how to make use of these data is becoming the focus of current research [Han et al 2011].

Personalized recommendation is a research field emerged with the increasingly sophisticated use of data mining techniques in recent years. It analyzes the preferences of users according to the user's access records to provide a personalized recommendation service to the user when they access the web site so that customers' satisfaction and loyalty can be improved [George et al 2007]. These systems have been successfully applied to various domains such as movies [Alspector et al 1997; Good et al 1999], news[Resnick et al 1994], and online e-commerce, such as Amazon.com and eBay[Schafer et al 2001], and it brings a lot of benefits to the users and service providers.

There are various kinds of algorithms that have been applied to personalized recommendation problems, and Collaborative Filtering (CF) is a main one among these methods [Su et al 2009]. In general, CF algorithm uses a database of users' preferences over items to predict additional topics or products that the target user might like. There are mainly three categories of CF algorithms, which are memory-based, model-based and hybrid based ones [Su et al 2009]. Although CF algorithms show their advantages in many applications, they still have some drawbacks [Badrul et al 2001], and thus need to be improved.

---

[*] Corresponding author.

L. Cao et al. (Eds.): BSIC/BSI 2013, LNAI 8178, pp. 165–177, 2013.

In some domains, the sequence of a user's behaviors can reflect his/her preferences over items [Cao 2010]. Taking the following case as an example, there are some movies shown in recent three weeks (See Fig. 1). Movies of same letter belong to the same type. User u_1 watched movies in the sequence of $<a_1, b_1, c_1, a_2, b_2>$, whereas user u_2 watched movies in the sequence of $<b_1, a_1, b_2, a_2>$, and user u_3 watched movies in the sequence of $<c_1, a_1, b_1, a_2, b_2>$. The reasons leading to the various behavior sequences may differs between different people. However, the order of movies watched will undoubtedly be affected by user's personal interests. Therefore, it is possible to find users with similar interests in terms of their Behavior Sequence Similarity Measures (BSSM).

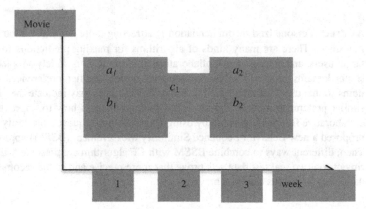

Fig. 1. Movie and Release Time

According to this fact, in this paper, we propose a model that combines BSSM with CF algorithm, and we present several ways to enhance the CF algorithm by applying BSSM.

The rest of the paper is organized as follows. In Section 2, we introduce the related work. In Section 3, we define the user behavior sequence and discuss how to select users who have similar preference with the target user based on BSSM. Then in Section 4 we propose several ways to combine the BSSM with the traditional CF algorithm. Experiments to evaluate the performance of our algorithm is demonstrated and discussed in Section 5. Finally, we conclude the paper and outline future research directions in Section 6.

2   Related Work

Recommendation systems have attracted many attentions nowadays in the field of web application system and on-line information retrieval systems. Traditionally, recommendation algorithms are partitioned into two main families: content-based filtering recommenders and collaborative filtering ones [Resnick et al 1997]. Content-based filtering recommenders make recommendation based on an evaluation of the user own past actions, as WebWatcher [Joachims et al 1997] and client-side agent Letizia [Lieberman et al 1995], while collaborative filtering is based on other similar users' preference. Our approach is an improvement to the traditional CF algorithm.

User behavior has become a research topic that tries to catch the sequence of user interactions at a higher level. These models will in general be hierarchical, as the workload requests at a lower level [Helmult et al 1999], such as WUM, which discover usage pattern from web log file and identify underlying user visit interest exhibited from user's navigational activity to satisfy the expert's criteria [Myra et al 1998], and LDA Model, which incorporating Web user access pattern based on Latent Dirichlet Allocation model to discover the associations between user sessions and multiple topics via probability inference so that to predict more preferable web pages for users via collaborative recommending technique [Guandong Xu et al 2008]. However, the research on user behavior mainly tries to predict future behavior for the original user. In this paper, we combine the user behavior analysis with the traditional CF algorithm to propose a new recommendation model, which can discover the user group that has similar preference with the target user and also take the advantages of a CF algorithm, so that the recommendation performance can be improved.

3   User Behavior Sequence Similarity Measurement

3.1   User Behavior Sequence

Based on social behavioristic theory, users' behaviors are influenced by users' objective preferences and subjective attributes such as age, occupation, area, etc, which has regularities that can reflect the characteristic and personal preferences of users. Based on this fact, users who have similar behaviors should have similar personal preferences.

User behavior sequence is the sequence of user's access behavior in the order of temporal precedence. Here we give the definition of user behavior sequence as follows.

Definition 1(User Behavior Sequence).
Given a user u, whose access behaviors within a time window can be represented as a temporal sequence $bs=<a_1, a_2, a_3,...., a_n>$, where a_i is the action of user u, then we call the sequence bs the user behavior sequence for user u.

Based on the definition of user behavior sequence, we can discover the user behavior pattern, which can be defined as:

Definition 2(User Behavior Pattern).
Given a user u whose user behavior sequence is $bs=<a_1, a_2, a_3,..., a_n>$, and a number $m(0\leq m \leq n)$, then all distinct sub-sequences whose length is m within a user behavior sequence form the user behavior pattern set for user u.

Here, the similarity between two users is measured by the similarity between their corresponding behavior sequences. Given two user behavior sequences, and given a length for constructing user behavior pattern set, the Behavior Sequence Similarity Measurement (BSSM) is the intersection of the user behavior pattern sets of two users. If we denotes W_{ij} as the similarity of behavior sequences between user u_i and user u_j, then W_{ij} is calculated by

$$W_{ij} = max(\frac{simiCount}{P^m_{length\_i}}, \frac{simiCount}{P^m_{length\_j}}) \tag{1}$$

Here, *simiCount* is the number of common user behavior patterns in both sequences. *length_i* and *length_j* is the number of actions in user behavior sequences, and m is the length of user behavior pattern.

For example, if user u_i has the user behavior sequence $<a_1, a_2, a_3, a_4, a_5>$, user u_j has the user behavior sequence $<b_1, a_2, b_3, a_4, a_5, b_6>$, and given the length of user behavior pattern is 2, then the similarity between the user sequences of u_i and u_j is

$$W_{ij} = max\left(\frac{3}{P_5^2}, \frac{3}{P_6^2}\right) = 0.3 \tag{2}$$

There are many ways to measure the similarity between user behavior sequences, such as comparing the frequency of items appearing in the sequences or comparing the common single items appearing in the sequences. Here, we choose to measure the similarity between user behavior pattern sets to compare the similarity between different users, because we believe that this can reflect the similarity of preference structures of different users over items.

In order to verify this intuition, we did some experiments on the real data set. For example, we did experiments on the dataset of MovieLens. Fig. 2 shows the normalized watching frequency distribution for an identified user group over the top ten most-watched movies. It can be observed that there is a common preference among users in the same group. This fact tells us it's possible to make use of BSSM to find users with similar preferences.

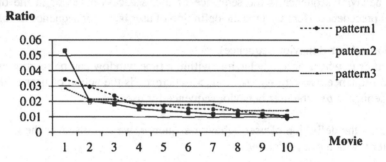

Fig. 2. Audience Ratio Distribution over Top Ten Movies

3.2   Analysis on the Length of User Behavior Pattern

BSSM relies on a parameter, i.e., the length of sub-sequence representing the user behavior pattern. Actually, when the length is 2, it can reveal the preference structure over any two items. When the length is 3, it reveals linear preference structure over any three items. In addition, this number also determines how many similar users could be found. When it is relatively short, the number of similar users will be relatively large. On the contrast, when this number is relatively large, the number of similar users will be relatively small. Obviously, the number of users in the group will influence the recommendation performance. Thus, we should find the best length for describing user behavior patterns.

In order to get reasonable result, an experiment dataset should have sufficient user numbers, so we first find out the movie that has been watched by most users, whose ID is 4196, recorded as M_1. In the first step ($n=1$), we select users who have watched movie 4196, recorded as *UserSet₁*. Then we treat *UserSet₁* as dataset for the next experiment, and find out the movie that has been seen most times, which is movie 424, recorded as M_2. Next we select users who have seen M_3 in *UserSet₂*, recorded as *UserSet₂*, and record this step as $n=2$. Similarly, we can get M_3, which is movie 1088 and corresponding user set *UserSet₃* for $n=3$. When performing on *UserSet₃* and obtain *UserSet₄*, we notice that there is an obvious decrease in the number of users in this group, which makes it contributes little to the experiment, so we stop at $n=3$. At last we get three user behavior patterns, which are (4196) noted as *pattern1*, (4196, 424) noted as *pattern2*, and (4196, 424, 1088) noted as *pattern3*.

For every user behavior pattern, we first find out the next movie which has been seen just after seeing the movies in the user behavior pattern, noted as after-movie, and the movie set we get is noted as after-movie-set. Then we make statistic on the frequency of movies in after-movie set, and rank them from large to small, noted as movie-count-list. Since the numbers of each user set are not same, we transform the result into movie-ratio-list, which avoids the influence caused by number difference. We calculate movie-ratio by the formula below,

$$\text{ratio} = \frac{\text{Count(MovieN)}}{\text{Count(UserSet)}} \tag{3}$$

where count(*MoiveN*) indicates the frequency distribution of movies, and count(*UserSet*) indicates the number of user in the user set.

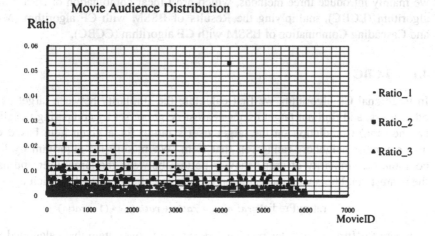

Fig. 3. Audience Ratio Distribution over all Movies

Fig. 2 and Fig. 3 show audience ratio distribution over movies. We set the length equals to 2, 3 and 4 respectively. It can be observed that the preference of users selected is most significant when the length of user behavior pattern is 2, which means the number of users that have similar preference in one user group set is the largest.

From the statistic chart, we can get this conclusion by noticing that the highest point belongs to the result of the user behavior pattern when the length is 2.

From the above observations we can get following result:

1. The preference of users in the same group does not become more obvious while the length of the behavior pattern increases. From the statistic chart above, the preference becomes most obvious when the length is 2. The reason for this result might due to the decrease of number in user group set while the length of the user behavior pattern increases.
2. The length of user behavior pattern also influences the dispersion of the result. While the length increases, the dispersion becomes small.

For different length user behavior patterns, the preference of every user group also different, which is reflected in the statistic chart by the different highest point in the normal distribution of the every result.

Based on above conclusions, we apply behavior patterns of length 2 to discover similar users and then combine BSSM with CF algorithm to support recommendation, which will be discussed in the next section.

4   Recommendation Based on BSSM

We tried several ways to combine BSSM with CF algorithm, and experimenting on the dataset to see whether the recommendation performance has been improved. Here we mainly introduce three methods, which are Linear combination of BSSM and CF algorithm (LCBC), multiplying the Results of BSSM with CF algorithm (MRBC), and Cascading Combination of BSSM with CF algorithm (CCBC).

4.1   LCBC

In traditional CF algorithm, we first calculate the similarity between target user and other users, and find out target user's nearest neighbor set by comparing the similarity, then make prediction on the target user's rating for a given item based on the user's nearest neighbors ratings on that item. We modify the algorithm by linearly combine the similarity of user behavior pattern between the target user and users in the nearest neighbors with the rating prediction calculating formula, which is

$$\text{ratingPredict} = rating_{NN} * ratio + rating_{NS} * (1 - ratio) \qquad (4)$$

where $rating_{NN}$ indicates predicted rating for a given item that calculated from a CF algorithm, and $rating_{NS}$ indicates predicted rating for the given item that comes from BSSM algorithm, which is calculated by

$$rating_{NS} = \sum \frac{W_n * rating(n,j)}{\sum W_n} \qquad (5)$$

where n is the number of nearest neighbor for the target user, and W_n is the similarity of behavior pattern between target user and user n in the nearest neighbor set.

By changing the value of ratio, we change the relative influences of these two algorithms on the final result, and get the predicted rating for each ratio. The experiment result is shown in Section 5.

4.2   MRBC

We consider another way to combine the two algorithms. After we get the nearest neighbor set for the target user by using CF algorithm, we calculate the BSSM between the target user and every user n in the nearest neighbor set, which is W_n .Then we calculate the predicting rating using the following formula

$$\text{ratingPredict} = \sum \frac{\frac{1}{distance[k]+1}*w_n*rating(k)}{\sum \frac{1}{distance[k]+1}} \qquad (6)$$

Here, the first item in the multiplication indicates the distance between the target user and the neighbor using CF algorithm, and n is the number of users in the nearest neighbor set. After getting the predicting ratings for the target user in this way, we compare the result with traditional CF algorithm, which is also shown in Section 5.

4.3   CCBC

Since traditional CF algorithm might have low efficiency when the number of user group is large, we consider first using user behavior pattern to select users who have similar preference with the target user, then using CF algorithm to select the nearest neighbor set for the target user, and making prediction for the target user.

First we need to find out users who have similar preferences with the target user using BSSM algorithm. We use the last n items of the target user to form the target user behavior sequence $(M_1, M_2, M_3,...,M_n)$, and set the user behavior pattern length to be 2 for filtering. We consider setting a threshold value while selecting similar preference user group by comparing the similarity between target user and other users. When the similarity of the behavior pattern between the target user and a candidate user exceeds the threshold value, we add the candidate user into the similar preference user group for the target user. After comparing all users with the target user, we get the similar preference user group for the target user, and run CF algorithm on this user set to get the predicting ratings. We set several different threshold values and compare the recommendation performance for each of them to select the best threshold value. We choose 0, 0.05, 0.1, 0.15 as the tested threshold value, and compare the recommendation performance between each other. The result of the experiment is also shown in Section 5.

5   Experiments and Results

5.1   Experiment Datasets

We use two datasets for our experiments. The first one is MovieLens dataset. MovieLens is a movie recommendation website (http://www.grouplens.org/node/73). It uses user's ratings to generate personalized recommendation for other movies user would like or not. In the experiment we use MovieLens 1M data set, which consists of 1 million ratings from 6000 users on 4000 movies. MovieLens gets users' preference information by letting users rate for the movie. Before using their service, the user need to rate for at least 15 movies. MovieLens data set is a widely applied dataset among experiments on recommendation algorithm, which has already become the basic data set for evaluating recommendation algorithm. The second dataset is book reading behavior information of users from website www.qidian.com. www.qidian.com is one of the largest online reading and writing website in China. We select one-month reading behavior data of users and tested our improved algorithm on it. We first use MovieLens dataset to compare the three ways of integrating BSSM with CF method with the traditional CF method. Then we select the best one based on the recommendation performance and use dataset from qidian website to do the test experiment.

5.2   Experiment on LCBC

We measure the difference between predicted rating with the actual result by calculating the deviation between the two, which is calculated by formula

$$MAE = \sum |ratingPre(i) - rating(i)|/n \qquad (7)$$

where *ratingPre(i)* is the predicted rating calculating from our algorithm, and *rating(i)* is the actual rating of the target user. n is the number of rating items. MAE reflects the recommendation precision of the algorithm.

The MAE of different ratio value is shown in Fig. 4.

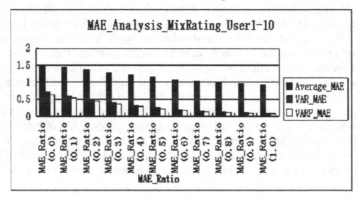

Fig. 4. MAE for LCBC

From the chart we can find that the recommendation precision is increased with the ratio increases, which means the modified algorithm performs worse than the collaborative filtering algorithm.

5.3 Experiment on MRBC

The MAE of different ratio value is shown in Fig. 5 and Fig. 6.

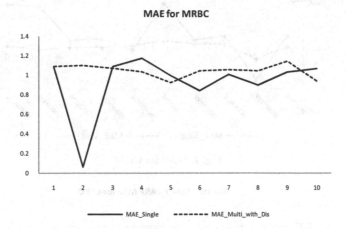

Fig. 5. MAE for MRBC

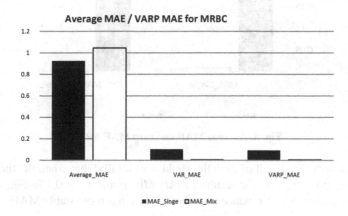

Fig. 6. Average MAE and varp MAE for MRBC

From the result, we can find the performance of modified algorithm has less rec-ommendation precision, but is more stable than the traditional CF algorithm, which has more stable MAE value.

5.4 Experiment on CCBC

The MAE of different ratio value is shown in Fig. 7 and Fig.8.

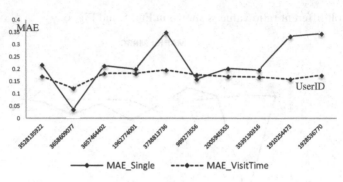

Fig. 7. MAE for CCBC

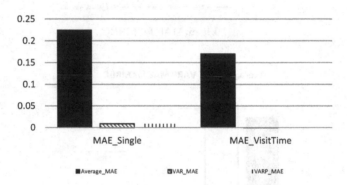

Fig. 8. Average MAE and varp MAE for CCBC

By comparing the result of each threshold, we can find that when the threshold value is 0.1, corresponding with the result of *MAE_Mix_simiRatio*>=0.1 in Fig. 7 and Fig. 8, the recommendation performance is the best, which has more stable MAE value.

5.5   Testing Experiment on CCBC

From the previous experiment, we find that the best way to integrate BSSM with the CF method is the third way, which uses user behavior pattern first before collabora-tive filtering algorithm. We use dataset from www.qidian.com as our test dataset to evaluate the performance of the algorithm. The experiment result is shown in Fig. 9 and Fig. 10.

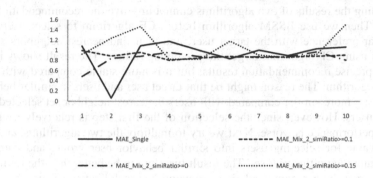

Fig. 9. MAE for CCBC

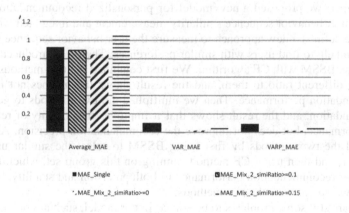

Fig. 10. Average MAE and varp MAE for CCBC

In Fig. 9, we used the CCBC method operating on the dataset from www.qidian.com and get the MAE value compared with single collaborative filtering method. From the result we can find that the user behavior pattern enhanced collaborative filtering method performs better than the traditional CF method, which have better precision and stability.

5.6   Experiment Results Analysis

We tried several ways to integrate the user behavior pattern algorithm into CF algorithm. We first add the two algorithm with different ratio assigned for each algorithm, and it turns out that the integration of the two algorithm does not improve the recommendation performance. This result might due to the fact that CF algorithm gets more precise result, while algorithm based on BSSM gets less precise result, and thus simply adding the results of two algorithms cannot improve the recommendation performance. Then we use BSSM algorithm before CF algorithm to select users who have similar preference with the target user, and then find nearest neighbors among these users using CF algorithm to get the predicting ratings. The result shows it produces less precise recommendation results, but it is more stable compared with traditional CF algorithm. The reason might be that target user and users in similar behavior user group are more similar compared with users in nearest neighbor set selected from the whole users. However, since the selection of the first step is relatively rough, so the whole performance is worse. Next we try to multiply the two algorithms, and set a threshold value for selecting users into similar behavior user group, and using CF algorithm running on this user set. The result turns out to be better than the traditional CF algorithm in both recommendation precision and stabilization. Thus, this is the best algorithm to combine BSSM and CF algorithm.

6   Conclusions

In this paper, we proposed a new model for personalized recommendation, which is based on user behavior sequence similarity measurement and integrated with CF algorithm. We defined a new approach to measure the user behavior sequence similarities, which can help to find users with similar preferences. Then we introduced three ways to combine BSSM with CF algorithm. We first combined the two methods parallel by assigning different ratio to them, and the result shows that it does not improve the recommendation performance. Then we multiplied the two methods to get the union recommendation, and the result shows that it improves the stability of recommendation performance, but does not improve the recommendation precision. After that we combined the two methods by first using BSSM to select the similar users for the target user, and then using CF method running on this group set, which turns out to have better recommendation performance in both precision and stability. Thus, this is the best way to integrate the two methods.

There are still some problems to be solved in our model, such as cool start problem and sparse data problem, which occurs in most CF methods. Also, we can improve our model by making combination between user behavior pattern methods with other recommendation algorithms. These issues will be the main focus in our future work.

Acknowledgments. This work is partially supported by China National Science Foundation (Granted Number 61073021, 61272438), Research Funds of Science and Technology Commission of Shanghai Municipality (Granted Number 11511500102, 12511502704), Cross Research Fund of Biomedical Engineering of Shanghai Jiaotong University (YG2011MS38).

References

1. [Alspector et al 1997] AL Spector, J., Koicz, A., Karunanithi, N.: Feature-based and Clique-based User Models for Movie Selection: A Comparative Study. User Modeling and User-Adapted Interaction 7(4), 279–304 (1997), doi:10.1023/A:1008286413827

2. [Badrul et al 2001] Sarwar, B., Karypis, G., Konstan, J., Riedl, J.: Item-based collaborative filtering recommendation algorithms. In: Proceedings of the 10th International Conference on World Wide Web (WWW 2001), pp. 285–295. ACM, New York (2001), doi:10.1145/371920.372071

3. [Cao 2010] Cao, L.: In-depth Behavior Understanding and Use: the Behavior Informatics Approach. Information Science 180(17), 3067–3085 (2010)

4. [George et al 2007] Lekakos, G., Giaglis, G.M.: A hybrid approach for improving predictive accuracy of collaborative filtering algorithms. User Modeling and User-Adapted Interaction 17(1-2), 5–40 (2007), doi:10.1007/s11257-006-9019-0

5. [Good et al 1999] Good, N., Ben Schafer, J., Konstan, J.A., Borchers, A., Sarwar, B., Herlocker, J., Riedl, J.: Combining collaborative filtering with personal agents for better recommendations. In: Proceedings of the Sixteenth National Conference on Artificial Intelligence and the Eleventh Innovative Applications of Artificial Intelligence Conference Innovative Applications of Artificial Intelligence (AAAI 1999/IAAI 1999), pp. 439–446. American Association for Artificial Intelligence, Menlo Park (1999)

6. [Guandong Xu et al 2008] Xu, G., Zhang, Y., Yi, X.: Modelling User Behaviour for Web Recommendation Using LDA Model. In: 2008 IEEE/WIC/ACM International Confernce on Web Intelligence and Intelligent Agent Technology (2008)

7. [Han et al 2011] Han, J., Kamber, M., Pei, J.: Data Mining: Concepts and Techniques, 3rd edn. Morgan Kaufmann (2011) ISBN-13: 978-0123814791

8. [Helmult et al 1999] Hlavacs, H., Kotsis, G.: Modeling User Behavior: A Layered Approach. In: Proceedings of the 7th International Symposium on Modeling, Analysis and Simulation of Computer and Telecommunication Systems (MASCOTS 1999), p. 218. IEEE Computer Society, Washington, DC (1999)

9. [Resnick et al 1994] Resnick, P., Iacovou, N., Suchak, M., Bergstrom, P., Riedl, J.: GroupLens: an open architecture for collaborative filtering of netnews. In: Proceedings of the 1994 ACM Conference on Computer Supported Cooperative Work (CSCW 1994), pp. 175–186. ACM, New York (1994), doi:10.1145/192844.192905

10. [Resnick et al 1997] Resnick, P., Varian, H.R.: Recommender systems. Communications of the ACM 40(3) (1997)

11. [Joachims et al 1997] Joachims, T., Freitag, D., Mitchell, T.: Webwatcher: A Tour Guide for the World Wide Web. In: The 15th International Joint Conference on Artificial Intelligence (IJCAI 1997), Nagoya, Japan, pp. 770–777 (1997)

12. [Lieberman et al 1995] Lieberman, H.: Letizia: An Agent that Assists Web Browsing. In: Proc. of the 1995 International Joint Conference on Artificial Intelligence, pp. 924–929. Morgan Kaufmann, Montreal (1995)

13. [Myra et al 1998] Spiliopoulou, M., Faulstich, L.C.: WUM: A Web Utilization Miner. In: Proceedings of EDBT Workshop WebDB9 (1998)

14. [Schafer et al 2001] Schafer, J.B., Konstan, J.A., Riedl, J.: Electronic-commerce recommender systems. J. Data Mining Knowl. Discov. 5(1), 115–152 (2001)

15. [Su et al 2009] Su, X., Khoshgoftaar, T.M.: A Survey of Collaborative Filtering Techniques. Advances in Atificial Intelligence 2009, Article ID 421425, 19 Pages (2009), doi:10.1155/2009/421425

Detecting Spam Community Using Retweeting Relationships – A Study on Sina Microblog

Bin Zhao*, Genlin Ji, Weiguang Qu, and Zhigang Zhang

School of Computer Science and Technology
Nanjing Normal University
Nanjing, P.R. China
{zhaobin,glji,wgqu}@njnu.edu.cn, zzg22936@gmail.com

Abstract. Microblog marketing is a new trend in social media. Spammers have been increasingly targeting such platforms to disseminate spam and promoting messages. Unlike the past behaviors on traditional media, they connect and support each other to perform spam tasks on microblogs. Therefore existing methods can't be directly used for detecting spam community. In this paper, we examine the behaviors of spammers on Sina microblog, and obtain some observations about their activities rules. Then we extract content features from tweet text and behavior features from retweeting interactions, perform machine learning to build classification models and identify spammers on microblogs. We evaluate our generated feature set used for detecting spammers under three classification methods, including Naive Bayes, Decision Tree and SVM. Extensive experiments show that our proposed feature set can make the classifiers perform well, and the crawler program combining the SVM classifier can effectively detect spam community.

1 Introduction

Microblog marketing is a new trend in social media. More and more business users broaden network business or promote their brands on microblogs. Unfortunately, spammers have been increasingly targeting the platform to conduct spam activities, including disseminating malware, spamming commercial messages and promoting phishing websites. Tremendous increase of spam has become a serious problem. Spammers are annoying individual users and threatening normal marketing, advertising and other business activities on microblogs [1].

There are existing works on spam detection, such as email spam filtering [1, 2, 3, 4], fake review detection [5, 6, 7] and social spam detection [8, 9, 10]. Usually social users are categorized into three main types: legitimate users, promoters and spammers [8]. Those who use social platforms to conduct business activities such as advertising or marketing and comply with associated rules (e.g., "The Twitter Rules" [2]) are called promoters; Those who post lots of duplicate or similar business messages, phishing links or unsolicited tweets in a short period are called spammers.

---

* Corresponding author.
[1] http://mashable.com/2011/10/26/warning-twitter-spam
[2] http://support.twitter.com/entries/18311-the-twitter-rules

L. Cao et al. (Eds.): BSIC/BSI 2013, LNAI 8178, pp. 178–190, 2013.
© Springer International Publishing Switzerland 2013

In this study, we focus on detecting spam community on microblogs, which can highly adversely affect user experience of normal users or violate individual interest and privacy. Research on spam community detection of microblogs is quite different from other works in two ways.

- Promoters are not targeted by spammer detection on microblogs. In the context of reviews, promoters who post no reviews and intend to promote their products and services are the target of spammer detection. But they are permitted and supported to launch marketing campaigns on microblogs. For example, Twitter will create its new advertising platform for companies of any size to grow their businesses using 'Promoted Tweets' and 'Promoted Accounts' products [3]. But promoters are sometimes harmful especially when they post marketing tweets in bulk. Therefore such promoters are also prohibited on microblogs.
- Spammer communities are treated as the target of detection approaches due to the coordination between them in spam activities. Spam accounts are usually created massively to avoid suspension, and cooperate in spam activities. Some spammers acting as supporters [9] tend to collect legitimate user profiles and expect them to follow back. Others spam marketing messages, malware and phishing links. They may switch spam roles after a period. Therefore, We seek to treat microblog spammer community as the target of detection. Such detection can remarkably enhance detection efficiency. However, there does not exist such coordination between spammers in the context of emails and reviews.

The recent approaches have started to study spammer detection in a community-level style. But they have the following limitations on spammer community detection.

- They utilize following relationships to represent social relationships of spammers. In [9], Yang et al. exploit the community nature of Twitter criminal accounts and propose spammer detection inference algorithms. However, social relationships based on following aren't accurate and believable. For example, it is observed that spammers may pose as legitimate users or popular users through following authenticated users so as to avoid being suspected, but actually they do not care about the following updates at all. In addition, the methods are very sensitive to the initial seed set of known spammers. These thus reduce the performance of spammer detection results. In our work, we prefer retweets within spammer community, which reflect social relationships more accurately, in order to enhance the quality of detection.
- Many previous work treats spam detection as classification. They focused on text features which are extracted from spam tweets and neglected spammers' behavior features [11] including following activities and '@' tags. These further increases the risk of spam on the platform.

---

[3] http://blog.twitter.com/2012/02/
coming-soon-twitter-advertising-for.html

In this paper, we focus on microblog spammer detection in the style of community-level. We extract representative content features from tweets, and extract spam behavior features from retweeting relationships to distinguish spammer from normal ones. We apply three kinds of classical classifiers (i.e. Naive Bayes, Decision Tree and SVM) on real-world dataset acquired from Sina microblog [4]. Throughout extensive experiments, we gain performance comparisons of detecting spammers under different classifiers. The results can provide practical advice for spammer detection on microblogs. The reason for using this microblog is that it is the largest microblog in China. According to 2013 Internet Trends Report [5], it has had more than 500 million users. The main contributions of this paper are summarized below.

- We extract both content features and behavior features from tweets, perform machine learning to build classification models and identify spammers on microblogs.
- We design and implement an online spammer detection system based on BFS strategy using retweeting behaviors so as to identify whole spammer communities.
- In the absence of ground truth, we collect the real-world dataset on microblogs. We perform extensive experiments to evaluate our proposed feature set and spam community detection.

The rest of the paper is organized as follows. Section 2 introduces spammer dataset of this study. Section 3 details supervised method for spammer detection. Section 4 presents the experimental results and analysis on the real microblog dataset. Section 5 provides a review of related work. Finally, we conclude in Section 6.

2   Microblog Dataset and Analysis

2.1   Microblog Dataset

Before discussing the methods of microblog spam detection, we collected a real-world dataset (**MDS**) acquired from Sina microblog. We first randomly pick up some promoters and spammers as seeds on Sina microblog. We then start from these seeds to crawl their followers and followings using the BFS (Breadth-first Search) algorithm. Finally we obtain **MDS** dataset, which consists of 10,180 accounts and 637,378 tweets. Those accounts consist of legitimate users, promoters and spammers. The duration of the dataset is from February 1st to March 31 in 2013.

Because promoters have also targeted microblogs to post a large number of advertisements and carry out commercial activities. Although the messages of promoters is less harmful than that of spammers, their posting behaviors may

---

also annoy normal users and affect user experience. Therefore we collect two kinds of microblog datasets (spammers and promoters) in this study.

We picked up spam and promotion tweets from **MDS** dataset and then obtained **MSpam** dataset and **MPromoter** dataset. Tweets of **MSpam** are manually chosen according to "Twitter Rules". The dataset consists of 174 spammers and 10,320 tweets. Most of the spammers are uncertified mechanical users from Taobao.com [6](a largest online shopping site in China). They usually post spam information (e.g. marketing activities or promotion advertisement) via Sina microblog.

The **MPromoter** dataset consists of 203 promoters and 11,921 tweets. Those users are mainly certified enterprise firms on Sina microblog. Although Both kinds of users may promote the same type of commodities, the posting ways of the promoters are completely different to those of spammers. Both **MSpam** and **MPromoter** datasets are summarized in Table 1, which lists the tweet number and the account number. We will demonstrate the effectiveness of our proposed methods based on these real-world datasets.

Table 1. Datasets used in our experiments

Dataset Name	# Tweets	# Users
MDS	637,378	10,180
MSpam	10,320	174
MPromoter	11,921	203

2.2   Data Statistics and Analysis

Each Sina tweet mainly consists of 6 parts, which are as follows:

- Account ID
- Tweet text content (up to 280 characters)
- Timestamp
- Reviewed number
- Retweeted number
- Retweet message (Optional)

Each tweet can contain text, '@' tag, short links and multimedia data (e.g. picture, video and music).

Before we introduce our proposed methods for spam detection, we present four kinds of feature distributions, including tweet length, '@' tag, link and hashtag. Figure 1, 2 and 3 show the length distributions of **MDS**, **MSpam** and **MPromoter** respectively. For each tweet length x, all figures show the number of tweets with x characters. **MDS**, **MSpam** and **MPromoter** datasets have

---

[6] http://www.taobao.com

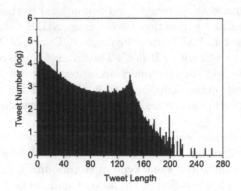

Fig. 1. Tweet length distribution of **MDS** dataset

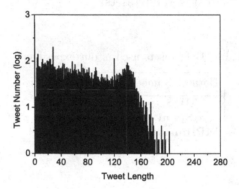

Fig. 2. Tweet length distribution of **MSpam** dataset

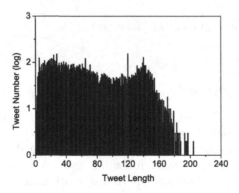

Fig. 3. Tweet length distribution of **MPromoter** dataset

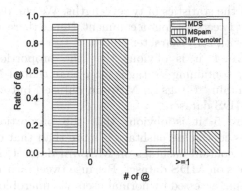

Fig. 4. @ distribution

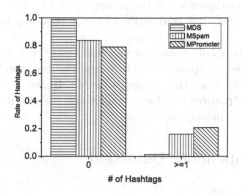

Fig. 5. Hashtag distribution

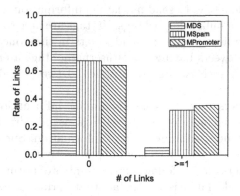

Fig. 6. Short link distribution

26.3%, 6.7% and 7.2% of tweets with zero character respectively, all of which are the largest number in the statistics of tweet lengths. We can observe that many users often retweet hot tweets without a comment. Hence there are a considerable proportion of tweets with zero character length.

As shown in figure 4, it is obvious that the proportion of **MSpam**'s (**MPromoter**) tweets containing '@' tag is more than that of **MDS**. For example, 17% of tweets contain '@' tags on **MSpam** dataset, but only 5% of tweets contain '@' tags on **MDS** dataset.

As shown in figure 5, it is obvious that the proportion of **MSpam**'s (**MPromoter**) tweets containing hashtags is more than that of **MDS**. For example, 16% of tweets contain hashtags on **MSpam** dataset, but only 1.2% of tweets contain hashtags on **MDS** dataset. Because tweets with hashtags have a high probability of being accessed by normal users via microblog search engines, spammers often post marketing tweets with hashtags.

As shown in figure 6, it is also obvious that **MSpam**'s (**MPromoter**) tweets have a high probability of containing links. The reason is that the links in tweets can take normal users to spam sites. For example, 32.4% of tweets contain hashtags on **MSpam** dataset, but only 5.5% of tweets contain hashtags on **MDS** dataset.

In terms of all features of tweets, we can find that the behaviors of promoters are similar to those of spammers. Only the hashtag number of promoting tweets is slightly higher than that of spam tweets. In Section 4.3, experiments on **MSpam** and **MPromoter** datasets will show insight into the differences between spammers and promoters.

3   Supervised Spammer Detection

3.1   Our Observations

Through our examination, we gain some following observations about spammer activities on Sina microblog.

- Microblog spammers tend to send marketing information, malware links and phishing websites in bulk using '@' tags. '@' tags are able to inform microblog users by attaching account-IDs to read tweets in time once users go online. But usually those tweets having the '@username' tags aren't subscribed by normal users, then such tweets are unsolicited tweets, called as microblog spam.
- Microblog spammers tend to send spamming information by retweeting. Retweet text may include as many '@' tags as possible because retweets don't need to include spamming content information. Such method can enhance the effectiveness and efficiency of spam activities.
- Microblog spammers tend to follow a large number of normal users in order to expect to follow back. There is a basic fact that normal users are hardly likely to subscribe spam ones. But some new users are unfamiliar with microblog usage, they may become the followers of spammers. Therefore, spammers

obviously have a large number of followings compared to the amount of followers.

- Microblog tweets tend to include links of marketing activities or shopping sites. Because tweets have up to 280 characters, users can access the detailed content using links.

The above observations are consistent with the posting style and spam strategies of spammers. Hence, we can model the behavior features of spammers, build the appropriate classifier for detecting spammers and distinguish from normal users and promoters.

3.2 Feature Set Extraction

We extract each of the following feature sets, which might be indicative of spam.

- Content features: text length, representative terms (e.g. brand name) , link number and image number.
- Behavior features: '@' number, the ratio of the follower number to the following number.

Note that representative terms are more important features compared to other features. For example, a tweet has a high probability of becoming spam or promoting tweet if it contains a band name (e.g. Nike Shoe or Samsung Galaxy S4). In order to construct the feature set of representative terms, we collected about 1,800 band terms, which are acquired from the shopping directory of Taobao.com and JD.com (famous shopping sites in China).

4 Experiment and Analysis

4.1 Dataset Description

We use two datasets (**DataSet1** and **DataSet2**) to evaluate our proposed feature set. **DataSet1** consists of 5,000 normal tweets and 5,000 spam tweets. **DataSet2** consists of 5,000 normal tweets and 5,000 promotion tweets. A microblog user is labeled spammer if he posts marketing messages in bulk or mention so many users via '@' tags. As a result his posting tweets are spam. A microblog user is labeled promoter if he posts marketing tweets with the normal frequency, which way of posting doesn't violate Sina microblog rules. Both datasets are summarized in Table 2.

4.2 Experiment Setting

We choose Naive Bayes, Decision Tree and SVM as the classifiers for spam detection. Both implements of Naive Bayes and Decision Tree are from WEKA [7], and that of SVM is from libsvm [8]. We evaluate our proposed feature set of spammer detection under three classification methods. All experiments have been carried out on Intel Core2 2.67 GHz Duo CPU with 4GB memory.

---

[7] http://www.cs.waikato.ac.nz/ml/weka/
[8] http://www.csie.ntu.edu.tw/~cjlin/libsvm/

Table 2. Training and test datasets used in our experiments

Dataset	Tweet type	# tweets
DataSet1	Normal	5,000
	Spam (MSpam)	5,000
DataSet2	Normal	5,000
	Promotion (MPromoter)	5,000

Table 3. Performances of different classifiers on both **DataSet1** and **DataSet2** datasets

dataset	Classifier	Precision (%)	Recall (%)	F1 (%)	Training (ms)	Test (ms)
	Naive Bayes	62.0%	81.0%	70.2%	**109**	47
DataSet1	Decision Tree	62.4%	82.1%	70.9%	1966	**15**
	SVM	**85.7%**	**83.1%**	**84.3%**	87493	1952
	Naive Bayes	72.4%	81.6%	76.7%	**94**	31
DataSet2	Decision Tree	73.6%	85.3%	79.0%	2215	**16**
	SVM	**90.6%**	**89.7%**	**90.1%**	90429	2934

4.3 Classification Comparison

For the performance comparison of classifiers, we utilize precision, recall and F1-measures to evaluate our proposed feature set and the those methods by performing repeated 5-fold cross validation on the dataset. For each fold, we use 80% of the dataset for training while the remaining 20% are used as test dataset. Meanwhile, both training runtime and test runtime will be also reported under the different methods.

As shown in Table 3, the performance of SVM is significantly better than the other methods. Most of experimental results on **DataSet2** are much better than those of **DataSet1**. The training runtime of Naive Bayes is shortest, while the test runtime of Decision Tree is achieved best. Considering the overall classification performance, SVM seems to be the best choice especially when the effectiveness is critical.

To further evaluate the contribution of different kinds of features, we compute the contribution rates which are based on precision in this study. Towards the feature f, the contribution C_f is defined as the following equation.

$$C_f = 1 - \frac{precision'_f}{precision_f} \tag{1}$$

where $precision'_f$ represents the precision of the classifier without feature f, $precision_f$ represents the precision of the classifier with feature f. Figure 7 reports that the following relationship (i.e. # follower/# following) is the top

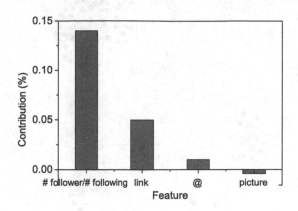

feature. Overall, the ratio of follower number to following number helps to boost the performance of classification.

4.4 Spam and Promoting Community Detection

According to [9], spammers and promoters tend to connect each other. We show a snapshot of the community of spammers and promoters on Sina microblog. We first choose an account (account name: 吴琼 ta_ta) as a seed, and then use BFS strategy to traverse its neighborhood. Each account is labeled by SVM classifier. We label each account using type tags. Some main accounts in the experiments are shown in Table 4. The results of community detection are shown in Table 5. Its precision is 94%, its recall is 96% and F1 is 94%. We can find that the SVM method based on our proposed feature set is practical and effective.

Table 4. Main accounts in Figure 8

ID	Account name	Tag
A	吴琼ta_ta	ad. account
B	森学文化宣传科	headset
C	点动广告	makeup
D	领先广告网络部	shoe
E	伟昌数码	shoe
F	斯杰传媒	shoe, headset
G	微博广告	ad. account
H	微博客服	n/a

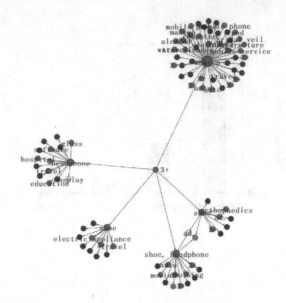

Fig. 8. Community detection of spammers and promoters starting from a specified seed

Finally, although the distribution of **MSpam** is similar to that of **MPromoter** in Section 2.2, Table 3 shows the promotion tweets are more easily detected than spam tweets.

5 Related Work

5.1 Review Spam

The problem of detecting review or opinion spam was introduced in [12], which analyzed such spam activities and utilized supervised learning to detect spam. [7] identified several characteristic behaviors of review spammers and modeled their rating behaviors to detect them. [13] proposed a novel relation-based approach to detecting spammer groups. [14] proposed a new method to detect singleton review spam via correlated temporal patterns. Considering common text features between reviews and microblogs, the techniques of review spam detection can also be utilized so as to address the microblog spam detection problem.

5.2 Microblog Spam

Spam detection on microblogs has been attracted much attention in recent years. [15] proposed a Supervised Matrix Factorization method with Social Regularization (SMFSR) for spammer detection in social networks. [16] proposed a machine learning method to detect microblog spam by each single tweet only. [17] proposed a scalable framework to detect both spam and promoting campaigns. [9]

Table 5. Results of spammer and promoter community detection in Figure 8

	True	False
Positive	47 (Red)	3 (Purple)
Negative	45 (Blue)	2 (Yellow)

performed an empirical analysis of the cyber criminal ecosystem on Twitter. [18] reported on a case study of rumor transmission during a nationwide scandal via Sina microblog.

6   Conclusions

In this paper, we examined the behaviors of spammers and promoters on Sina microblog, and gain some observations about their activities rules. Then we extracted content features from tweet text and behavior features from retweeting interactions, performed machine learning to build classification models and identified spammers and promoters on microblogs. We evaluated our generated feature set used for detecting both spammers and promoters under three classification methods, including Naive Bayes, Decision Tree and SVM. Extensive experiments show that our proposed feature set can make the classifiers perform well, and crawler based on such feature set and SVM classifier can effectively detect spam and promoting community.

Acknowledgments. This work is partially supported by the Natural Science Foundation of the Jiangsu Higher Education Institutions of China (Grant No. 13KJB520014), , National Science Foundation of China (Grant No. 61272221) , Social Science Foundation of Jiangsu Province (Grant No. 12YYA002) and Key Program of Science Foundation of Jiangsu Province (Grant No. BK2011005).

References

[1] Dasgupta, A., Gurevich, M., Punera, K.: Enhanced email spam filtering through combining similarity graphs. In: WSDM, pp. 785–794 (2011)

[2] Cormack, G.V., Kolcz, A.: Spam filter evaluation with imprecise ground truth. In: SIGIR, pp. 604–611 (2009)

[3] Wei Chang, M., Tau Yih, W., Meek, C.: Partitioned logistic regression for spam filtering. In: KDD, pp. 97–105 (2008)

[4] Fette, I., Sadeh, N.M., Tomasic, A.: Learning to detect phishing emails. In: WWW, pp. 649–656 (2007)

[5] Ott, M., Choi, Y., Cardie, C., Hancock, J.T.: Finding deceptive opinion spam by any stretch of the imagination. In: ACL, pp. 309–319 (2011)

[6] Wang, G., Xie, S., Liu, B., Yu, P.S.: Review graph based online store review spammer detection. In: ICDM, pp. 1242–1247 (2011)

[7] Lim, E.P., Nguyen, V.A., Jindal, N., Liu, B., Lauw, H.W.: Detecting product review spammers using rating behaviors. In: CIKM, pp. 939–948 (2010)

[8] Benevenuto, F., Rodrigues, T., Almeida, V.A.F., Almeida, J.M., Gonçalves, M.A.: Detecting spammers and content promoters in online video social networks. In: SIGIR, pp. 620–627 (2009)

[9] Yang, C., Harkreader, R.C., Zhang, J., Shin, S., Gu, G.: Analyzing spammers' social networks for fun and profit: a case study of cyber criminal ecosystem on twitter. In: WWW, pp. 71–80 (2012)

[10] Lee, K., Caverlee, J., Webb, S.: Uncovering social spammers: social honeypots + machine learning. In: SIGIR, pp. 435–442 (2010)

[11] Cao, L.: In-depth behavior understanding and use: the behavior informatics approach. Information Sciences 180(17), 3067–3085 (2010)

[12] Jindal, N., Liu, B.: Opinion spam and analysis. In: WSDM, pp. 219–230 (2008)

[13] Mukherjee, A., Liu, B., Glance, N.S.: Spotting fake reviewer groups in consumer reviews. In: WWW, pp. 191–200 (2012)

[14] Xie, S., Wang, G., Lin, S., Yu, P.S.: Review spam detection via temporal pattern discovery. In: KDD, pp. 823–831 (2012)

[15] Zhu, Y., Wang, X., Zhong, E., Liu, N.N., Li, H., Yang, Q.: Discovering spammers in social networks. In: AAAI (2012)

[16] Liu, L., Jia, K.: Detecting spam in chinese microblogs - a study on sina weibo. In: CIS, pp. 578–581 (2012)

[17] Zhang, X., Zhu, S., Liang, W.: Detecting spam and promoting campaigns in the twitter social network. In: ICDM, pp. 1194–1199 (2012)

[18] Liao, Q., Shi, L.: She gets a sports car from our donation: rumor transmission in a chinese microblogging community. In: CSCW, pp. 587–598 (2013)

Cooperative Community Detection Algorithm Based on Random Walks

Mingwei Leng, Weiming Lv, Jianjun Cheng, Zhao Li, and
Xiaoyun Chen*

School of Information Science and Engineering, Lanzhou University
Lanzhou, 730000,China,
lengmw@163.com, chenxy@lzu.edu.cn

Abstract. Community Detection is a significant tool for understanding the structures of real-world networks. Although many novel methods have been applied in community detection, as far as we know, cooperative method has not been applied into community detection to improve the performance of discovering community structure of social networks. In this paper, we propose a cooperative community detection algorithm, named cooperative community detection algorithm based on random walks. Firstly, it uses random walks to calculate the similarities between adjacent nodes, and then translates a given unweighted networks into weighted networks based on the similarities between adjacent nodes. Secondly, it detects community structures of networks by activating the neighbors a node whose community label is known. Thirdly, it cooperates running results of many times of our community detection algorithm to improve its accuracy and stability. Finally, we demonstrate our community detection algorithm with three real networks, and the experimental results show that our cooperative semi-supervised method has a higher accuracy and more stable results compared with other random community detection algorithms.

Keywords: Social Networks, community detection, random walks, linear threshold model, cooperative method.

1 Introduction

Community detection is the key issue in behavior computing [14] of finding the structure and understanding the function of complex networks. Generally, community is identified as a set of nodes whose links inside are more densely than links outside. Community detection has been studied for a long time and it is closely related to the graph partitioning theory.

Most of community detection algorithms can be divided into three classes: agglomerative method, divisive method and label propagation method. Since Girvan and Newman proposed the GN algorithm based on the iterative removal of edges with maximum edge betweenness[1], a large number of algorithms have

---

* Corresponding author.

L. Cao et al. (Eds.): BSIC/BSI 2013, LNAI 8178, pp. 191–203, 2013.

been proposed to be applied to complex networks. Clauset et al. introduced a fast algorithm (CNM) based on the greedy optimization of the quality[2]. Most of those modularity methods and there variations use modularity as the evaluation metric to evaluate the quality of the finally detected community structure. However, some researchers such as Steinhaeuser and Chawla found that the maximum modularity does not necessarily mean the correct community structure of some complex networks.

Raghavan et al. proposed a label-propagation algorithm (LPA) with a linear time complexity, which initials each node with a unique numeric label and then replaces the label for each node with the most frequent label from its neighbor nodes[3]. Some variations of LPA such as LPAm[4], LPAm+[5], SHARC[6] are proposed. LPA and its these variations are nondeterministic algorithms, difference between the detecting results of different running times is larger in some complex networks.

Sine maximum modularity does not necessarily mean the correct community structure of some complex networks, LPA and its these variations are nondeterministic algorithms. In this paper, we introduce cooperation into community detection, and we propose a cooperative community detection approach based on random walks. Firstly, we use random walks' method[8] to calculate the relationship between any two adjacent nodes, and this translates an unweighted networks into weighted one. Secondly, we find out two most similar nodes as the first community and iteratively expand them by adding all their neighbor nodes that can be activated by them till there has no node to be activated by this community, then find out two most similar nodes in the rest nodes as the second community, and repeat the process until all nodes are activated. Here, the activation is a linear threshold (LT) model[9] and more details is given in section 2. Thirdly, since we use random walks to calculate the similarity between adjacent nodes, the weight of each edge maybe different in different running time, and this leads the performance of our community detection algorithm is unstable. We utilize cooperative method[10] to improve the performance of our community detection algorithm and achieve to a stable results.

The rest of the paper is organized as follow. Section 2 gives some definition. Section 3 introduces Random-Walks Algorithm and presents our algorithm. Section 4 demonstrates our algorithm with tree real-world networks and gives the experimental results. The conclusion and future works are given in Section 5.

2   Some Definition

In order to give more simple description of this paper, we give some definitions used in the rest of the paper. Formally, given a network $G =< V, E >$ with $n = |V|$ nodes and $m = |E|$ edges, we have some definitions as below:

Definition 1. Node Strength, For a given node u , the node strength of node u is defined as:

$$K(u) = \sum_{v \in N(u)} w(u, v) \tag{1}$$

Where $N(u)$ is the neighbor nodes set of node u and $w(u, v)$ is calculated by random walks algorithm, the calculating method of $w(u, v)$ is given as algorithm 1 in section 3.

Definition 2. Belonging Degree, For a given community C and a given node u, the belonging degree $B(u, C)$ between u and C is defined as:

$$B(u, C) = \frac{\sum_{v \in (N(u) \cap C)} w(u, v)}{K(u)} \tag{2}$$

where $w(u, v)$ and $N(u)$ are the same as in Eq.(1). $B(u, C)$ is used to measure how tight between the node u and community C.

Definition 3. Community Strength, For a given community C, the community strength is defined as:

$$S(C) = \frac{\sum_{u \in C} \sum_{v \in (N(u) \cap C)} w(u, v)}{\sum_{u \in C} K(u)} \tag{3}$$

where $w(u, v)$ and $N(u)$ are the same as in Eq.(1).

3 Cooperative Community Detection Algorithm Based on Random Walks

In this section, we give our community detection algorithm, cooperative community detection algorithm based on random walks. It can be divided into three stages: (i) calculating the degree of influence relationship between neighbors by using random walks, (ii) Using the idea of LT model to detect the community structure and (iii) improving the detected result via cooperative method. The conceptions of random walks, linear threshold model and cooperative method are given as follows.

• **Random walks** have been applied to graph clustering for a long history and have attracted a lot of attentions. It can be computed efficiently and be used in hierarchical clustering algorithm[11]. Van Dongen introduced an algorithm called Markov cluster algorithm (MCL) whose underlying intuition stems from the idea of random walks[12]. The author supposes that a random walker placed in a network would spend more time to cross different communities than to walk around the same community. Hence, starting from a node i, if another node j has a high probability to visit it during the given steps, we can assert that nodes i and j have a high probability of belonging to the same community. Steinhaeuser et al. implemented a new method that applied directly the idea of actually taking random walks[8]. In our paper, we use this random walk algorithm to calculate the degree of influence relationship between neighbors.

• **LT** model is one of the two basic influence cascade models in the field of influence maximization which were proposed by Kempe et al.[9]. In the LT model, a node in the network is influenced by its neighbors. Therefore, for a given initial set of active nodes, the diffusion process unfolds the active neighbors iteratively which the total weight of their active neighbors exceed the threshold. LT model as a diffusion model has a lot of applications in the field of influence maximization. The authors presented a greedy algorithm without scalable in large datasets[9]. Narayanam et al. also proposed a heuristic SPIN algorithm for the LT model[13]. In this paper, we introduce LT model into community detection to find community structure of complex networks.

- **Cooperative Method.** Kashef et al. introduced a novel cooperative clustering (CC) model[10]. CC model is based on the common sense that no clustering method can adapt to all types of datasets and based on a cooperative methodology utilizing multiple clustering algorithms with the goal of achieving better clustering quality than individual approaches. Unlike other hybrid algorithms [15,16], CC model allows synchronous execution of multiple sub-algorithms to get a better performance. In this paper, we utilize the idea of CC model to improve the performance of our community detection algorithm.

3.1   Calculation Similarity between Nodes via Random Walks

Steinhaeuser et al.[8] introduced a method to calculate the similarity of nodes based on random walks. The idea is that the encountered nodes, which starting from a node and randomly walking with short steps, belong in the same community with a relatively large probability. We use this method to calculate the degree of influence relationship between neighbors. However, the similarity matrix is unstable due to the method of random walks, in this paper, we adopt the average value of similarity matrix of several running times as the final similarity matrix. The pseudo-code is given in Algorithm 1.

Algorithm 1. Calculation Similarity between Nodes via Random Walks

1. Input:$G = <V, E>$, *loops*
2. $W = \{\}$
3. $W[u][v] = 0$ for $u \in V, v \in N(u)$
4. $numSteps = G.diameter$
5. for $i = 1$ to *loops*:
6.   for each node p in V:
7. $curNode = p$
8. $metNodes = \{curNode\}$
9.   for *step* in range($numSteps$):
10. $curNode = random.choice(N(curNode))$
11. $metNodes = metNodes \cup \{curNode\}$
12.   for each node u in $metNodes$:
13.   for each node v in $(metNodes \cap N(s))$:
14. $W[u][v] += 1.0$
15. $W[u][v] = W[u][v]/loops;\ \forall u \in V, v \in N(u)$
16. return W

At first we define an adjacent matrix and initialize each element to zero. For each loop, each node in V is used as a starting node for a random walk. Each random walk jumps for $numSteps$ times with the strategy that selecting the next node from current node's neighbor nodes random (line 9). Then elements in the adjacent matrix corresponding to the path in random walk are incremented (line11-13). After all loops are complete, we format the similarity matrix by calculating the average of all $loops$ (line 14). The number of steps $numSteps$ in our method is fixed to the diameter of G.

3.2 Community Detection Method

This subsection gives our community detection algorithm, and it can be divided into two steps: (i) selecting the pair nodes with maximum degree of influence relationship as an initial community C and (ii)expanding community C by using the activating mechanism of LT model to expand the community label of a node in C to its neighbors. Firstly, we select two nodes which are the most similar in the network, and they are the initial nodes as the first community C. Secondly, we calculate belonging degree $B(u, C)$, where u is the neighbor of some node in C and u is not in C, if $B(u, C)$ is larger than a given threshold θ, then add u into C. Repeat this process until the $B(v, C)$ of any neighbor v which is not in C of nodes in C is less than or equal to θ, then the expanding process of community C is finished. Thirdly, select two nodes which are the most similar from the rest nodes in the network, and they are the initial nodes as the second community, expand this community by using the same method above. Finally, we repeat the above method until there no one node in network which does not belong to any community. More details of community detection are shown in algorithm 2 as the lines 2-13.

(RCD) denotes our community detection based on random walks. We generate community structure via the method above-mentioned at first (lines 2-13). However, our method may leave some isolated nodes and generate some communities that are too small. It often generates many overlapping nodes on the boundary especially when the threshold θ is less than 0.5. We define these three cases and propose the solutions respectively.

(i) Isolated Node: The node isn't contained by any community in network. Suppose that the number of communities which have been identified is m, then the formulaic definition is:

$$Isolated\_node(INs) = \{u | u \notin \bigcup_{i=1}^{m} C_i\} \tag{4}$$

For each isolated node, we select the community with maximum belonging degree between isolated node and community, and then assign this isolated node to it, and the lines 24-27 of algorithm 2 deal with isolated nodes.

(ii) Isolated Community: Suppose that C is a community, C is isolated community if and only if $S(C) < 0.5$

For these communities, we traverse the array of communities to find a community with the largest growth of community strength after merging them.

Algorithm 2. Community Detection (**RCD**)

---

1. Input:$G =< V, E >$, W and θ
2. $communities = []$
3. $expandeds = []$
4. $simItem \leftarrow \arg_{u,w} \max_{u,w}(W(u,w))$
5. **while** $(W(simItem) > 1)$
6. $newC = [simItem.nodes]$
7. $NC \leftarrow (\cup_{u \in newC} N(u)) \backslash newC$, order them according to belonging degree
8.   **while** $(B(NC.firstNode, new) > \theta)$
9. $new \leftarrow NC.firstNode$
10.   update the list of NC
11. $expandeds = expandeds \cup newC$
12. $communities \leftarrow newC$
13. $simItem \leftarrow \arg_{u,w} \max_{u,w \in V \backslash expandeds}(W(u,w))$.
14. $ICs \leftarrow \{C | S(C) < 0.5\}$
15. for each C in ICs
16. $targetC \leftarrow \arg_{C'} \max_{C' \in communities}(\Delta S(C, C'))$
17.   if $(\Delta S(C, targetC) > 0)$, merge C into $targetC$
18   else: else: remove community C from $communities$
19. $ONs \leftarrow \{u | u \in C_1 \wedge u \in C_2\}$
20. for u in ONs
21. $coms \leftarrow \{C | u \in C\}$
22. $com \leftarrow \arg_C \max_{C \in coms} B(u, C)$
23.   remove u from $coms \backslash com$
24. $INs \leftarrow V \backslash communities$
25. for u in INs
26. $com \leftarrow \arg_C \max_{C \in communities} B(u, C)$
27. $com \leftarrow u$
28. return $textbf communities$

The growth is defined as:

$$\Delta S(C_1, C_2) = S(C_1 \cup C_2) - \max\{S(C_1), S(C_2)\} \tag{5}$$

If the maximum of ΔS is positive, then merge two communities. Otherwise, we let the nodes in this isolated community to be isolated node and delete this community, and the lines 14-18 of algorithm 2 deal with isolated nodes

(iii) Overlapping Node: The node is contained by two or more than two communities. The formulaic definition:

$$Overlapping\_Nodes(ONs) = \{u | u \in C_i \wedge u \in C_j\} \tag{6}$$

where C_i and C_j are arbitrary two different communities which have been detected. For each overlapping node u, we assign u to the community which has more belonging degree between them, and the lines 19-23 of algorithm 2 deal with isolated nodes.

3.3   Performance Improving via Cooperative Method

Our community detection algorithm is unstable according to calculating similarities between nodes by using random method just like LPA algorithm, although most of the results are superior to LPA algorithm. The key problem is calculating method of similarity matrix in Algorithm 1. Although we have adopted some approaches in Algorithm 1 to weaken the randomness, the problem of some boundary nodes can not be solved. In this subsection, we use cooperative method to improve the performance of our community detection algorithm.

In our cooperative method, we run our community detection algorithm many times, more details are given as algorithm 3.

Algorithm 3. Cooperation Community Detection **CCD**)

---

1. Input:$G = <V, E>$, *loops* and *reliability*
2. $NR = \{\}$
3. $NR[i][j] = 0; \forall i, j \in V$
4. for *loop* in range (*loops*):
5.   *communities* ←call community detection algorithm
6.   for *com* in *communities*:
7. $NR[i][j]+ = 1; \forall i, j \in com$
8. remove the elements in NR whose values are less than *loops* * *reliability*
9. *communities* = []
10. for *rowNode* in NR
11. $NC = [rowNode]$
12.   Remove the row and column of *rowNode*
13.   *willExtends* ← all elements in $NR = [rowNode]$
14.   while(*willExtends* is not *null*):
15.   remove the most similar node from *willExtends* to *simNode*
16. $NC.add(simNode)$
17. $willExtends \cap = NR[simNode]$
18   Remove the row and column of *simNode* from NR
19.   *communities* ← NC
20. *isolatedNodes* ← the communities whose sizes equal to one
21. search and merge each isolated node to the community with maximum belonging degree
22. return *textbfcommunities*

---

4   Experimental Results

In this section, we demonstrate our method with three classical real-world social networks: Zachary's karate club network[17], bottlenose dolphin community[18] and the network of American college football[1]. They are used to demonstrate the performance of community detection algorithms popularly by many authors. Although the maximum modularity does not necessarily mean the correct community structure of some complex networks, the maximum modularity is popularly used to measure performance of community detection algorithms. In this section, we use accuracy and modularity to show that our cooperative community detection algorithm(CCD) has higher accuracy and more stable results in many running times compared with LPA, CNM, RCD.

4.1   Accuracy

For a given community structure $P = \{C_1, C_2, \cdots\}(C_i \cap C_j = \emptyset, i \neq j)$, node in C_i is labelled as l_{C_i}. Steinhaeuser et al. [12] defined the accuracy as the fraction of all nodes whose labels are correctly predicted:

$$Accuracy = \frac{\sum_i \sum_{v \in C_i} (l_{C_i} = l_v)}{|V|} \tag{7}$$

where l_{C_i} is the predicted label of node v and l_v is the true label of v.

4.1.1   Zachary's Network of Karate Club Members

This dataset contains the network of friendships between the 34 members of an American college karate club, and was described by Wayne W. Zachary in 1977[17]. Due to the conflict between the club's administrator and instructor, the club split into smaller ones. The network and its community structure show in Fig. 1, and the club's administrator and instructor are node 1 and 33 respectively. Fig.1 shows community structure of the network.

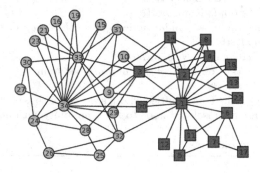

Fig. 1. Community structure in Karate Club network

We do 100 experiments on this network, and each experiment of our cooperative community detection algorithm(CCD) is cooperated with 50 running results of our community detection algorithm(RCD). The accuracies of four algorithms are shown in Fig. 2. Although RCD is higher than that of LPA in most case, RCD is not stable. The accuracies of our community detection algorithm CCD and RCD are higher than that of LPA and CNM in the 100 experiments. In addition, CCD is a stable algorithm on this networks.

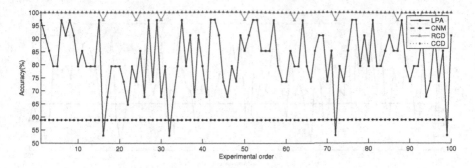

Fig. 2. Experimental Results of LPA, CNM, RCD and CCD on Karate Club network

4.1.2 Dolphins Network

The bottlenose dolphin network was described by Lusseau et al. at first[18]. It denotes the frequent associations between 62 bottlenose dolphins in a community living off Doubtful Sound, New Zealand. This network can split into two large communities based on dolphins' age, and the larger one also can split into three smaller communities[19]. This network with four communities is shown in Fig. 3.

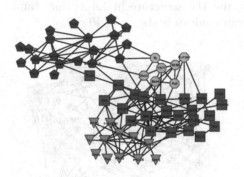

Fig. 3. Community structure in Dolphins Network

We do 100 experiments on this network, and each experiment of our cooperative community detection algorithm(CCD) is cooperated with 50 running results of our community detection algorithm(RCD). The accuracies of LPA, CNM, RCD and CCD on Dolphins network are shown in Fig.4. The experiments show that the accuracies of two our algorithms CCD and RCD are higher than that of LPA and CNM in the 100 experimental results, and this is the same as that of in Zachary's Network of Karate Club Members. The accuracy of RCD is larger than 0.9 in the worst experimental result, and CCD is a stable on this network.

4.1.3 Football Network

The network of college football introduced by Girvan and Newman[1] is also usually used as a benchmark for the community detecting. It describes the schedule

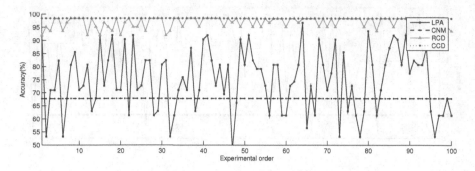

Fig. 4. Experimental Results of LPA, CNM, RCD and CCD on Dolphins Network

of the US college football between Division I for the 2000 season, and contains 115 vertices represented teams and 616 edges represented regular-season games between the two teams they connect. This network can be divided into 12 communities[1] or 13 communities[20]. Even though the structure in[1] is relatively real, communities in the community structure of[20] are tighter than they in[1] . Therefore we use the structure in[20] as our standard. The community structure with 13 communities is shown in Fig. 5.

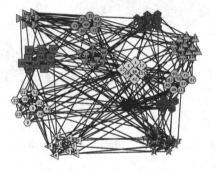

Fig. 5. Community structure in Football Network

We do 100 experiments on this network, and each experiment of our cooperative community detection algorithm(CCD) is cooperated with 50 running results of our community detection algorithm(RCD). The accuracies of LPA, CNM, RCD and CCD on Dolphins network are shown in Fig.6. Although the accuracy of RCD is less than that of CNM in some experiments, there are only 5 experimental results in which the accuracies of CCD are less than those of CNM. There are only 3 experimental results in which the accuracies of CCD are less than those of LPA. The experiments show that the performance of our algorithm CCD is better than those of LPA and CNM.

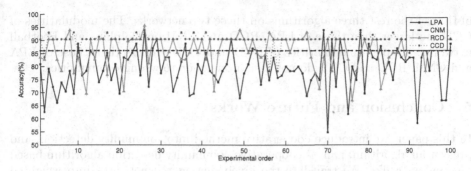

Fig. 6. Experimental Results of LPA, CNM, RCD and CCD on Football Network

4.2 Modularity

The modularity greedy algorithm, originally is described by Newman, ranges from 0 to 1. The modularity is viewed as a index to quantify how good a particular division of a network is, a larger value of modularity implies a better division of a complex network. Let e_{ij} be one-half of the fraction of edges in the network that connect vertices in group i to those in group j. e_{ii}, which are equal to the fraction of edges that fall within group i. The modularity is is described as,

$$Q = \sum_i (e_{ii} - a_i^2)$$ (8)

where a_i is the fraction of all ends of edges that are attached to vertices in group i, and $a_i = \sum_j e_{ij}$. Here, we use the modularity Q to measure the performances of community detection algorithms LPA, CNM, RCD and CCD. The statistical results are shown in Table 1. Std in table 1 denotes standard deviation of modularities of LPA, CNM, RCD and CCD in the 20 running times.

Table 1. Modularity

Networks	LPA	CNM	RCD	CCD
Karate	0.3416	0.3789	0.3715	0.3715
Dolphins	0.4593	0.4898	0.5238	0.5265
Football	0.5858	0.5668	0.5981	0.6009

Here, we demonstrate the performances of LPA, CNM, RCD and CCD with modularity. We use the average of modularities of each algorithm in the 100 experimental results to show that our cooperative community detection algorithm is a better and more stable community detection algorithm. The statistical result is shown in Table 1. CNM is a stable community detection algorithm, but its modularity is lower than that of the rest three algorithms on Dolphins and Football networks, this shows that the performance of CNM is worse than that of that of the rest three algorithms on these two networks. The modularities of CCD are larger than those of LPA, RCD and CNM on Dolphins and Football networks. although modularities of RCD and CCD are less than those of LPA and CNM, RCD and CCD do not assign one node to wrong communities.

5   Conclusion and Future Works

In this paper, we introduce cooperative method into community detection, and present an algorithm, named cooperative community detection algorithm based on random walks. We translate the given unweighted networks into weighted networks by using random walks method, and then select two nodes which are most similar in the nodes which are not assigned to any community as the initial community and expand this community by activating their neighbors until there no node can be activated. Since we adopt random walks to calculate the similarities between nodes, the community structure detected is unstable. In order to get more stable algorithm, we use cooperative method to achieve this goal. We demonstrate our algorithm with three real networks which are well known to test the community detection algorithms popularly, and the experiments show that our cooperative algorithm has a better performance and more stable results compared with LPA, CNM and RCD. Since our cooperative method requires running RCD many times, the time-consuming is larger than LPA, CNM and RCD. We will work on paralleling method for our cooperative community detection algorithm.

Acknowledgments. This paper is Supported by the Fundamental Research Funds for the Central Universities (lzujbky-2012-212).

References

1. Girvan, M., Newman, M.E.J.: Community Structure in Social and Biological Networks. Proc. Natl. Acad. Sci. 99, 7821–7826 (2002)
2. Clauset, A., Newman, M.E.J., Moore, C.: Finding Community Structure in Very Large Network. Phys. Rev. E 70, 066111 (2004)
3. Raghavan, U.N., Albert, R., Kumara, S.: Near Linear Time Algorithm to Detect Community Structures in Large-scale Networks. Phs. Rev. E 76, 036106 (2007)
4. Barber, M.J., Clark, J.W.: Detecting Network Communities by Propagating Labels under Constraints. Phys. Rev. E 80, 026129 (2009)
5. Liu, X., Murata, T.: Advanced Modularity-specialized Label Propagation Algorithm for Detecting Communities in Networks. Physica A 389, 1493–1500 (2010)
6. Herbiet, G.J., Bouvry, P.: SHARC: Community-based Partitioning for Mobile Ad Hoc Networks Using Neighborhood Similarity. In: IEEE International Symposium on "A World of Wireless, Mobile and Multimedia Networks", pp. 1–9. IEEE Press, New York (2010)
7. Newman, M.E.J., Girvan, M.: Finding and Evaluating Community Structure in Networks. Physical Review E - Statistical, Nonlinear, and Soft Matter Physics 69, 026113 (2004)

8. Steinhaeuser, K., Chawla, N.V.: Identifying and Evaluating Community Structure in Complex Networks. Pattern Recognition 31, 413–421 (2010)
9. Kempe, D., Kleinberg, J., Tardos, E.: Maximizing the Spread of Influence Through a Social Network. In: 9th ACM SIGKDD International Conference on Knowledge Discovery and Data Mining, KDD 2003, pp. 137–146. ACM Press, New York (2003)
10. Kashef, R., Kamel, M.S.: Cooperative Clustering. Pattern Recognition 43, 2315–2329 (2010)
11. Lovász, L.: Random Walks on Graphs:A Survey. Combinatorics, Paul Erdos is Eighty 2, 353–397 (1993)
12. van Dongen, S.M.: Graph Clustering by Flow Simulation. Ph.D.Thesis, Universiteit Utrecht, Utrecht, The Netherlands (May 2000)
13. Narayanam, R., Narahari, Y.: A Shapley Value Based Approach to Discover Influential Nodes in Social Networks. IEEE Transactions on Automation Science and Engineering 8, 130–147 (2011)
14. Cao, L.: In-depth Behavior Understanding and Use: the Behavior Informatics Approach. Information Science 180(17), 3067–3085 (2010)
15. Eng, Y., Kwoh, C., Zhou, Z.: On the Two-level Hybrid Clustering Algorithm. In: International Conference on Artificial Intelligence in Science and Technology, pp. 138–142 (2004)
16. Xu, S., Zhang, J.: A Hybrid Parallel Web Document Clustering Algorithm and its Performance Study. Journal of Supercomputing 30, 117–131 (2004)
17. Wayne, W.: Zachary: An Information Flow Model for Conflict and Fission in Small Groups. Journal of Anthropological Research 33, 452–473 (1977)
18. Lusseau, D., Schneider, K., Boisseau, O.J., Haase, P., Slooten, E., Dawson, S.M.: The Bottlenose Dolphin Community of Doubtful Sound Features a Large Proportion of Long-lasting Associations. Behavioral Ecology and Sociobiology 54, 396–405 (2003)
19. David, L., Newman, M.E.J.: Identifying the Role That Animals Play in Their Social Networks. In: Proc. R. Soc. B, pp. S477–S481. Royal Society Publishing, London (2004)
20. Chen, D., Shang, M., Lv, Z., Fu, Y.: Detecting Overlapping Communities of Weighted Networks via a Loacal Algorithm. Physica A 389, 4177–4187 (2010)

An Actor Network-Based Approach to Pirates Community Discovery in Peer-to-Peer Network

Xiancheng Hou[1], Bing Shi[1], Wenjia Niu[2], Qi Feng[3], and Ying Qi[2]

[1] Shandong University, Jinan, China
[2] High Performance Network Lab, Institute of Acoustics, Chinese Academy of Science, Beijing
[3] Newcastle University, UK
{niuwj,qy,houxiancheng}@hpnl.ac.cn
springbell.feng@gmail.com
shibing@sdu.edu.cn

Abstract. Due to the potential content sharing applications in civilian environment, peer-to-peer (P2P) network has received considerable attention. Unfortunately, the problem of pirates widely exists in P2P network as the absence of content supervision. Piracy propagation shares high similar piracy contents frequently to constitute the pirates community. Therefore in the P2P network, pirate community discovery is one of the most important research topics. Interest-based and random walk-based approaches have been developed for community discovery in the P2P network, but they work ineffectively in pirates community discovery. Because they fail to simultaneously consider the message similarity and the message passing frequency. This paper argued that these factors should not be ignored in the pirates community discovery. Based on the analysis, we proposed an actor network-based approach and extended the Girvan-Newman (GN) algorithm for pirates community analysis. The experimental evaluation confirms the effectiveness of the approach.

Keywords: pirates community discovery, P2P network, content similarity, actor network, GN algorithm.

1   Introduction

Unlike traditional distributed application architecture systems, the rapid development of P2P network [1], such as Gnutella, Freenet and Napster [2, 3, 4], lies in its decentralized nature, self-organization, and scalability. Unfortunately, the popularity of P2P network suffers from a rampant piracy propagation problem due to the lack of strict content authorization and third-party supervision. Pirates distributed and reproduced copyrighted contents or illegal pornography without authorization. When pirates frequently share similar piracy contents with each other, they naturally form the pirates community.

Community is one significant network structure with each set of nodes densely connected internally [5]. The study usually contains community structure and the community discovery [6]. The community structure reflects how the nodes are

L. Cao et al. (Eds.): BSIC/BSI 2013, LNAI 8178, pp. 204–213, 2013.
© Springer International Publishing Switzerland 2013

connected in the network, while community discovery aims to partition the network into different communities. The interest-based and random walk-based methods have been employed for community structure; GN algorithm has been proposed for community discovery. Both concepts have been well studied in many fields [7, 8, 9, 10]. Naturally, the theory would apply to discover the pirates community.

However, discovering the pirates community has meet many challenges for pirates community feature [11]. Not merely the pirates are highly similar to each other, the frequent messages communicated between pirates also have high similarity. And links in same community have a higher message passing frequency, while links in different one are less frequent. Consequently, both the message similarity and the passing frequency might help to discover pirates community accurately.

Hence, we proposed an effective approach on pirates community structure and discovery, while simplifying the large scale P2P network Our efforts mainly focus on two aspects. Firstly, to simplify the model of the P2P network, we provide an actor network-based model (ANM) based on the actor-network theory (ANT) and the content similarity graph (CSG). The proposed model takes both the message similarity and the message passing frequency into account for pirates community structure and uses the actor-network theory corresponding to the process for pirates community discovery. Secondly, we design a divisive algorithm ANMGN (ANM-based GN algorithm) that can remove more edges in one recalculation based on GN algorithm.

After partitioning the network to different communities, we supervise the contents that are shared in the same one. If they are piracy contents, we can decide that the community belongs to the pirates community. Then the piracy propagation problem will be prevented efficiently. So partitioning the network to communities is the premise work.

The rest of this paper is organized as follows. Section 2 discusses the related work, followed by the detailed approach and the whole process of pirates community discovery in Section 3. Section 4 presents experimental results that illustrate the benefits of the proposed scheme. Section 5 concludes the paper and envisions the future work.

2   Related Work

In order to complete the pirates community discovery in P2P network, we have been inspired by a variety of related work [12, 13, 14]. Several studies have demonstrated that the network is constituted by different types of nodes. The same type of nodes exist a large number of connections, and connections between different types of nodes are less. In the P2P network, nodes with the same type and the edges connecting them compose one subgraph is called the community. We can separate communities from one another and uncover the underlying community structure of the network.

For community structure, the interest-based and random walk-based methods are used to community structure, among which the interest-based approach considers the similarity between two nodes, while the random walk-based method utilizes the message passing probability (MPP) between two nodes. When the similarity or the MPP exceeds the threshold determined in advance, a graph containing many communities is formed by joining the two nodes reiteratively.

Few of existing the methods consider both the two characters of the pirates community. In the interest-based method, the similarity between two nodes is based on the numbers of same contents shared by them. The random walk-based method utilizes the sum of message passing probability between two nodes. Using the two methods on pirates community will results in a noticeable problem. For instance, there are three users; each of them has 10 same piracy files. In one condition, user A and B exchange message in the high frequency, while user C receives the message passively and never delivers it. Obviously, A and B are exactly in one pirates community and C is not. But they have the same similarity and will be in one community by the interest-based methods. In another condition, user A and B exchange message in the high frequency, but the mash massages are unrelated. They should not belong to the same class, while they will be divided into one community through random walk-based method.

For community discovery, GN algorithm has been successfully used to divide communities. All shortest paths between different communities must go along one of these few intergroup edges. Thus, the edges connecting communities will have high edge betweenness. GN algorithm removes only one edge with the highest betweenness in each recalculation running in O (m2n) time on an arbitrary network with m edges and n nodes. The GN algorithm demands heavy computational resources. It is not efficient that applying the algorithm in large scale P2P network directly. Although this algorithm has been applied successfully to community analysis in a variety of networks giving the modularity to quantify the strength of community structure, it does not offer a strategy to break the recalculation loop. Here we apply the increment of modularity to break the loop which will reduce the runtime.

3   Actor Network-Based Model

In this section, the content similarity graph (CSG) and the actor-network theory are introduced. And then we will present the detail works on ANM. Finally, the pirates community discovery process and ANMGN algorithm are presented.

3.1   Content Similarity Graph and Actor-Network Theory

To quantify the message similarity, the CSG [15] is imported to the ANM. As the crawling data is organized as a bipartite graph that connects users to files, the contents similarity can be well calculated by the number of users that both contains two contents at one time. Then, this bipartite graph is transformed into CSG, where the weight of a link is the content similarity. However, one kind of special case will appear that two contents have high similarity but one of them has rarely frequency of occurrence in network. Hence a precise and normalized calculate model is needed here. Let $N_{i,j}$ be the number of users that hold both contents, and M_i be the number of times for i or j appears in network respectively.

$$S(i, j) = \frac{N_{i,j}}{\sqrt{M_i \cdot M_j}} \tag{1}$$

The overall goals of pirates community discovery are thus: using ANM to semantically simply the P2P network and analyzing the network structure. We introduce the ANT to support these goals. The ANT is a material-semiotic approach in social theory [16], exploring how relations between artifacts and actors who generate and distribute the artifacts are formed. It consists of three prime components: heterogeneous network, network consolidation and network ordering. We implement P2P network and CSG to construct a heterogeneous network, actors presenting the pirates, and artifacts presenting the piracy contents. The simplification process of ANM for pirates community structure is network consolidation; using the ANMGN algorithm to pirates community discovery corresponding with network ordered in the ANM.

3.2 ANM Architecture

Actor Network-based Model is an approach to simplifying the P2P network before analyzing the network. The primary attributes in the ANM is shown below:

- ETS (Edge Timestamp): A field distinguishing message from the source nodes;
- CID (Content ID): A field distinguishing content from the source nodes;
- EW (Edge Weight): The weight carried by edges between two actors;
- MW (Message Weight): The weight carried by message from the linked actors.

These attributes are used to compute the message passing frequency and the message similarity as followed. The ETS is recorded when a message is generated between two actors (i, j), ETS (i, j) is used in the equation.

$$EW = \sum ETS(i, j) \tag{2}$$

The MW is based on the similarity of contents (i, j). Let A_{ij} be an element of the adjacency matrix such that $A_{ij} = S(i, j)$, obtained from the CSG and set $A_{ii} = 0$.

$$MW = \sum \sum A_{ij}/2 \tag{3}$$

Furthermore, a threshold is set to filter the edges with smaller EW and MW. It is showed in the equation, in which a, b are constant value depending on the network):

$$T = a \cdot EW + b \cdot MW \tag{4}$$

Based on the ANM, pirates community structure has been formed. Both the EW and MW belonging to one link with the larger value in one pirates community, while the intergroup edges connecting communities will have little value. By removing these edges, we discover the community structure of the P2P network.

3.3 Pirates Community Discovery Process

Based on ANM, the whole pirates community discovery process contains three stages: data preprocessing, community structure and community discovery. Fig. 1 shows the target of each stage. In the data preprocessing stage, the preliminary data cleaning on the large scale P2P network removed the irrelevant dataset, which will be leveraged for the construction CSG in stage 2. Next, EW is calculated through the ETS recorded using equation two. And MW considering the content similarity is calculated that based on the CSG. So far, the ANM is structured with the attributes, EW and MW, which has been simplified the mess P2P network to an undirected graph by the second filtration process in the community structure stage.

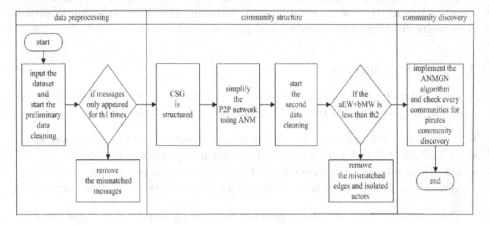

Fig. 1. The pirates community discovery process

Actually, the ANM can be considered one big community by deleting the isolated actors. Finally, the divisive algorithm ANMGN can be used to analysis the graph for pirates community discovery.

3.4 ANMGN Algorithm

The target of ANMGN algorithm is to discover communities in the graph noted by G = (V, E), where G is the network, V is the pirates and E is the links between them. It focuses on the edges that are most "between" communities. The basic idea is simply stated as follows: 1. calculating the each edge betweenness; 2. removing the edge with the highest betweenness; 3. removing edges for which the EW and MW are less than the removed edge; 4. Recalculating the edge betweenness for all edges and repeat the step 2 until the increment of modularity less than zero.

Let vector Ck = (C1, C2, C3... Ck) be the community sequence. When new community is generated, noted as m and n, the Ck becomes to Ck+1= (C1, C2, C3...Ck, Ck+1). a_m^{k+1} and a_n^{k+1} present the fraction of edges that connect to vertices inside community m and n respectively; e_{mn}^{k+1} present the fraction of edges that interconnect community m and n. If $\Delta Q < 0$, the modularity has reach the maximum, and the algorithm will stop, outputting the community sequence Ck. The following is a formal description:

```
Preliminaries:
ΔQ: modularity increment, initially set to infinity
spb: the shortest-path betweenness
ew: edge weight; mw: message weight
begin
while ΔQ ≥ 0 do
for every edge eᵢ∈ E
set spb to 1 initially
calculate the spb using the breadth-first search methods
select the edge with highest spb
marked as e(e.spb, e.ew, e.mw)
remove e from E
end for
for every edge eᵢ∈{E-e}
if eⱼ.ew ≤ e.ew and eⱼ.mw ≤ e.mw remove eᵢ from {E-e}
end if
end for
calculate ΔQ
end while
end
```

Note that before the second "for" statement, the ANMGN algorithm resembles the general GN algorithm, and the mentioned betweenness is calculated using the breadth first search methods. The second "for" statement makes ANMGN distinctly stand out, with the EW and MW. If two communities connected by more than one edge, then there is no guarantee that it has the high betweenness in all of those edges. In general GN, we cannot choose which one to remove, whereas, many of the edges may have lesser EW or MW than the one with highest betweenness.

Therefore, the main advantage of ANMGN is that it can successfully remove more than one edge in terms of $e_j. ew \leq e. ew$ and $e_j. mw \leq e. mw$ in one recalculation, for which the general GN algorithm cannot carry out without considering them

To evaluate the quality of community structure, modularity Q [15] is yielded as the quantitative measure. e_{ii} presents the fraction of edges in one community; a_i presents the interconnect ones. Modularity is widely used and is defined as:

$$Q = \sum(e_{ii} - a_i^2) \qquad (5)$$

Furthermore, ANMGN reduce the running time by breaking the "while" loop according to increment of modularity, which plays a vital role in large scale P2P networks. We implement the increment of modularity ΔQ to break the loop [17]. The increment of modularity is calculated as:

$$\Delta Q = 2a_m^{k+1}a_n^{k+1} - e_{mn}^{k+1} \qquad (6)$$

All these advantages make ANMGN efficient than GN algorithm, which will be proved by experiment in next section. As mentioned before, some of the communities that are divided by the proposed approach have the characters of the pirates community. Based on this work, we can judge whether a community belongs to the pirates community by supervising the contents in it.

4   Experimental Evaluation

We use two applications to evaluate the performance of the proposed algorithm and the accuracy in the pirates community discovery.

4.1   Tests on Karate Club Network of Zachary

In the first part, we simulate an execution on the karate club network of Zachary [18] to compare the performance with interest-based and random walk-based methods. The karate club is a social network of friendship between 34 numbers in US University, which is a classic study in community discovery with 34 nodes and 78 edges. In order to simulate the pirates community, each edge is assigned with a given MW and EW.

To be compared with the typical existing method, we use the MW to present the node similarity to interest-based method and EW to present the message frequency to random walk-based method respectively for community structure. Then the GN algorithm is implemented for community discovery. Finally, we use ANMGN to divide the network based on ANM. We use the serviceable network visualization tool, Geghi, to display the community discovery result, in which communities are rendered in different colors.

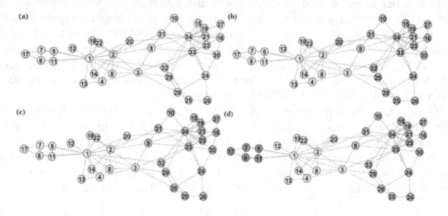

Fig. 2. Division of the network by GN and ANMGN Algorithm

The original karate club network of Zachary is shown in Fig.2 (a), which is one network initially. In Fig.2 (b) and (c), the network is divided by interest-based method and three communities based on random walk-based method respectively. Fig.2 (d) utilizes ANMGN algorithm based on ANM. The value of modularity Q: 0.485, 0.525, and 0.547 respectively. It shows that the AMNGN provides a more subtle perspective on the underlying structure of the network. For the whole karate club network, the complete result is shown in Fig.3.

The number of the recalculation and runtime in different methods is used to evaluate the computing efficiency. One method that removed more edges but used less recalculation should be better for the runtime (runtime metric is 10ms) is shorter. The edge-removed process is also presented in the experiment.

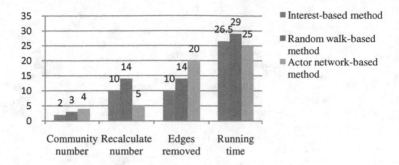

Fig. 3. Performance analysis of the three methods on karate club network

Fortunately, as shown in Fig.3, the ANMGN algorithm deleted 20 edges by 5 re-calculations with our method. Although, the ANMGN algorithm has to compare the $e_i.ew \leq e.ew$ and $e_i.mw \leq e.mw$ before the next recalculation process, the performance has increased significantly. Experiment results show that our method outperforms the former methods both in modularity Q and the efficiency, by taking both the message similarity and the message passing frequency.

4.2   Working with Computer Generated Network

As a simulated test on how well our approach performs, we generated the network with the known pirates community structure, to see if the approach can analyze the network and discover the pirates community properly.

In this experiment, we generated a large number of graphs with 65 nodes that present the users. In order to simulate the pirates community discovery, we select 4 users to share piracy contents just with each other and another 6 users to do the same thing. So far, there have been two pirates communities in the graph. During the simulation process, each user passes message to his neighbors with a given probability. Initially, the largest message passing frequency M is set to 50; the contents number N is set to 500. The contents include pirated ones and authorized ones. Each user selects a random message passing frequency from [1, M] and the corresponding number of contents. Pirates have the tendency to select a large message passing frequency. When one message is generated, the number of ETS increased by 1, and the CID is recorded as well. Then, we will compute the EW and MW to structure the ANM. We also use the MW to present the node similarity to interest-based method and EW to present message frequency to random walk-based method for community structure.

The original network is shown in Fig.4 (a). The network is divided into 6 communities based on interest-based method, 7 communities based on random walk-based method and 8 communities based on our method shown in (b), (c), (d) with the value of modularity Q: 0.507, 0.541, and 0.664 respectively. After we detect the piracy contents percentage in each community, we found that green-community 1 (62, 63, 64, 65) and red-community 2 (24, 25, 26, 28, 29, 32) have the high 80%, 90% piracy contents respectively; others have the piracy contents percentage under 20%. We can see that community 1 and 2 are the pirates communities.

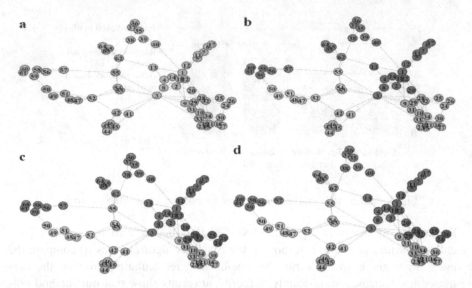

Fig. 4. Performance analysis on computer generated network

Experiments show that our method outperforms the former methods both in community modularity and accuracy, which has taken the message similarity and the message passing frequency into consideration.

5   Conclusion

In this paper, we propose an actor network-based approach to discover the pirates community in P2P network, which can prevent pirates from piracy propagation. Based on the content similarity and message passing frequency, the pirates community will be discovered more accurately. Furthermore, we design ANMGN for pirates community discovery, which had achieved better performance in the experiment.

In fact, in an actual P2P network, there are several future challenges in pirates community discovery. Firstly, in this work, we ignore the scale of pirates community that may affect the precision of division performance. Secondly, one user may exist in different communities, while the current version of the proposed algorithm cannot solve the overlapping community problem. Future work will be carried out along this line.

Acknowledgement. This research is supported by the National Nature Science Foundation of China (No.61103158), Guangxi Key Laboratory of Trusted Software, the National S&T Major Project (No.2010ZX03004-002-01), the Securing CyberSpace Research Lab of Deakin University, the Sino-Finnish International S&T Cooperation and Exchange Program (No.2010DFB10570), the Strategic Pilot Project of Chinese Academy of Sciences (No.XDA06010302), National Science S&T Technology Pillar Program of China (No.2012BAH01B03).

References

1. Parameswaran, M., Susarla, A., Whinston, A.B.: P2P Networking: An Information-Sharing Alternative. Computer 34(7), 31–38 (2001)
2. Ripeanu, M.: Peer-to-peer architecture case study: Gnutella network. Technical report, University of Chicago (2001)
3. Clarke, I., Miller, S.G., Hong, T.W., Sandberg, O., Wiley, B.: Protecting Free Expression Online with Freenet. IEEE IC 6(1), 40–49 (2002)
4. Saroiu, S., Gummadi, K.P., Gribble, S.D.: Measuring and analyzing the characteristics of napster and gnutella hosts. Multimedia Syst. 9, 170 (2003)
5. Newman, M.E.J.: Fast algorithm for detecting community structure in networks. Phys. Rev. E69, 066133 (2004)
6. Clauset, A., Newman, M.E.J., Moore, C.: Finding community structure in very large networks. Phys. Rev. E70, 066111 (2004)
7. Palla, G., Derényi, I., Farkas, I., Vicsek, T.: Uncovering the overlapping community structure of complex networks in nature and society. Nature 435, 814–818 (2005)
8. Clémençon, S., De Arazoza, H., Rossi, F., Tran, V.-C.: Visual mining of epidemic networks. In: Cabestany, J., Rojas, I., Joya, G. (eds.) IWANN 2011, Part II. LNCS, vol. 6692, pp. 276–283. Springer, Heidelberg (2011)
9. Barnard, K., Forsyth, D.A.: Learning the semantics of words and pictures. In: International Conference on Computer Vision, pp. 408–415 (2001)
10. Redmond, U., Harrigan, M., Cunningham, P.: Mining dense structures to uncover anomalous behaviour in financial network data. In: Atzmueller, M., Chin, A., Helic, D., Hotho, A. (eds.) MSM/MUSE 2011. LNCS (LNAI), vol. 7472, pp. 60–76. Springer, Heidelberg (2012)
11. Kwok, S.H., Gao, S.: Knowledge Sharing Community in P2P Network and its Application Features A Study of Motivation Perspective. In: Pacific Asia Conference on Information System, pp. 10–13 (2003)
12. Newman, M.E.J., Girvan, M.: Finding and evaluating community structure in networks. Phys. Rev. E69, 026113 (2004)
13. Khambatti, M., Ryu, K.D., Dasgupta, P.: Structuring peer-to-peer networks using interest-based communities. In: Aberer, K., Koubarakis, M., Kalogeraki, V. (eds.) VLDB 2003 Ws DBISP2P. LNCS, vol. 2944, pp. 48–63. Springer, Heidelberg (2004)
14. Ramaswamy, L., Gedik, B., Liu, L.: A Distributed Approach to Node Clustering in Decentralized Peer-to-Peer Networks. IEEE Transactions on Parallel and Distributed System 16(9) (2005)
15. Shavitt, Y., Weinsberg, E., Weinsberg, U.: Mining musical content from large-scale peer-to-peer networks. IEEE Multimedia 18(1), 14–23 (2011)
16. Reinhardt, W., Wilke, A., Moi, M., Drachsler, H., Sloep, P.: Mining and visualizing Research Networks using the Artefact-Actor Network approach. Computational Social Networks, 233–267 (2013)
17. Pujol, J.M., Bejar, J., Delgado, J.: Clustering algorithm for determining community structure in large networks. Physical Review E 74, 016107 (2006)
18. Zachary, W.W.: An information flow model for confict and fission in small groups. Journal of Anthropological Research 33, 452–473 (1977)

Suggestions for Fresh Search Queries by Mining Mircoblog Topics

Lin Li[1], Xing Chen[1], and Guandong Xu[2]

[1] School of Computer Science & Technology, Wuhan University of Technology, China
{cathylilin,rebecca_lymx}@whut.edu.cn
[2] University of Technology, Sydney, Australia
Guandong.Xu@uts.edu.au

Abstract. Query suggestion of Web search has been an effective approach to help users quickly express their information need and more accurately get the information they need. All major web-search engines and most proposed methods that suggest queries rely on query logs of search engine to determine possible query suggestions. However, for search systems, it is much more difficult to effectively suggest relevant queries to a fresh search query which has no or few historical evidences in query logs. In this paper, we propose a suggestion approach for fresh queries by mining the new social network media, i.e, mircoblog topics. We leverage the comment information in the microblog topics to mine potential suggestions. We utilize word frequency statistics to extract a set of ordered candidate words. As soon as a user starts typing a query word, words that match with the partial user query word are selected as completions of the partial query word and are offered as query suggestions. We collect a dataset from Sina microblog topics and compare the final results by selecting different suggestion context source. The experimental results clearly demonstrate the effectiveness of our approach in suggesting queries with high quality. Our conclusion is that the suggestion context source of a topic consists of the tweets from authenticated Sina users is more effective than the tweets from all Sina users.

1 Introduction

Web search engines have greatly changed the way that people acquire information during the last ten years. Web searching is a typical kind of user behavior, which involves not only a user behaviors but also the behaviors of other online users [7]. As an end-user starts typing a query in a search engine's query box, most search engines assist users by providing a list of queries that have been proven to be effective in the past [20]. The user can quickly choose one of the suggested completions (in some cases, alternatives) and thus, does not have to type the whole query herself. Feuer et al. [11] analyzed approximately 1.5 million queries from the search logs of a commercial search engine and found that query suggestions represented nearly 30% of the total queries and the engine with phrase suggestions performs better in terms of precision and recall than

L. Cao et al. (Eds.): BSIC/BSI 2013, LNAI 8178, pp. 214–223, 2013.
© Springer International Publishing Switzerland 2013

the same search engine without suggestions. Furthermore, Kelly et al. [14] observed that the use of offered query suggestions is more for difficult topics, i.e., topics on which users have little knowledge to formulate good queries. Yang et al. [21] presented an optimal rare query suggestion framework by leveraging implicit feedbacks from users in the query logs. Sumit et al. [3] put forward a probabilistic mechanism for generating query suggestions from a corpus without using query logs and utilized the document corpus to extract a set of candidate words.

Traditional methods rely on some other users who searched for the same information before, and then utilize these large amounts of past usage data to offer possible query suggestions. Although there are many works using query logs to suggest queries [1,2,4,6,9,13,17,18,21], there still exist some difficulties.

First, query logs may not always be accessible in some applications due to privacy and legal constraints. Second, even in the case of general-purpose web search engines, end-users sometimes pose queries that are not in query logs or are not very frequent. Third, with the rise of social network, there has been emerging a group of new network vocabulary. When these newly appeared words formulate search queries, they always have few search history in query logs. Thus they are insufficient in context. Both the queries that in the absence of query logs and the newly appeared queries together constitute a kind of search queries, so called fresh queries. They may cause a great amount of search traffic potentially affecting the performance of search engines significantly. Therefore, how to offer an effective query suggestion for fresh search queries is a challenging research problem, which we discuss in this paper.

At present, as a widely used medium platform, microblog's diverse features meet the people's information, interpersonal information and other aspects of the new requirements. Compared with the traditional media, microblogging as a new service has the following characteristics and advantages.

(1) Its information propagation is convenient and rapid.
(2) Its information dissemination is of high efficiency.
(3) It has great potential business value.

Among the three features, the second one motivates our work. Nowadays the speed of information propagation through the microblog service is faster than most of media products, and more people pay attention to it. The intuitive, convenient, and efficient communication makes microblog popular and the micoblog information updated quickly, which is the reason that we choose the microblog topics as our study background. The key idea of our work is that extracting and analyzing fresh queries by mining microblog topics in order to give query suggestions to web search users. Our main contribution is that the suggestion context source of a topic consists of the tweets from authenticated Sina users is more effective than the tweets from all Sina users.

The rest of the paper is organized as follows. In Section 2, we provide an overview of the prior work on query suggestion along with explaining how our approach differs from the previous methods. In Section 3, we give a suggestion flowchart to describe our whole query suggestion process. In Section 4, we further describe the specific approach of offline processing in details. Experiments and results are presented in Section 5. Section 6 concludes the paper and outlines future research directions.

2 Related Work

2.1 Query Suggestion

There are a variety of research works about query suggestion. Initial works focus on identifying past queries similar to a current user query. Baeza-Yates et al. [1] cluster queries presented in search logs. Given an initial query, similar queries from its cluster are identified based on vector similarity metrics and are then suggested to a user. Barouni-Ebrahimi and Ghorbani utilize words frequently occurring in queries submitted by past users as suggestions [2]. Gao et al. describe a query suggestion mechanism for cross lingual information retrieval where for queries issued in one language, queries in other languages can also be suggested [12]. By utilizing clickthrough data and session information, Cao et al. propose a context aware query suggestion approach [6]. In order to deal with the data sparseness problem, they use concept based query suggestions where a concept is defined as a set of similar queries mined from the query-URL bi-partite graph.

Lately, Broder et. al propose an online expansion of rare queries in [5]. Their framework starts by training an offline model that is able to suggest a ranked list of related queries to an incoming rare query. The rare query is then expanded by a weighted linear combination of the original query and the related queries according to their similarity. Yang et al. [21] also work on rare query suggestion by using implicit feedbacks, while Sumit et al. [3] make use of a corpus instead of query logs. To the best of our knowledge, our work makes the fist to study the query suggestion of fresh queries (both newly appeared queries and queries absent from query logs).

2.2 Social Media

The rising popularity of online social networking services has spurred research into microblogs and their characteristics. There are a number of research works which explore and study microblog., especially English microblogging, i.e., twitter. Newman et al. [19] make the first quantitative study on the entire Twitter sphere and information diffusion on it. They study the topological characteristics of Twitter and its power as a new medium of information sharing and have found a non-powerlaw follower distribution, a short effective diameter, and low reciprocity, which all mark a deviation from known characteristics of human social networks. In 2010, the work in [15] further discusses the topological characteristics of Twitter and its power as a new medium of information sharing. Chen et al. [8] compare two kinds of approaches, traditional cosine-based approach and WordNet-based semantic approach, when computing similarities between microblogs to recommend top related ones to users.

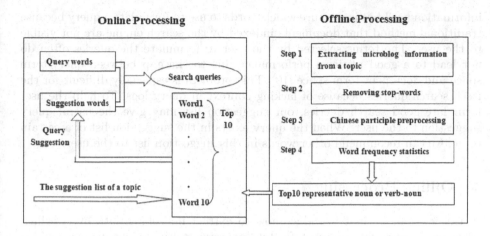

Fig. 1. Suggestion Flowchart for A Search Query

With the prevalence of Sina microblogging, some researchers begin to study the new Chinese microblog media. Liu et al. [16] combine a translation-based method with a frequency-based method for keyword extraction. They extract keywords for microblog users from the largest microblogging website in China, Sina Weibo. Different from them, we present how to extract and analyze microblog topics to produce effective suggestions to fresh queries, and experimentally discuss the selection of suggestion context sources in terms of precision and efficiency.

3   Suggestion Flowchart

As shown in Figure 1, the whole suggestion process is divided into two modules: offline processing and online processing.

First, let us look at the offline module. It consists of the following four steps. Step 1 extracts microblog information from a topic. Here we not only get the tweets from all Sina users for each topic, but also extract the microblog tweets from authenticated Sina users. Then we can take the two types of data as two different suggestion context sources. Step 2, step 3 and step 4 make a text preprocessing for our selected suggestion context sources, including removing stop-words, Chinese participle preprocessing and word frequency statistics. After completing these four steps, we extract the top 10 representative nouns or verb-nouns in the sequence according to the results of word frequency statistics. Nouns and verb-nouns can represent the meaning of a topic. Last, the produced words are put into the suggestion list in turn.

We give an example to describe our online processing. When a user has an information need, she will transform the information need into a query and start typing the query in the query box of a search engine. The user has some information need but is not sure which words to use to formulate a query because traditional method that documents indexed by the search engine are not visible to the user. The terms selected by the user to formulate the queries often do not lead to a good retrieval performance due to the gap between query-term space and document-term space [10]. This problem is especially difficult for the fresh search queries because of lacking context in query logs. To help the user formulate good search queries, our suggestion list may give the useful query suggestion to the user. When the query exists in the suggestion list of a certain topic, we can recommend other words in this suggestion list to the user.

4   Offline Processing

In this section, we first introduce how to extract microblog data by crawling. Then we describe our approach for text processing. Finally, we make some discussions.

4.1   Extracting Microblog Data by Crawling

For benefiting from our professional point of view of computer science technology, we select the technology/IT Internet as our data source. The chosen 14 topics all are the most popular topics at the crawling time as our experimental data. We extract the tweets of these 14 topics. Sina microblog only gives 10 pages space capacity to display the tweets of each micro-topic and each page only exists 20 tweets. From the end of March 2012, we start collecting micro-topic data. In order to ensure nonduplication of data, nearly every two days, we download the html webpages of each Micro-topic, and then save them in the local disk folder as .txt file format. By the end of June 2012, we obtain almost 3750 web pages. But how to extract our needed information from these html files? Here we use HtmlParser [1]. HtmlParser is an open-source project used to parse the HTML document. It is small, fast, simple and has a powerful function.

4.2   Text Processing

First, we need to point out that so-called the authenticated users mainly includes the users of Sina microbog VIP, Sina approved Sina agencies and authenticated Sina individuals. These users are certified by Sina microblog with a certain authenticity and authority. Then we have collected profiles of users who mentioned about 14 Sina microblog trending topics from March 25th to June 17th, 2012 by crawling. We separately extracted tweets information from all users and from authenticated users for each topic among 14 topics. Under our preliminary statistics, there are 63,354 tweets form all users. The number of tweets by the authenticated users is about 22,724, accounting for about 35.9% of total users' tweets.

---

[1] http://htmlparser.sourceforge.net/

To complete text processing, two NLP tools (i.e., *MyTxtSegTag* and *MyZiCiFreq*) is used [2]. The next step is to remove all stopwords. We remove the words in our tweets for each topic that appeared in a stopwords list. After making stopwords processing for authenticated tweets and the whole tweets of each topic, we make Chinese participle preprocessing for the filtered tweets by a set of word segmentation and POS tagging tool which is named *MyTxtSegTag*. The big advantage of this software is that it can identify proper and newly appeared nouns and minimize the word granularity, such as the new word of Mirco-Letters, weixin(a mobile phone chat software) which is a new application launched by Tencent company in 2011. If the option of starting proper nouns is not selected, then after making participle processing,the word of weixin will be divided into two words that "Micro" and "letters". So using this software can improve the precision and accuracy of participle processing results.

Last, we save these produced words in a .txt formatted file, making a preparation for word frequency statistics and analysis. We adopt a word frequency statistic tool named MyZiCiFreq. This software can not only make character frequency statistics but also make word frequency statistics. Furthermore, we also observe that the processing times for the same topic from two different sets of users' tweets are significantly different. Averagely, it takes about 4 hours for all users' tweets of a certain topic, but for processing authenticated users' tweets, it just take about 30 minutes less than an hour.

4.3 Discussions

What we will discuss is about why we collected microblog data by crawling not using Sina API (Application Programming Interface). As we all know it will greatly shorten the time so as to improve the efficiency if we collect data using API. But there are many limiting factors, such as only a part of API, not all API is provided. Moreover, some API just can be used by senior member users, making that we cannot crawl and collect data in time and completely.

To help the user formulate effective queries, a suggestion list is produced after text processing. When the query exists in the suggestion list of a certain topic, we can recommend other words in this suggestion list to the user. In this step, we can adopt computing semantic similarity between query word and other words that appeared in the suggestion list based on the path length similarity, in which we treat taxonomy as an undirected graph and measure the distance between them in HowNet which serves as a base of research in knowledge processing and multilingual NLP [3]. This method will be used in our future work.

5 Experiment

In this section, we first introduce the data sets and evaluation method. Then we present the experimental results. Finally, a dicussion is given.

---

[2] They are recommended by the website of
http://www.china-language.gov.cn/index.htm

[3] http://www.keenage.com

Table 1. Explanation for the abbreviations in Table 2

	Meaning
Authenticated tweets	The tweets that from authenticated users
Total tweets	The tweets that from all of users involved in a topic
Authenticated/Total	Authenticated tweets/ Total tweets
Atop10 precision	The precision of top 10 words produced by authenticated tweets
Ttop10 precision	The precision of top 10 words produced by total tweets

5.1   Data Set and Evaluation Method

We collected a sample of almost three months tweets between March 25th and June 17th from Sina microblogging platform. We got 22,724 tweets from authenticated users and 63,354 tweets from total users. For each of topics and each of tweets, we conduct the preprocessing of removing stopwords and chinese participle preprocessing. Then word frequency statistics are done and top 10 representative nouns or verb-nouns are extracted.

For a given query, the precision of a query suggestion method is defined as the fraction of suggestions generated that are meaningful. Note that since an exhaustive set of all possible suggestions for a given query is not available, recall cannot be computed. Also, for the query suggestion task, precision is a much more important metric than recall as the number of suggestions that can be offered is limited by the screen space. Precision is defined as

$$Precision@N = \frac{\#related\ words\ in\ a\ suggestion\ list}{N}. \tag{1}$$

In Equation 1, we take the extracted top 10 representative nouns or verb-nouns as the words that can represent a certain topic. We manually judge whether these words can be considered to accurately reflect the topic. The precision value of each topic is computed.

5.2   Experimental Results

Here, in Table 1, we have made a specific explanation for all abbreviations appeared in Table 2 which show the results of each microblog topic. Using the tweets from all users as suggestion context source is our baseline. The average results of all the 14 topics are listed in Table 3.

From the results that presented in Table 2, it seems that the differences between Atop10 precision and Ttop10 precision are not particularly obvious in terms of precision. For further observation, we decide to make an average for the precision values of 14 topics. To our surprise, the precision value of top 10 words that produced by the tweets that from authenticated users is higher than that produced by the tweets from all of users involved in a topic on average.

Before conducting experiments, we think that the number of the total tweets for one topic actually not only contains the tweets from authenticated users, but also contain others tweets from common users. In comparison, it has the

Table 2. The precision values of each topics

Topics	New ipad sale	Iphone news	Ipad show	Apple ceo salary	App Store
Authenticated tweets	2079	471	2420	1831	3005
Total tweets	6043	1242	6889	5600	6760
Authenticated/Total	0.344	0.3792	0.3513	0.327	0.4445
ATop10 precision	0.4	0.6	0.4	0.5	0.4
TTop10 precision	0.5	0.6	0.4	0.5	0.4
ATop5 precision	0.3	0.4	0.3	0.2	0.3
TTop5 precision	0.3	0.3	0.3	0.4	0.4
Topics	CES2012	HTC	Tablet pc	Kodak bankrupt	Huawei for new life
Authenticated tweets	1866	487	443	2472	340
Total tweets	6126	1237	1283	7137	1116
Authenticated/Total	0.3046	0.3937	0.3453	0.3464	0.3047
ATop10 precision	0.4	0.5	0.4	0.4	0.4
TTop10 precision	0.3	0.5	0.4	0.4	0.4
ATop5 precision	0.3	0.4	0.4	0.4	0.4
TTop5 precision	0.2	0.5	0.4	0.2	0.2
Topics	Iphone 4s sale	Windows 8	iOS jailbreak	Facebook	
Authenticated tweets	2491	2454	604	1761	
Total tweets	6714	6516	1645	5046	
Authenticated/Total	0.371	0.3766	0.3672	0.3489	
ATop10 precision	0.3	0.5	0.6	0.3	
TTop10 precision	0.3	0.4	0.6	0.3	
ATop5 precision	0.3	0.4	0.6	0.3	
TTop5 precision	0.3	0.3	0.5	0.2	

Table 3. The average precision values of all the 14 topics

	Average
Authenticated/Total	0.3575
Atop10 precision	0.4357
Ttop10 precision	0.4286
Atop5 precision	0.3286
Ttop5 precision	0.3214

larger suggestion context source and the richer content information. Thus, it should output higher precision scores. However, the results run adversely to what we might intuitively expect the average precision value of top 10 words that produced by the tweets that authenticated users, i.e., slightly higher.

So what does this show? It illustrates that we do not need to select all tweets of a topic as our suggestion context source. Considering the final result, the tweets that from authenticated users could be on behalf of the entire tweets under a topic. During the preprocessing, we observed that under the background of computer configuration with a 32-bit operating system, dual-core CPU and 3.00GB memory, it takes about 4 hours for all users' tweets of a certain topic, but for processing authenticated users' tweets, it just takes about 30 minutes. Taking tweets that from authenticated users as our suggestion context source saves not only the processing time, but also the storage space. How much storage space does it save at all? From experimental data, we can see that average Authenticated/Total is about 0.3575. In other words, the authenticated context accounts for around 1/3 in total tweets and almost saves 2/3 storage space.

5.3   Discussions

There are some limitations in our approach. That is, for the words of a query that do not appear in the suggestion list of a topic, we cannot give a suggestion. In other words, our approach is based on the query that has already appeared in microblog topics, but they are little or even no in the history record of search engine. That is the so-called fresh query. The characteristic of high efficiency of information dissemination in microblog is our motivation to do this research.

6   Conclusions and Future Work

In this paper, we have introduced our approach for the suggestion of fresh search queries by mining microblog topics. We gave out the whole process that how to be access to microblog topics data and how to do text processing for these tweets until the words produced. It is worth mentioning that we not only extracted the tweets that from all of users involved in a topic, but also extracted the tweets that from authenticated users. Through the final experimental results, we can see that the average precision value of the top 10 words that produced by the tweets that from authenticated users is actually slightly higher. In addition, taking tweets that from authenticated users as our suggestion context source saves both the processing time and the storage space. In the future, an interesting topic is how to combine other social evidence to enhance query suggestion quality.

Acknowledgments. This research was undertaken as part of Project 61003130 funded by National Natural Science Foundation of China and Project 2011CDB254 founded by Ministry of Education of China.

References

1. Baeza-Yates, R., Hurtado, C.A., Mendoza, M.: Query recommendation using query logs in search engines. In: Lindner, W., Fischer, F., Türker, C., Tzitzikas, Y., Vakali, A.I. (eds.) EDBT 2004. LNCS, vol. 3268, pp. 588–596. Springer, Heidelberg (2004)
2. Barouni-Ebrahimi, M., Ghorbani, A.A.: A novel approach for frequent phrase mining in web search engine query streams. In: Proceedings of Fifth Annual Conference on Communication Networks and Services Research (CNSR 2007), pp. 125–132. IEEE Computer Society (2007)
3. Bhatia, S., Majumdar, D., Mitra, P.: Query suggestions in the absence of query logs. In: Proceeding of the 34th International ACM SIGIR Conference on Research and Development in Information Retrieval, SIGIR 2011, pp. 795–804. ACM (2011)
4. Boldi, P., Bonchi, F., Castillo, C., Donato, D., Vigna, S.: Query suggestions using query-flow graphs. In: Proceedings of the 2009 workshop on Web Search Click Data, WSCD 2009, pp. 56–63. ACM (2009)
5. Broder, A.Z., Ciccolo, P., Gabrilovich, E., Josifovski, V., Metzler, D., Riedel, L., Yuan, J.: Online expansion of rare queries for sponsored search. In: Proceedings of the 18th International Conference on World Wide Web, WWW 2009, pp. 511–520. ACM (2009)

6. Cao, H., Jiang, D., Pei, J., He, Q., Liao, Z., Chen, E., Li, H.: Context-aware query suggestion by mining click-through and session data. In: Proceedings of the 14th ACM SIGKDD International Conference on Knowledge Discovery and Data Mining, pp. 875–883. ACM (2008)
7. Cao, L.: In-depth Behavior Understanding and Use: the Behavior Informatics Approach. Information Science 180(17), 3067–3085 (2010)
8. Chen, X., Li, L., Xu, G., Yang, Z., Kitsuregawa, M.: Recommending related microblogs: A comparison between topic and wordnet based approaches. In: Proceedings of the Twenty-Sixth AAAI Conference on Artificial Intelligence, AAAI 2012. AAAI Press (2012)
9. Cucerzan, S., White, R.W.: Query suggestion based on user landing pages. In: SIGIR 2007: Proceedings of the 30th Annual International ACM SIGIR Conference on Research and Development in Information Retrieval, pp. 875–876. ACM (2007)
10. Cui, H., Wen, J.-R., Nie, J.-Y., Ma, W.-Y.: Probabilistic query expansion using query logs. In: Proceedings of the Eleventh International World Wide Web Conference, WWW 2002, pp. 325–332. ACM (2002)
11. Feuer, A., Savev, S., Aslam, J.A.: Evaluation of phrasal query suggestions. In: Proceedings of the Sixteenth ACM Conference on Information and Knowledge Management, CIKM 2007, pp. 841–848. ACM (2007)
12. Gao, W., Niu, C., Nie, J.-Y., Zhou, M., Hu, J., Wong, K.-F., Hon, H.-W.: Cross-lingual query suggestion using query logs of different languages. In: SIGIR 2007: Proceedings of the 30th Annual International ACM SIGIR Conference on Research and Development in Information Retrieval, pp. 463–470. ACM (2007)
13. Jones, R., Rey, B., Madani, O., Greiner, W.: Generating query substitutions. In: Proceedings of the 15th International Conference on World Wide Web, WWW 2006, pp. 387–396. ACM (2006)
14. Kelly, D., Gyllstrom, K., Bailey, E.W.: A comparison of query and term suggestion features for interactive searching. In: Proceedings of the 32nd Annual International ACM SIGIR Conference on Research and Development in Information Retrieval, SIGIR 2009, pp. 371–378. ACM (2009)
15. Kwak, H., Lee, C., Park, H., Moon, S.B.: What is twitter, a social network or a news media? In: Proceedings of the 19th International Conference on World Wide Web, WWW 2010, pp. 591–600. ACM (2010)
16. Liu, Z., Chen, X., Sun, M.: Mining the interests of chinese microbloggers via keyword extraction. Frontiers of Computer Science in China 6(1), 76–87 (2012)
17. Ma, H., Yang, H., King, I., Lyu, M.R.: Learning latent semantic relations from clickthrough data for query suggestion. In: Proceedings of the 17th ACM Conference on Information and Knowledge Management, CIKM 2008, pp. 709–718. ACM (2008)
18. Mei, Q., Zhou, D., Church, K.W.: Query suggestion using hitting time. In: Proceedings of the 17th ACM Conference on Information and Knowledge Management, CIKM 2008, pp. 469–478. ACM (2008)
19. Newman, M.E.J., Park, J.: Why social networks are different from other types of networks. Phys. Rev. E 68, 036122 (2003)
20. Silvestri, F.: Mining query logs: Turning search usage data into knowledge. Foundations and Trends in Information Retrieval 4(1-2), 1–174 (2010)
21. Song, Y., Wei He, L.: Optimal rare query suggestion with implicit user feedback. In: Proceedings of the 19th International Conference on World Wide Web, WWW 2010, pp. 901–910. ACM (2010)

Learn to Rank Tweets by Integrating Query-Specific Characteristics

Xin Zhang, Ben He, and Tiejian Luo

School of Computer and Control Engineering
University of Chinese Academy of Sciences
zhangxin510@mails.ucas.ac.cn, {benhe,tjluo}@ucas.ac.cn

Abstract. Current approaches to real-time Twitter search usually deploy a learning to rank (LTR) algorithm that incorporates diverse sources of tweet features, such as the content-based relevance score and the number of reposts, to find fresh and relevant tweets in response to user queries. In this paper, we argue that the user's information need is a query-dependent notion, which is yet to be exploited for retrieval from tweets. To this end, we propose a learning to rank framework to improve the retrieval performance for real-time Twitter search by capturing the query-specific features. In particular, the proposed approach consists of two components: (1) a general ranking model learned from the training instances represented by features common to all queries; (2) a query-specific model learned by making use of LTR to select the most benefical expansion terms for each query. Finally, the query-specific model that reforms the original query topics with the extracted terms is combined with the general ranking model to produce the ranked list of documents in response to the given target query. Extensive experiments on the standard TREC Tweets11 collection show that the combined learning to rank approach outperforms the strong baseline, namely the conventional application of Ranking SVM.

Keywords: Real-time Twitter search, Query-specific, Learning to rank.

1 Introduction

Both fresh and informative tweets are favored in real-time Twitter search to a given query, whereby a user's information need is represented by a query issued at a specific time. Previous research has shown the benefits brought by applying learning to rank in real-time Twitter search as multiple intrinsic features, such as content-relevance scores, user authority, retweets, mentions, hashtags, etc, can be integrated to learn a ranking model. Such approaches usually rely on a set of training queries to learn a ranking model, which is assumed to be generalized to the test data, as the features used are common to different queries.

However, the user's information need, a query-dependent notion, indicates the desire to locate and obtain information to satisfy a conscious and unconscious need. Ignoring of characteristics and aspects unique to the given queries during the learning process may hinder the retrieval performance as the usual learning to rank methods do [17,14,15]. Indeed, there have been research to take query differences into consideration to improve the effectiveness of learning to rank, for instance [27,22,6,19,25].

L. Cao et al. (Eds.): BSIC/BSI 2013, LNAI 8178, pp. 224–236, 2013.
© Springer International Publishing Switzerland 2013

Motivated by the above studies on query differences, in this paper, we put forward a combined learning to rank framework to improve the retrieval performance by combining the general ranking model and the query-specific model that reforms the original query with the unique features, e.g. the most benefical expansion terms. More specifically, the general ranking model is learned through the application of conventional learning to rank algorithm, where the training instances are represented by the predifined common features. Besides, a query-specific ranking model is proposed to expand the original queries with terms selected by applying learning to rank approach with features unique to each given query. For the given query, the final ranked list is produced by the combination of the general ranking model and the query-specific ranking model.

The major contributions of the paper are two-fold. First, we propose a query-specific model by utilizing LTR method with a variety of features for implying the particular characteristics of a given query. Inspired by the idea of pseudo relevance feedback, we reform the query topic with the selected expansion terms obtained by applying the LTR approach to enhance the retrieval performance. Second, a learning to rank framework that combines a general ranking model and the query-specific ranking model is proposed. Experiments on the standard TREC Tweets11 collection demonstrate the effectiveness of the proposed method.

The rest of the paper is organized as follows. In Section 2, we survey the existing LTR research on Twitter search. Section 3 gives a detail description about our proposed algorithm and the features exploited for the tweet representation, which is evaluated in Section 4. Finally, we conclude this research and suggest future research directions.

2   Related Work

Learning to rank approaches have been widely used in real-time Twitter search, where users are interested in fresh relevant messages. In the TREC 2011 Microblog track [17], Metzler and Cai use ListNet to combine the evidence from multiple features, where recency is represented by the difference in time between the query's temporal point and tweet's timestamps [14]. Miyanishi et al. apply an unspecified learning to rank method by clustering the tweets retrieved for given topics [15]. In addition to the above described approaches in the Microblog track, Hong et al. propose to apply affinity propagation, a non parametric clustering algorithm, to cluster the initial ranked list of tweets [8]. Li et al. apply the Word Activation Force algorithm and Term Similarity Metric algorithms to mine the connection between the expansion terms and the given topic [10]. Louvan et al. apply query expansion from dataset with different weighting schemes and then incorporate timestamps of the tweets for real-time search [13]. We refer to [17] for an overview of all the other techniques and approaches evaluated in Microblog track 2011. Besides, there are research studies that apply semi-supervised learning algorithms to facilitate learning to rank with only limited training data available [24,4].

However, most of learning to rank approaches treat all the queries equally during the learning and ranking processes. As a result, the unique aspects of different queries are ignored, which may potentially hurt the retrieval effectiveness. Recently, there have been efforts to take query differences into consideration during the learning process to improve the ranking functions. Zheng et al. put forward a minimum effort optimization method by considering all the entire training data within a query during each iteration by using functional iterative methods where the update in each iteration is computed through the approach of solving a isotonic regression problem [27]. Wu et al. propose a listwise query-level regression method, called ListReg, by using the neural network to model the ranking function and gradient descent for optimization [22]. Geng et al. point the owing to the great variety of queries, and argue that the rerank task should be conducted by using different models based on different properties of queries, Hence, a K-Nearest Neighbour method is put forward to learn different ranking functions [6]. Veloso et al. propose a novel method to uncover the patterns or rules in the training data in which documents are associated with features of relevance to the given query by generating association rules on a demand-driven basis at the query time [19]. Besides, the semi-supervised learning algorithm is used in Twitter search, where a query-biased model is learned by applying the transductive learning [25].

We argue that the improvement brought by learning to rank can be further improved if the differences that exist in the diverse queries are considered during the retrieval process. To address this problem, in this paper, we propose a combined framework that makes use of both the common features and query-specific features for learning to rank, as introduced in the next section. Different from [25,26], instead of using a semi-supervised learning algorithm to buid a query-specific model, in this paper, we adopt a supervised pairwise learning to rank approach to capture the particular characteristics of a given query.

3   Combined LTR by Integrating Query-Specific Aspects

In this paper, both the common features of Twitter messages, and the query-specific aspects that differentiate between queries are utilized to construct the combined learning to rank framework. The proposed framework combines a general ranking model and a query-specific ranking model. More specifically, the general ranking model is learned from the training instances, represented by the features common to different queries. The query-specific model is learned from the query-specific features by applying RankSVM to select the most useful expansion terms. The two models are integrated by a linear combination as follows:

$$Score_{final}(d, Q) = \beta \cdot Score_{LTR}(d, Q) + (1 - \beta) \cdot Score_{QSR}(d, Q) \qquad (1)$$

where $Score_{final}(d, Q)$ is the final score of tweet d for the given query Q; $Score_{LTR}(d, Q)$ is the score given by the general ranking model; $Score_{QSR}(d, Q)$ is the score given by the query-specific model. The setting of the parameter β is obtained by grid search on training queries.

To deploy our proposed learning to rank framework in practice, we firstly learn a general ranking model from a set of training queries with their associated relevance assessments information. Next, for the given target queries, we learn a query-specific ranking model using the unique features in response to the query to expand the inital query with the selected terms benefical for boosting the retrieval effectiveness. Finally, the two models are combined to produce the final relevance scores for the target queries.

Sections 3.1 and 3.2 present details on the general and the query-specific ranking models, respectively.

3.1 General Model

Pre-defined Tweet Features

Our features are organized around the basic entities for each query-tweet tuple to distinguish between the relevant and irrelevant messages, some of which have been widely used in previous work on Twitter search [3,15,14,24]. More specifically, in addition to the five types of features which were defined in [24], we exploit the sentiment features in this paper.

Sentiment refers to those features that indicate the opinions embodied in the given tweet. In our model, we extract the number of negative, positive, neural sentiment words and their total ratio in the content of the tweet. All these sentiment words are defined in the dictionary of OpinionFinder system [21], which can automatically identify the subjectivity of a sentence conveying opinions and sentiments.

3.2 Query-Specific Ranking Model

Section *KL-divergence Method to Select Candidate Terms* introduces the method to select the candidate expansion terms. Section *Term Features Extracting* gives a detailed description of the features that are used to represent the candidate expansion terms. In Section *Evaluation of Term Quality* presents the method of labeling the candidate expansion terms. When the candidate terms are selected, we apply RankSVM to rank the candidate terms. Once the ranked list is produced, the top-ranked 10 terms will be used to reform the inital query. Our arbitrary choice of selecting the top-10 terms from the top-30 tweets is mainly due to the fact that this setting was found to provide the best query expansion effectiveness in the TREC 2011 Microblog track, as reported in [1]. Figure 1 gives a description of the query-specific model.

KL-divergence Method to Select Candidate Terms

The purpose of the query-specific ranking model is to utilize the most benefical expansion terms through the application of learning to rank algorithm to reform the inital query. Therefore, how to select the appropriate terms unique to the given query becomes a challenging issue. Since queries submitted by users often contain very few keywords and phrases, query expansion has been widely used to further describe the user's information need. Pseudo-relevance feedback, which hypothesizes the top-ranked documents in the initial retrieval results convey many useful terms helping describing the true information need better, has shown great benefits in many information retrieval tasks. Basing on the similar assumption, in this, in this paper, the terms with highest KL divergence weights are chosen as the candidate terms to expand the original query topic, as illustrated in Figure 2. The KL divergence weight of a candidate term t in the top-k ranked tweets in the initial retrieval is computed as follows:

$$w(t, R_k) = P(t|R_k) \log_2 \frac{P(t|R_k)}{P(t|C)} \qquad (2)$$

Input
    T: a set of the candidate expansion terms for
    each query
    N: the predifined number of expansion terms that
    will be used
    F: the features to represent each candidate term

Output
    T: the final selected expansion terms for each
    given query
    L: the retrieval list obtained by the reform topics

Algorithm

    Do the following for each query
        (1) Represent each candidate term in T with F
        (2) Using Ranking SVM to learn a ranking
    query model M
        (3) Get the most N benefical terms to expand
    each query by utilizing the model M
        (4) Return the retrieval list L by reforming the
    original query with the selected terms

Fig. 1. The query-specific ranking model

where $P(t|R_k)$ is the probability of generating the candidate term t from the set of top-k ranked tweets R_k, and $P(t|C)$ is the probability of generating t from the entire collection C.

Note that all the features exploited in Section *Pre-defined Features* are taken as common features to learn a general ranking model, which is generalized to the test queries. In the query-specific model, the most weighted terms as attributes are treated as unique terms to represent the unique query-specific characteristics of the given target queries.

Evaluation of Term Quality

The basic idea of the query-specific ranking model is that we can effectively predict the useful expansion query terms for a novel query by learning a ranking model from the exsisted training candidate terms. Therefore, it needs to create a ground truth for each candidate expansion term in the training set to imply whether it is good enough to improve the retrieval effectiveness.

Intuitively, a candidate term is considered to be good if it provides an improvement in MAP (mean average precision) when compared to the inital retrieval results obtained by applying the content-based model. Simply, we add each candidate term with the same weight into the original query to examine its impact on the retrieval effectiveness, as defined in Equation 3. If Δ defined in Equation 3 below is larger than zero, we consider

```
Input
    R: initial retrieved tweets returned by the
    content-based model e.g. DFRee for a
    batch of query topics
    N: the maximum candidate terms that are used
    to expand each query
    K: the number of top-ranked tweets for each
    given query

Output
    T: Candidate terms to expand each given query
    W: the KL divergence weight of each term

Algorithm
    For each query, do the followings
        (1) Extract the top-ranked K tweets for each
        given query
        (2) Get and stem every term occuring in each
        tweet excepting the stopping words
        (3) computed the KL weight of each term
        according to Equation 2 for the given query
        (4) return the terms with the highest weight as
        the candidate expansion terms
```

Fig. 2. The algorithm of candidate expansion terms selection

the candidate term e to be a good expansion term for the given query, and a bad one otherwise.

In our experiment, the standard TREC Tweets11 with 49 official queries is used. We randomly divide these queries into three groups . In the training dataset, each query has a term list which ranks the candidate expansion terms according to Δ. The term features used to repesent each candidate term will be discussed in the next section.

$$\Delta = \frac{MAP(Q \cup e) - MAP(Q)}{MAP(Q)} \tag{3}$$

where $MAP(Q)$ is the MAP of the inital query Q; e is the candidate expansion term.

Term Features Extraction
This section describes the statistical features exploited to represent each candidate terms obtained by computing the KL divergence weights. These features include KL divergence weights, term frequency (TF), document frequency (DF), as well as the co-occurrences of the candidate terms and the query keywords. Among all the features, many of them have been used in previous research studies [7,11], such as TF and DF. Additionaly, a set of query term co-occurrence features is exploited in [11] to evaluate the potential of social annotations as a resource of expansion terms. However, different from [11], the whole content of the tweet is considered as the text window.

- KL divergence weight as computed by Equation 2.
- Sum TF: the total occurrences of a given term in the top-ranked results.

- DF: the number of top-ranked documents in which the candidate term occurs.
- Term co-occurrence as defined in Equation 4: co-occurrence with a single query keyword, measuring how often the terms occur together in a text.

$$termCooc(t_i, q_j) = \frac{\sum_{f \in S} log(tf(t_i) + 1) \cdot (log(tf(q_j) + 1)}{log(N)} \qquad (4)$$

where N is the sum tweets in the retrieval results of each query, $tf(t_i)$ is the term frequency of the candidate term t_i, and $tf(q_j)$ is the term frequency of the query term q_j.
- Query co-occurrence as defined in Equation 5:
measures how often the given term occurs together with a given query that contains a few words.

$$queryCoof = \sum_{q_j \in Q} \{idf(q_j) \cdot idf(t_i) \cdot \qquad (5)$$
$$(log(termCooc(t_i, q_j) + 1))\}$$

where idf is the inverted document frequency, and it is computed as follows.

$$idf = log(\frac{N}{df}) \qquad (6)$$

where N is the sum tweets in the Tweets11, df is the document frequency, namely the number of tweets containing the term.
- Query neighbour co-occurrence as defined in Equation 7: measures the how often the given term occurs with the neighbouring query terms of the whole given query.

$$queryNeighCoof(t_i, Q) = \sum_{j=1}^{n-1} \{idf(q_j) \cdot idf(q_{(j} + 1)) \cdot idf(t_i) \cdot \qquad (7)$$
$$log(termCooc(t_i, q_j) + 1) \cdot log(termCooc(t_i, q_{j+1}) + 1)\}$$

Intuitively, term dependency is usual in many queries, which indicates that if one term occures, the other will occure simultaneously. In Equation 5, all the terms are considered independently without taking the inherent term dependency into account. Thus, Equation 7 improve Equation 5 by hypothesizing the terms in each query topic are somewhat independent if they are neighbours.
- Combined co-occurrence as defined in Equation 8:

$$coof(t_i, Q) = (1 - \alpha) \cdot queryCoof(t_i, Q) + \alpha \cdot queryNeighCoof(t_i, Q) \qquad (8)$$

4   Experiments

4.1   Experimental Settings

Section *Dataset and Indexing* gives an introduction to the dataset and preprocessing of Tweets11. Section *Parameter Tuning* describes how to obtain the optimized parameters for RankSVM which are used in general LTR stage. Section *Evaluation Design* introduces the baselines of evaluating our proposed methods.

Dataset and Indexing

We experiment on the Tweets11 collection, which consists of a sample of tweets over a period of about 2 weeks spanning from January 24, 2011 to February 8, 2011 [17]. In the TREC 2011 Microblog track, this collection is used for evaluating the participating real-time Twitter search systems over 50 official topics. Participants are required to download the tweets from Twitter.com using the feeds distributed by the track organizers. Our crawl of the Tweets11 collection consists of 13,401,964 successfully downloaded unique tweets. Note that because of dynamic nature of Twitter, there is a discrepancy between the number of tweets in our crawl and the figures reported by other participants in the Microblog track 2011. This does not affect the validity of the conclusions drawn from our experiments as the proposed approach and the baselines are evaluated on the same dataset with consistent settings.

Standard stopword removal and Porter's stemmer are applied during indexing and retrieval. All of the indexing and retrieval experiments are conducted on an in-house extension of the open source Terrier3.0 [16]. The official measure in the TREC Microblog Track, namely precision at 30 (P30), is used as the evaluation metric in our experiments.

Parameter Tuning

It is known, the choice of the hyperparameter C, the regularization parameter for RankSVM, plays an important role in the retrieval performance. C can be selected by carrying out cross-validation experiments through a grid search by scaning 0.05, 0.1, 0.3, 1, 3 and 4 on the training queries.

Evaluation Design

The aim of our experiments is to evaluate the effectiveness of the proposed query-specific learning to rank framework. The proposed approach is evaluated at the follwing two levels.

1. Comparing the proposed method, denoted as **CLTR** to the learning to rank approaches [12] with the use of the relevance judgments (**LTR**), which represents the conventional application pair-wise learning to rank algorithms.
   Many learning to rank approaches, including pointwise, pairwise and listwise, have been proposed in the literature [12,23,5,9,2], which can be applied for learning the ranking model. In the experiments, we choose RankSVM as the learning to rank algorithm to rank the candidate expansion terms and the tweet lists in the general ranking model. Extensive experiments are conducted using RankSVM [9,2], where

the ranking models are learned from the official relevance assessments from the Microblog track 2011. RankSVM [9,2] is a classical pairwise learning to rank approach, which adopts the traditional formulation of the SVM optimization problem by taking the document pairs and their preferences as the learning instances. Using the LTR approaches, we conduct experiments in 3-fold (**LTR_3**) cross-validation. While carrying out the 3-fold cross-validation experiments, we divide the queries into three groups randomly, and then learn a ranking model from two groups, while testing it on the queries in the remaining group.

2. Comparison to the query-specific ranking model, denoted as **QSR**, which is also proposed in our paper. Through the extensive experiments, we measure the effectiveness of our proposed CLTR framework when just considering the query differences during the retrieval process.

4.2 Results and Discussion

Firstly, the combined framework CLTR is compared to the conventional LTR approach, which learns the ranking models from the official relevance assessments. We examine to which extent our proposed combined framework is able to improve the retrieval effectiveness by taking query differences into consideration. The 3-fold cross-validation experiments using CLTR are compared to the general LTR approach which utilizes the relevance assessment information as shown in Table 1. We can see that comparing to RankSVM, CLTR outperforms the baseline, which suggests the effectiveness of the query-specific ranking model. Besides, we examine how CLTR performs while comparing with QSR model, namely the query-specific model. Results in Table 2 indicate significant differences between the two models. In all the tables, a $*$ indicates a significant improvement over the baseline according to the two sided paired randomization tests [18] at the 0.05 level.

Besides, Figure 3 plots the results obtained by our proposed approach with different settings of β defined in Equation 1 . As shown by the results, β also has an important impact on the retrieval effectiveness of our proposed approach.

Table 1. Comparison of the combined framework (CLTR) with the learning to rank algorithm (LTR))

LTR.	CLTR
0.3850	**0.4048, +5.14%** $*$

Table 2. Comparison of the combined framework (CLTR) with the query-specific model (QSR) using RankSVM

QSR.	CLTR
0.3823	**0.4048, +5.89%** $*$

Table 3. Candidate expansion terms for query MB001 and MB013

MB001: "BBC World Service staff cuts"
friend, work, cuerpo , ichanurbani, *compani, enriquepenalosa*, kendi28, *concertforhop, nonprofit*, push, asamiaudreylov, *twitter, 04*, lean, *03*, momo, a1nonlykavalon
MB013: "Oprah Winfrey half-sister"
vinkyyohann, reibniz, concertforhop, aerf, compani, sulpin, traderandym, pleeeas, higher, new, twitter, ichanurbani, kendi28, muslim, friend, eunhyuk, lunchless, push, nonprofit, nursemom90

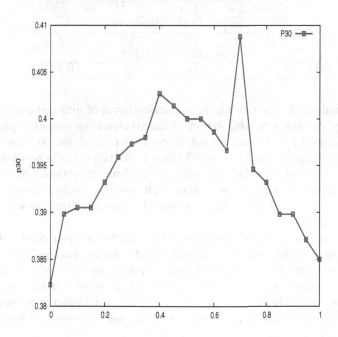

Fig. 3. The retrieval effectiveness obtained with different settings of β defined in Equation 1. Other parameters are obtained by training in each fold of the cross-validation.

Moreover, we investigate the impact of the expansion terms selected by the query-specific model. Table 3 shows the candidate expansion terms for query MB001 "BBC World Service staff cuts" and MB013 "Oprah Winfrey half-sister" by making use of KL

Table 4. Term qualities selected by applying the query-specific model (QSR) for query MB001 and MB013

MB001: "BBC World Service staff cuts"	
Good	friend, work, 04
Bad	compani, twitter, cuerpo, concertforhop nonprofit, enriquepenalosa, 03
MB013: "Oprah Winfrey half-sister"	
Good	vinkyyohann, reibniz, concertforhop, aerf, compani,sulpin, traderandym, pleeeas higher, new
Bad	

Table 5. The number of queries with changes in P30 at different percentage levels.

$\leq -10\%$	$-10\% \sim -1\%$	$-1\% \sim 1\%$	$1\% \sim 10\%$	$\geq 10\%$
Compare CLTR to RankSVM				
7	5	21	3	13
Compare CLTR to QSR				
11	4	10	5	19

divergence method. It turns out that the expansion terms of different queries behavior [20] diversely. As shown in Table 4, each of the 10 expansion terms for query MB013 boosts the retrieval performance (*Good*, in contrast to *Bad* that decreases the P30), while for MB001 query, only 3 of the 10 terms prove helpful to improve the retrieval effectiveness. It is believed that the initial retrieval results obtained by the content-based retrieval model for MB001 is good enough, thus there is little room for potential improvement; while for MB013, the most useful expansion terms are selected by the query-specific model.

Finally, Table 5 gives a detail description of the numbers of queries, of which precise at 30 are changed slightly, decreased or unchanged when comparing the proposed CLT with the general ranking model and the query-specific model (QSR). It appears that CLTR has led to more queries with improved P30 than those with decreased P30. On the other hand, the table also indicates the possibility for further improvement if the queries with decreased effectiveness brought by the query expansion can be predicted.

5   Conclusions and Future Work

In this paper, we have proposed a combined learning to rank framework that utilizes both the general and query-specific evidence of relevance for the real-time Twitter search. In particular, a query-specific ranking model is learned by applying the learning algorithm in order to better capture the characteristics of the given queries. Such a query-specific ranking model is combined with a general ranking model given by the conventional learning to rank approach to produce the final ranking of the Twitter messages, namely the tweets, in response to the user information need. Extensive experiments have been conducted on the standard Tweets11 dataset to evaluate the effectiveness of our proposed approach. Results show that our proposed combined learning to rank approach is able to outperform the strong baseline, namely the state-of-the-art learning to rank algorithm.

As shown by the experimental results, there still exist some useful expansion terms in the abandoned candidate term collection, due to the experimental setting of the final expansion term number, namely only 10 terms will be chosen to reform the inital query topic. In the future, we plan to improve the effectiveness of the query-specific ranking model by intelligently determining the number of the expansion terms for each given query. Finally, the results in Table 5 indicate that our proposed approach can also lead to the marked decreased in the effectiveness ($\geq 10\%$) for appropximately one fifth of the queries. We plan to investigate a prediction mechanism to foresee failures of CLTR, which prevents the loss of retrieval effectiveness, and improve the robustness of our proposed approach in this paper.

Acknowledgements. This work is supported in part by the National Natural Science Foundation of China (61103131/F020511), the President Fund of GUCAS (Y15101FY00/Y25102HN00), and the National Key Technology R&D Program of China (2012BAH23B03).

References

1. Amati, G., Amodeo, G., Bianchi, M., Celi, A., Nicola, C.D., Flammini, M., Gaibisso, C., Gambosi, G., Marcone, G.: Fub, iasi-cnr, univaq at trec 2011. In: TREC (2011)
2. Cohen, W.W., Schapire, R.E., Singer, Y.: Learning to order things. Journal of Artificial Intelligence Research 10, 243–270 (1998)
3. Duan, Y., Jiang, L., Qin, T., Zhou, M., Shum, H.-Y.: An empirical study on learning to rank of tweets. In: COLING, pp. 295–303. Tsinghua University, Beijing (2010)
4. Duh, K., Kirchhoff, K.: Learning to rank with partially-labeled data. In: SIGIR, pp. 251–258 (2008)
5. Ganjisaffar, Y., Caruana, R., Lope, C.: Bagging gradient-boosted trees for high precision, low variance ranking models. In: SIGIR, pp. 85–94. ACM (2011)
6. Geng, X., Liu, T.-Y., Qin, T., Arnold, A., Li, H., Shum, H.-Y.: Query dependent ranking using k-nearest neighbor. In: SIGIR 2008, pp. 115–122. ACM, New York (2008)
7. He, B., Ounis, I.: Finding good feedback documents. In: CIKM 2009, pp. 2011–2014. ACM, New York (2009)
8. Hong, D., Wang, Q., Zhang, D., Si, L.: Query expansion and message-passing algorithms for TREC Microblog track. In: TREC (2011)
9. Joachims, T.: Optimizing search engines using clickthrough data. In: KDD, pp. 133–142. ACM (2002)
10. Li, Y., Zhang, Z., Lv, W., Xie, Q., Lin, Y., Xu, R., Xu, W., Chen, G., Guo, J.: PRIS at TREC 2011 Micro-blog track. In: TREC (2011)
11. Lin, Y., Lin, H., Jin, S., Ye, Z.: Social annotation in query expansion: a machine learning approach. In: SIGIR 2011, pp. 405–414. ACM, New York (2011)

12. Liu, T.: Learning to rank for information retrieval. Foundations and Trends in Information Retrieval (3), 225–331 (2009)
13. Louvan, S., Ibrahim, M., Adriani, M., Vania, C., Distiawan, B., Wanagiri, M.Z.: University of Indonesia at TREC 2011 Microblog track. In: TREC (2011)
14. Metzler, D., Cai, C.: USC/ISI at TREC 2011: Microblog track. In: TREC (2011)
15. Miyanishi, T., Okamura, N., Liu, X., Seki, K., Uehara, K.: TREC 2011 Microblog track experiments at Kobe university. In: TREC, Gaithersburg, MD (2011)
16. Ounis, I., Amati, G., Plachouras, V., He, B., Macdonald, C., Lioma, C.: Terrier: A high performance and scalable information retrieval platform. In: SIGIR OSIR, Seattle, WA (2006)
17. Ounis, I., Macdonald, C., Lin, J., Soboroff, I.: Overview of the TREC 2011 microblog track. In: TREC, Gaithersburg, MD (2011)
18. Smucker, M.D., Allan, J., Carterette, B.: A comparison of statistical significance tests for information retrieval evaluation. In: Proceedings of the Sixteenth ACM Conference on Information and Knowledge Management, CIKM 2007, pp. 623–632. ACM, New York (2007)
19. Veloso, A.A., Almeida, H.M., Gonçalves, M.A., Meira Jr., W.: Learning to rank at query-time using association rules. In: SIGIR 2008, pp. 267–274. ACM, New York (2008)
20. Cao, L.: In-depth Behavior Understanding and Use: the Behavior Informatics Approach. Information Science 180(17), 3067–3085 (2010)
21. Wilson, T., Hoffmann, P., Somasundaran, S., Kessler, J., Wiebe, J., Choi, Y., Cardie, C., Riloff, E., Patwardhan, S.: Opinionfinder: a system for subjectivity analysis. In: Proceedings of HLT/EMNLP on Interactive Demonstrations, HLT-Demo 2005, pp. 34–35. Association for Computational Linguistics, Stroudsburg (2005)
22. Wu, J., Yang, Z., Lin, Y., Lin, H., Ye, Z., Xu, K.: Learning to rank using query-level regression. In: SIGIR 2011, pp. 1091–1092. ACM, New York (2011)
23. Wu, Q., Burges, C., Svore, K., Cao, J.: Ranking boosting and model adaptation. Technical report, Microsoft (2008)
24. Zhang, X., He, B., Luo, T.: Transductive learning for real-time twitter search. In: ICWSM (2012)
25. Zhang, X., He, B., Luo, T., Li, B.: Query-biased learning to rank for real-time twitter search. In: Wen Chen, X., Lebanon, G., Wang, H., Zaki, M.J. (eds.) CIKM, pp. 1915–1919. ACM (2012)
26. Zhang, X., Lu, S., He, B., Xu, J., Luo, T.: UCAS at TREC-2012 Microblog track. In: TREC (2012)
27. Zheng, Z., Zha, H., Sun, G.: Query-level learning to rank using isotonic regression (2008)

Exploration on Similar Spatial Textual Objects Retrieval

Yanhui Gu[1], Zhenglu Yang[1], Miyuki Nakano[1], and Masaru Kitsuregawa[1,2]

[1] Institute of Industrial Science, University of Tokyo,
4-6-1 Komaba, Meguro-ku, Tokyo, Japan
[2] National Institute of Informatics,
2-1-2 Hitotsubashi, Chiyoda-ku, Tokyo, Japan
{guyanhui,yangzl,miyuki,kitsure}@tkl.iis.u-tokyo.ac.jp

Abstract. Effective and efficient retrieval of similar spatial textual objects plays an important role for many location based applications, such as Foursquare, Yelp, and so forth. Although there are many studies exploring on this issue, most of them focus on how to integrate spatial and textual information to efficiently retrieve top-k results yet few of them address the effectiveness issue. In this paper, we propose a semantic aware strategy which can effectively and efficiently retrieve the top-k similar spatial textual objects based on a general framework. Extensive experimental evaluation demonstrates that the performance of our proposal outperforms the state-of-the-art approach.

1 Introduction

Retrieval of similar spatial textual objects is an important issue and has been supported in many location based applications, e.g., Foursqure services[1], Facebook Places[2], and Yelp[3], where location aware contents can be discovered. For example, in Fig. 1, it represents a map with eight objects and each object is associated with a textual description. For a query Q, the task is to retrieve the most similar spatial textual objects by considering both the spatial proximity and the textual similarity. In recent years, many techniques have been introduced for efficient processing spatial textual queries. These strategies can be categorized based on the spatial indices they utilize: (a) R-tree based techniques [4,12,19,18]; (b) grid based techniques [10]; and (c) space filling curve based techniques [1,3]. According to the text indexing strategies employed, these works can be classified as inverted file based techniques [4,12] and signature file based techniques [6]. To address the issue of similar spatial textual objects retrieval, an intuitive idea is to integrate the spatial index and the textual index. The difference between them is that which index is as the skeleton of the framework: (1) spatial index oriented [1]; and (2) text index oriented [15]. However, these techniques employ

---

[1] http://foursqure.com
[2] http://www.facebook.com/placesband
[3] http://www.yelp.com

L. Cao et al. (Eds.): BSIC/BSI 2013, LNAI 8178, pp. 237–249, 2013.

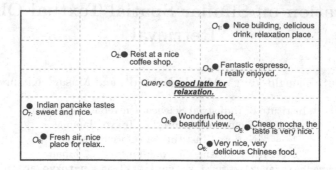

Fig. 1. The illustration of similar spatial textual objects

the loose combination strategy which consumes more space and has poor performance on retrieval efficiency. To tackle this problem, the tight combination scheme was introduced [4,3,12].

The tight hybrid indexing strategy seamlessly combines two kinds of the indices (i.e., spatial and textual) into a unified framework, in which the node is calculated as the integral value by taking into account both spatial proximity and textual similarity. Specifically, in [4,12], the authors introduced the IR-tree, that each node n of R-tree is associated with a summary of the content based on the objects in the corresponding subtree of n.

However, the textual description is always short and with high probability there are few or even no common words existing. As a result, the naïve term frequency based strategy [4,12] is inappropriate on measuring similarities between short texts. For the example illustrated in Fig. 1, suppose the query as "*Good latte for relaxation*" and the user is interested in the top-1 similar object. Based on the traditional strategies, o_1 is the result because some common word exists (i.e., relaxation) and the spatial distance is relative small. However, if the semantic similarity is taken into account, a more reasonable object, i.e., o_2, should be discovered. This problem was also observed in [14,11], which confirmed that the semantic similarity between short texts should be concerned. Therefore, semantic aware strategy is more appropriate for similar spatial textual objects retrieval compared with the traditional term frequency approach.

In this paper, we introduce effective and efficient strategies on extracting the top-k similar spatial textual objects. The basic idea is to construct an integral structure, that seamlessly combines the semantic similarity aware index and spatial index. Thorough experiments are conducted to evaluate the performance of the proposed strategies. The results show that the introduced techniques outperform the state-of-the-art approach. Our contributions of this paper are as follows:

- We propose to tackle the issue of effective and efficient retrieval of top-k similar spatial textual objects. This is an important and practical problem because users are more interested in semantically similar objects in many real applications.

- We propose a semantic similarity aware strategy to build a comprehensive index, which seamlessly integrates the spatial and textual information together.
- We conduct thorough experiments and evaluate the performance of the proposed strategies. The results show that the introduced techniques outperform the state-of-the-art approach.

2   Preliminaries

2.1   Problem Definition

Formally, let O be a spatial textual data collection. Each spatial object $o \in O$ is defined as a pair $(o.\rho, o.\varphi)$, where $o.\rho$ is a 2-dimensional geographical point location (illustrated by longitude and latitude) and $o.\varphi$ is a textual description. The issue we aim to tackle is to extract the top-k similar spatial textual objects to a query. For a query $Q = <Q.\rho, Q.\varphi, k>$, finding a set of k objects P in a given object collection O which are ranked according to a score that takes into consideration both spatial proximity and textual similarity, i.e., $\forall o \in P$ and $\forall r \in (O - P)$ will yield $sim_{dist}(Q, o) \leq sim_{dist}(Q, r)$. Specifically, the ranking score of object P for a top-k query is defined in the following equation:

$$Sim_{dist}(o, Q) = \alpha \cdot S_S(o.\rho, Q.\rho) + (1 - \alpha) \cdot S_T(o.\varphi, Q.\varphi)$$

where $S_S(o.\rho, Q.\rho)$ is the spatial Euclidian distance between ojbects $o.\rho$ and $Q.\rho$, $S_T(o.\varphi, Q.\varphi)$ is the text distance (inverted text similarity) between $o.\varphi$ and $Q.\varphi$, and $\alpha \in [0, 1]$.

2.2   Spatial Proximity and Textual Similarity

The spatial proximity S_S is defined as the normalized Euclidean distance: $S_S = \frac{dist(o.\rho, Q.\rho)}{dist_{max}}$, where $dist(o.\rho, Q.\rho)$ is the Euclidian distance between all objects $o \in O$ and Q. The text similarity can be evaluated by kinds of similarity strategies, e.g., language mode [4], cosine similarity strategy [15] or BM25 [3]. So, the textual distance can be defined as $S_T = 1 - Sim(o.\varphi, Q.\varphi)$. From the analysis before, we can see that, the real texts of the spatial objects are short. Existing co-occurrence based strategies have been introduced based on an intuitive assumption that many common words exist in similar texts. However, these methods are inappropriate for measuring similarities between short texts, e.g., sentences, because for short texts common words are few or even null. To tackle such problem, many approaches have been applied to evaluate the semantic similarity between short text, i.e., sentences which can be classified into: knowledge based strategy [17], corpus based strategy [9], syntax based strategy [9] or hybrid based strategy [9,11].

To measure the semantic text similarity $S_T(Q.\varphi, o.\varphi)$ between two short texts, we apply the state-of-the-art strategies by assembling multiple similarity metric features together [9,11]. Note that a short text is composed of a set of words and

	good	latte	relaxation			good	latte	relaxation
rest	0.0541	0.2345	0.6739		rest	0.0541	0.2345	**0.6739**
nice	0.4255	0.0184	0.1696	→	nice	0.4255	0.0184	0.1696
coffee	0.1950	0.4545	0.2126		coffee	0.1950	0.4545	0.2126
shop	0.1252	0.2325	0.2021		shop	0.1252	0.2325	0.2021
	(a)					(b)		

0.4255	0.0184		**0.4255**		
0.1950	**0.4545**		0.1950		
0.1252	0.2325		0.1252		
(c)			(d)		

Fig. 2. Semantic similarity measurement between two texts

therefore, the similarity score between two texts is the overall scores of all the word pairs whose components belong to each text, respectively [9]. As such, they apply three different kinds of *string* similarity [4] and corpus based *semantic* similarity strategy to evaluate the word semantic similarity. We have introduced how to measure the similarity between words. Here we illustrate how to obtain the similarity between sentences. Let us take two texts of Q and o_3 from Fig. 1 as an example. Here, we denote $S = Q.\varphi$ and $P = o_2.\varphi$. After removing all stop words and lemmatizing, we obtain $S=Good\ latte\ relaxation$. $P=Rest\ delicious\ coffee\ shop$. Through similarity measuring on each combination of word pair for the S and P, we construct a similarity matrix and each element represents the overall similarity score of the word pair, i.e., aggregation of semantic similarities, e.g., string-based and corpus-based similarities. To obtain the score between texts, we first find the maximal-valued element (i.e., representative word). Then the related row and column which include this element are removed. This process is recursively executed and finally all the similarities of the representative words have been extracted (i.e., Fig. 2. The similarity between texts is computed as follows: $Sim(S, P) = \frac{\sum_{i=1}^{|min(|S|,|P|)|} \rho_i(|S|+|P|)}{2|S|*|P|}$, where ρ_i is the value of the representative word of round i. Therefore we have $Sim(S, P)=\frac{(0.6739+0.4545+0.4255)(3+4)}{2*3*4}=0.4532$ and $S_T(S, P) = 1 - Sim(S, P) = 0.5468$.

2.3 A General Framework

To efficiently retrieve the top-k objects, a number of indexing techniques has been applied, in which we select one representative technique [4]. The authors proposed a hybrid indexing structure, i.e., IR-tree, that utilizes both the spatial and textual information. The IR-tree is essentially an R-tree and each node is enriched with reference to an inverted file for the objects contained in the subtree rooted at the node. The IR-tree augments each node of the R-tree with a summary of the text content of the objects in the corresponding subtree which is applied to describe all the texts in the entries of the child node. It estimates a bound of the text relevancy to a query of all texts contained in the subtree.

---

[4] Three representative strategies, i.e., $NLCS$, $NMCLCS_1$, and $NMCLCS_n$, have been applied. Refer [9] for detail.

The top-k objects are retrieved by applying the best first search strategy and the priority queue.

3   Proposed Approach

We propose efficient strategies for extracting the top-k similar spatial textual objects by considering semantic information. Before introducing the proposed approach, we discuss how to exploit existing techniques for top-k similar spatial textual retrieval.

3.1   Baseline Strategy

To efficiently retrieve the top-k objects, the main challenge is how to index for both spatial and textual information. A naïve strategy [13] is to compute the spatial proximity using a R-tree and measure the text similarity by applying an inverted list. Then we can combine them to obtain the top-k objects. However, evaluating all the candidate objects in the data collection is time consuming. Another simple approach is to use the inverted list/R-tree to generate a set of top candidate objects based on textual similarity/spatial proximity and then evaluate the spatial proximity/textual similarity of the candidates using R-tree/inverted list. However, this approach is not efficient neither. There is no intuitive way to determine the number of candidate objects that is needed in the first stage to ensure all the top-k objects are discovered.

Therefore, an integrated index structure [4,12] is necessary for efficient top-k similar spatial textual objects retrieval. As far as we know, most of the previous works apply word frequency based strategy. This is the first study that takes into account the semantic similarity to deal with the retrieval of similar spatial textual objects. The intuitive idea is that the textual information is always short and the traditional term frequency based text similarity measurement strategy is not effective. In this paper, we choose some strategies which are introduced in [4,12] as a baseline framework.

3.2   Semantic Aware Strategy

Our goal is to incorporate semantic information into a hybrid index structure, that the spatial proximity and textual similarity are taken into account together. A state-of-the-art work, i.e., [4]), tightly combines the inverted list and R-tree. From the similarity measurement strategy in Sec. 2.2, we can see that, given two texts S and P, $Sim(S, P)$ is related to the representative word pair of these two texts. We set $t_1^S, t_2^S, ..., t_n^S$ and $t_1^P, t_2^P, ..., t_m^P$ are terms of S and P, respectively. Suppose we have $n \leq m$, and then $Sim(S, P) = \sum_i^n Sim_r(t_i^S, P)$, where Sim_r indicates the similarity score between the representative word pair[5] (term in S and term in P). From the analysis, we can see that, the similarity score between

---

[5] $Sim_r = Sim \cdot \frac{1+|P|}{2*1*|P|}$ for length of a term is "1" and $| P |$ is the length of text P.

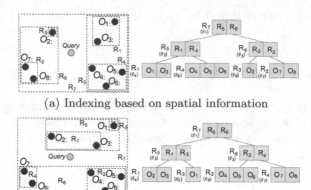

(a) Indexing based on spatial information

(b) Indexing based on both spatial and textual information

Fig. 3. The illustration of spatial and textual indexing

two texts by gathering the representative word similarity pair. The inverted list for textual information is built as follows: (1) all terms in the data collection are identified; and (2) a set of posting lists, each of which relates to a term t which is a sequence of pairs $< Sim(t, t'), textID >$ based on the descending order of similarity $Sim(t, t')$ between terms t and t'.

However, if the query text Q contains several terms $t_1^Q, t_2^Q, ..., t_n^Q$, how to obtain the order of the related texts? Since we obtain the ranked list from the inverted list, each term $t_i^Q (i \in n)$ corresponds to a ranked list. Therefore, we can easily apply the threshold algorithm [5] to obtain the order of top related texts to a query text Q.

In [4], the authors combine the spatial index and textual index in a hybrid index structure. Based on the strategy of index construction, we apply two methods and incorporate semantic information into index construction.

3.2.1   Index Structure Construction

IRS **Strategy:** The *IRS* index structure is to incorporate semantic information into IR-tree [4] (i.e., IR-tree with semantic similarity). The tree structure of *SIR* is essentially R-tree and each node of which is enriched with reference to an inverted list for the spatial objects contained in the sub-tree rooted at the node. The tree structure of *IRS* is constructed by means of an insert operation which is adapted from R-tree [7]. The operation includes ChooseLeaf and Split which augments each node of the R-tree with a summary of the text content of the objects in the corresponding subtree. Specifically, each node contains a pointer to an inverted list that describes the objects in the subtree rooted at the node. In index structure of *IRS*, a leaf node contains a number of entries of the form $(O, R, O.\varphi)$, where O is the objects in the data collection, R is the bounding rectangle of object O, and $O.\varphi$ is the textual description of object O. A pointer to an inverted list for the text of the objects is stored in a leaf node.

A non-leaf node R contains a number of entries of the form $(D, R, D.\varphi)$, where D is the address of a child node of R, R is the minimum bounding rectangle of all rectangles in the entries of the child node and $D.\varphi$ is the identifier of a textual summary. In this paper, we incorporate semantic information into the textual description of objects. In an inverted list, each term corresponds to a list of texts of objects with similarity score based on the descending order of the score between the term and the text. In IRS, the textual summary represents all texts in the entries of the child node, enabling us to estimate a bound of the text similarity with a query. In this paper, we apply maximum weight of each term in the textual summary referenced by $D.\varphi$ since the semantic similarity between two texts is related with the maximum similarity of all word pairs. Based on the objects which are illustrated in Fig. 1, we construct a indexing structure which is presented in Fig. 3(a). Each inverted list is corresponds a node, il_4, il_5, il_6 and il_7 correspond leaf node and il_1, il_2 and il_3 correspond non-leaf node.

$DIRS$ **Strategy:** From the analysis on construction of IRS index, we can see that the construction of tree structure only takes the spatial information into consideration, i.e., the rectangle enclose the most closing objects based on the spatial information. We take an example to illustrate the procedure. In Fig. 1, o_1, o_2 and o_3 are spatially related. For IRS strategy, objects o_1 and o_3 is spatially related for $S_S(o_1, o_3) = 0.10$ which is larger than $S_S(o_1, o_2) = 0.23$ and $S_S(o_2, o_3) = 0.17$. From the textual information, $o_3.\varphi$ is much more semantically similar to $o_2.\varphi$ but not $o_1.\varphi$. By taking both spatial and textual information, we find that $Sim_{dist}(o_2, o_3)$ is closed among the Sim_{dist} pairs of o_1, o_2 and o_3. Therefore, object o_2 and o_3 are enclosed in the same rectangle.

Unlike the tree construction method of IRS strategy, this $DIRS$ strategy aims to take both spatial and textual information into consideration during tree construction (which is similar to DIR in [4]). The structure of leaf node has the same format as R-tree. A non-leaf node R contains a number of entries of the from $(D, R, D.\varphi)$. To choose an appropriate insertion path fro a new coming object, the $DIRS$ strategy takes into account both the spatial and textual information. We describe how to incorporate textual information. We denote $En_1, En_2, ..., En_k$ be the entries in the current node, and let o_{new} be the object to be inserted. In R-tree, the area enlarging of inserting o_{new} into $En_i, 1 \leq i \leq k$, we use a metric $EnlargeRec(En_k)$ to describe the area enlarging, here $EnlargeRec(En_k) = Rec(En_k^{new}.R) - Rec(En_k.R)$. where $Rec(En_k^{new}.R)$ is the new entry of rectangle En_k after inclusion of new object o_{new}. By considering textual information, the area enlarging could be:

$$EnlargeRec_{\rho\varphi}(En_k) = (1 - \delta) \cdot \frac{Rec_{En_k}}{Rec_{max}} + \delta \cdot S_T(En_k, O.\varphi)$$

where δ is a parameter to adjust the effect of spatial information and textual information, Rec_{max} is the area of the minimum bounding rectangle enclosing all objects.

The construction of $DIRS$ index differs from R-tree on the insertion operation. When choosing the subtree, the strategy finds at every level the most

Table 1. Distance value of objects and rectangles to query Q

O	$Sim_{dist}(Q, o)$	R	$min_{\rho\varphi}(Q, R)$	
			(a) IRS strategy	(b) $DIRS$ strategy
o_1	0.26			
o_2	0.23	R_1	0.22	0.32
o_3	0.32	R_2	0.42	0.20
o_4	0.50	R_3	0.30	0.17
o_5	0.39	R_4	0.11	0.45
o_6	0.49	R_5	0.05	0.06
o_7	0.69	R_6	0.27	0.50
o_8	0.56	R_7	0.00	0.00

(a)distance value of IRS strategy; (b)distance value of $DIRS$ strategy.

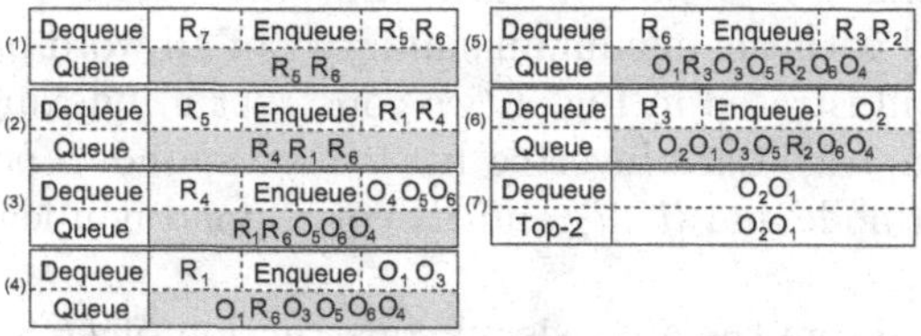

(a) Query processing based on IRS strategy

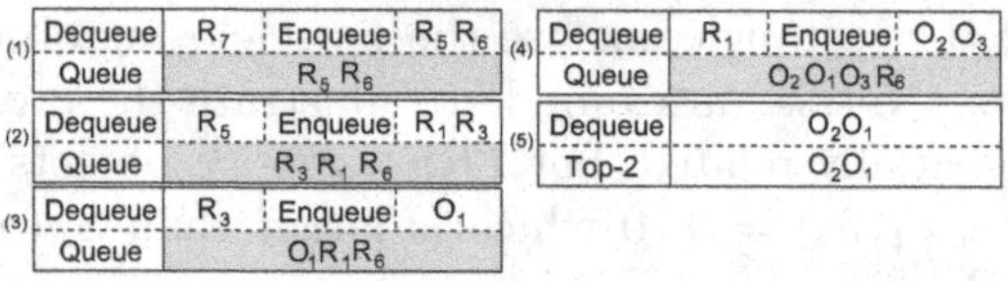

(b) Query processing based on $DIRS$ strategy

Fig. 4. Illustration on top-2 objects retrieval

suitable subtree to enclose the new entry until a leaf node is reached, i.e., it chooses subtrees that minimize the value of $EnlargeRec_{\rho\varphi}$. The split operation also incorporates text semantic similarity into consideration which leads all the objects in the related rectangle has the most similar Sim_{dist}.

3.2.2 Query Processing

Before we present the query processing, we introduce a variable, $min_{\rho\varphi}$. Given a query Q and a node N in the index, the variable $min_{\rho\varphi}$ offers a lower bound on the actual spatial textual distance between Q and objects enclosed in the rectangle of the current node. The bound can be used to order and efficiently prune the paths of the search space in the spatial textual index. The $min_{\rho\varphi} = \alpha \cdot S_Smin(Q.\rho, N.R.\rho) + (1 - \alpha) \cdot S_T(Q.\varphi, N.\varphi)$, where $S_Smin(Q.\rho, N.R.\rho)$ is the minimum Euclidian distance between $Q.\rho$ and $N.R.\rho$. When searching the index for k objects to a query Q, one must decide at each visited node of the hybrid index which entry to search first. Therefore, $min_{\rho\varphi}$ can guarantee every objects $o \in O$ whose distance $Sim_{dist}(o, Q) < min_{\rho\varphi}$. The illustration is presented in Fig. 3(b).

The best first traversal algorithm [8] has been exploited and a priority queue is applied to keep track of the nodes and objects that have yet to be visited. We

Table 2. Dataset statistics

size	Different size of data collection							
	1k		5k		10k		20k	
Type	(A)	(B)	(A)	(B)	(A)	(B)	(A)	(B)
Avg. length	7.32	6.12	7.54	6.03	7.29	6.45	7.63	6.10
Min. length	5	2	5	2	5	2	5	2
Max. length	21	10	21	10	21	10	21	10

Note:

* (A) is the original text and (B) denotes after preprocessing, i.e., removing stopword, lemmatization.

denote $min_{\rho\varphi}(Q, R)$ as the bound between the query Q and rectangle R, and $Sim_{dist}(o, Q)$ as the distance between each object with Q in Table. 1. Note here the algorithm only evaluates the scores between Q and the objects or rectangles traversed by the algorithm, not all the scores in Table. 1. We take an example to illustrate the algorithm that retrieves the top-2 objects. The IRS strategy starts firstly enqueueing R_7 and then follows the steps illustrated in Fig. 4(a).

From the illustration of IRS strategy, we know that the top-2 objects o_2,o_1 are retrieved by accessing R_5,R_6,R_1,R_2,R_3,R_4, which means large percentage of rectangles have been accessed to find the top results. This is due to the reason that the index structure of IRS is built on the heuristic of minimizing the area of each enclosing rectangle in the inner nodes. However, each node corresponds a textual description which means we should take the textual information into consideration. The query processing of $DIRS$ strategy is presented in Fig. 4(b). Considering textual information, the minimal rectangle bound has been changed. Therefore, the index structure is built not only based on the spatial proximity but also the textual similarity. Objects which are spatially and textually close are enclosed in the same rectangle. In the query processing, some unnecessary nodes are avoid to be accessed. Therefore, the top-2 results o_2 and o_1 are retrieved by accessing only R_5, R_1, and R_3 which is efficient than the IRS strategy.

4   Experimental Evaluation

In this section, we evaluate the performance of the proposed strategies based on two aspects, i.e., effectiveness and efficiency. We conducted experiments using 16-core Intel(R) Xeon(R) E5530 server which runs Debian 2.6.26-2. All the algorithms were written in C and compiled by GNU gcc.

Dataset Description. We conducted experiments on the dataset which was first used in [2]. It includes the spatial textual information, that there are totally 225,098 users and 22,506,721 unique objects (texts). The textual information is from Twitter, and the spatial data is extracted from Foursquare, Twitter, Gowalla, Echofon, and Gravity [2]. To evaluate the scalability of the proposed strategy, we randomly extracted varying size of data collection as $1k$, $5k$, $10k$, and $20k$ objects. The statistics of the dataset is presented in Table. 2.

Evaluation Metrics: To evaluate the effectiveness and efficiency, we compare the following strategies, i.e., *baseline* (IR-tree with no semantic incorporated),

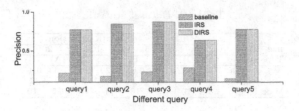

Fig. 5. Effectiveness comparison

IRS (IR-tree with semantic incorporated) and $DIRS$ (textual enhanced IR-tree with semantic incorporated). We randomly extracted 5 objects from the dataset as queries and 50 objects from the data collection. Each Sim_{dist} has been evaluated by human. For each query, the average value of Sim_{dist} is regarded as the ground truth. The precision is defined as the Pearson Correlation Coefficient between the evaluated results and human ground truth.

4.1 Effectiveness Evaluation

There are two parameters employed. One is the fusion parameter that combines spatial proximity and textual similarity, i.e., α. Another is the textual impact factor δ which is used in $DIRS$. We conducted cross-validation experimental evaluation on different parameter setting for α and δ in $[0.1, 0.9]$ with varying granularity 0.1. After the test, we obtained the optimal values, i.e., $\alpha=0.71$ for *baseline*; $\alpha=0.68$ for IRS; $\alpha=0.68$ and $\delta=0.2$ for $DIRS$.

The comparison on effectiveness of the three different strategies is illustrated in Fig. 5. We can see that, the semantic similarity oriented strategies, i.e., IRS and $DIRS$, have higher precision compared with the *baseline*. The reason is that for short text (i.e., sentences), the similarity is mainly determined by the semantic similarity, which is in accordance with the previous work [14,11]. This paper is the first work that explores how to effectively integrate the spatial proximity and semantic similarity together.

4.2 Efficiency Evaluation

To evaluate the efficiency, we set the parameters as the optimal values that have been explained in Sec. 4.1. We conducted experiments to evaluate the scalability, i.e., varying the size of data collection and the value of k. To test the effect on the size of data collection, we randomly extracted 10 queries for each data collection and reported the average execution time, as shown in Fig. 6(a). We can see that $DIRS$ is faster than IRS strategy. The reason is that $DIRS$ does not need to traverse many useless candidate nodes by summarizing both the spatial and textual information into single node.

To evaluate the effect of the value of k, we randomly extracted 10 queries and reported the average results based on different k, as illustrated in Fig. 6(b). For a small value of k, both IRS and $DIRS$ are fast because the top objects

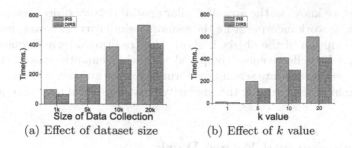

(a) Effect of dataset size   (b) Effect of k value

Fig. 6. Efficiency comparison

can be output by accessing only a small number of nodes. When k increases, the execution time of both strategies increases. However, the $DIRS$ strategy obtains is faster than the IRS approach because the seamless tight hybrid strategy used in $DIRS$ is more efficient than the loose combination technique employed in IRS.

5 Related Work

Many types of index techniques have been proposed to tackle the efficiency issue, e.g., suffix array, signature file, or inverted list. Inverted list is competitive with other index techniques that has been applied in many large-scale IR system. Some works concentrate on improving the query efficiency [16] while others aim at reducing the index cost [20]. These techniques can be applied in our work but it beyonds the scope of this study.

Recently, much attention has been given to the issue of similar spatial textual objects retrieval. In [19], the authors deal with the problem of web document retrieval as keyword based search in a predefined region. They build an index which loosely combines the inverted list and R*-tree. When the number of the query words increase, the algorithm needs to access multiple R*-trees and intersect the results. In addition, building an inverted list and a R*-tree for each keyword requires substantial storage.

To tackle this issue, tight hybrid indexing techniques have been proposed. In [19], the authors introduce to combine the two aspects (i.e., spatial and textual) in two stages. However, it is not suitable for top-k search because we cannot determine the value of k in the first stage. In [4,12], they tightly combine the inverted list and R-tree. Therefore, the comprehensive value of the spatial and textual information can be used to prune the search space at query time. In [20], the authors compute the text similarity and spatial proximity independently and then combine the two ranking scores. An index structure that integrates signature file and R-tree to enable keyword search on spatial data has been proposed in [18]. The hybrid index structure combines the R*-tree and bitmap index to process the m-closet keyword query which requires spatially closest objects matching m keywords. However, all these strategies are not competitive with the strategy in [4,12].

As far as we know, in the area of similar spatial textual object retrieval, there is no previous work incorporating the semantic similarity. However, because the textual description of the object is short, the traditional term frequency based strategy has low effectiveness compared with the semantic based strategy. In this paper, we incorporate semantic information into an integral index structure which is capable of measuring the similarity between spatial textual objects more precisely.

6   Conclusion and Future Work

In this paper, we proposed a semantic aware strategy by incorporating semantic information in textual similarity which is important in top-k similar spatial textual objects extraction. In addition, we improve the efficiency by taking spatial and textual information into consideration when indexing the data. Extensive experimental evaluation demonstrates that our proposal is more effective and efficient than the baseline strategy. In the future, we will concentrate on applying different techniques for index construction and enhance our proposed techniques for various of access patterns.

References

1. Chen, Y.-Y., Suel, T., Markowetz, A.: Efficient query processing in geographic web search engines. In: SIGMOD, pp. 277–288.
2. Cheng, Z., Caverlee, J., Lee, K., Sui, D.Z.: Exploring millions of footprints in location sharing services. In: ICWSM, pp. 81–88 (2011)
3. Christoforaki, M., He, J., Dimopoulos, C., Markowetz, A., Suel, T.: Text vs. space: efficient geo-search query processing. In: CIKM, pp. 423–432 (2011)
4. Cong, G., Jensen, C.S., Wu, D.: Efficient retrieval of the top-k most relevant spatial web objects. PVLDB 2(1), 337–348 (2009)
5. Fagin, R., Lotem, A., Naor, M.: Optimal aggregation algorithms for middleware. In: PODS, pp. 102–113 (2001)
6. Felipe, I.D., Hristidis, V., Rishe, N.: Keyword search on spatial databases. In: ICDE, pp. 656–665 (2008)
7. Guttman, A.: R-trees: a dynamic index structure for spatial searching. In: SIGMOD, pp. 47–57 (1984)
8. Hjaltason, G.R., Samet, H.: Distance browsing in spatial databases. TODS 24(2), 265–318 (1999)
9. Islam, A., Inkpen, D.: Semantic text similarity using corpus-based word similarity and string similarity. TKDD 2(2), 1–25 (2008)
10. Khodaei, A., Shahabi, C., Li, C.: Hybrid indexing and seamless ranking of spatial and textual features of web documents. In: Bringas, P.G., Hameurlain, A., Quirchmayr, G. (eds.) DEXA 2010, Part I. LNCS, vol. 6261, pp. 450–466. Springer, Heidelberg (2010)
11. Li, Y., McLean, D., Bandar, Z., O'Shea, J., Crockett, K.A.: Sentence similarity based on semantic nets and corpus statistics. TKDE 18(8), 1138–1150 (2006)
12. Li, Z., Lee, K.C.K., Zheng, B., Lee, W.C., Lee, D.L., Wang, X.: Ir-tree: An efficient index for geographic document search. TKDE 23(4), 585–599 (2011)

13. Martins, B., Silva, M.J., Andrade, L.: Indexing and ranking in geo-ir systems. In: GIS, pp. 31–34 (2005)
14. Mihalcea, R., Corley, C., Strapparava, C.: Corpus-based and knowledge-based measures of text semantic similarity. In: AAAI, pp. 775–780 (2006)
15. Rocha-Junior, J.B., Gkorgkas, O., Jonassen, S., Nørvåg, K.: Efficient processing of top-k spatial keyword queries. In: Pfoser, D., Tao, Y., Mouratidis, K., Nascimento, M.A., Mokbel, M., Shekhar, S., Huang, Y. (eds.) SSTD 2011. LNCS, vol. 6849, pp. 205–222. Springer, Heidelberg (2011)
16. Strohman, T., Turtle, H., Croft, W.B.: Optimization strategies for complex queries. In: SIGIR, pp. 219–225 (2005)
17. Tsatsaronis, G., Varlamis, I., Vazirgiannis, M.: Text relatedness based on a word thesaurus. JAIR 37(1), 1–40 (2010)
18. Zhang, D., Chee, Y.M., Mondal, A., Tung, A.K.H., Kitsuregawa, M.: Keyword search in spatial databases: Towards searching by document. In: ICDE, pp. 688–699 (2009)
19. Zhou, Y., Xie, X., Wang, C., Gong, Y., Ma, W.Y.: Hybrid index structures for location-based web search. In: CIKM, pp. 155–162 (2005)
20. Zobel, J., Moffat, A.: Inverted files for text search engines. ACM Comput. Surv. 38(2) (2006)

Indicating Important Parts in Searched Web Pages by Retrieval Keywords

Shunichi Yokoo and Noriaki Yoshiura

Department of Information and Computer Sciences, Saitama University
255, Shimo-ookubo, Sakura-ku, Saitama, Japan
{syokoo,yoshiura}@fmx.ics.saitama-u.ac.jp
http://www.fmx.ics.saitama-u.ac.jp

Abstract. Users cannot always find retrieval keywords immediately in web pages that are obtained by search engines. There are several reasons, one of which is that the retrieval keywords are hidden in searched web pages. To solve the problem, this paper develops software that indicates important HTML elements in searched web pages. The software finds HTML elements that are the most closely related with the retrieval keywords and indicates important part in searched web pages. This paper also evaluates the software by experiments. The results of the experiments show that the software can indicate important parts more correctly than existing similar software and reduce time taken to find the retrieval keywords in searched web pages.

1 Introduction

Development of information technology provides varieties of web page designs. In addition to HTML[11], Cascading Style Sheets (CSS)[6] or JavaScript enables to create many kinds of designs of web pages. However, the variety of web page designs has several negative effects; it is difficult to find retrieval keywords for search engines in the complicated web pages that are found by search engine with the retrieval keywords. One of such complicated web pages is tab menu web page. Figure 1 is one of tab menu web pages in Japanese. To click the tab that is within the frame in Figure 1 changes the contents that are displayed on the web page, but the HTML file for the web page does not change. The HTML file contains all contents for all tabs and web browsers display the content that corresponds to each tab on the web page; the displayed content is a part of the HTML file and to view all parts of the HTML file requires to click all tabs in the web pages.

Search engines such as Google collect many HTML files of many web pages to construct web page database, which is used to search web pages by keywords. Search engines also collect HTML files of tab menu web pages. All parts of HTML files reflect the web page database; if retrieval keywords exist on a HTML file of a tab menu web page, the web page can appear on the search results of the retrieval keywords. However, all contents in the HTML file of the tab menu web page do not appear on web browsers and the retrieval keywords are not always

L. Cao et al. (Eds.): BSIC/BSI 2013, LNAI 8178, pp. 250–263, 2013.

found on web browsers. Web browsers have a function of searching keywords in displayed contents, but the retrieval keywords for search engines do not exist on web browsers. Users that search web pages by the retrieval keywords may have to click tab buttons manually to find the keywords on web pages. Users that are unfamiliar with PCs cannot always find the keywords on web pages. Thus, it is useful to point out the places of retrieval keywords. In Figure 1, to click "Mac support products" changes displayed web pages as Figure 2. If the word that appears on Figure 2 but not on Figure 1 is used as a retrieval keyword, the search results include the web page of Figure 1, but the retrieval keyword does not appear on Figure 1.

This paper implements software that points out the place of searched keywords on web pages. The software is plug-in software of web browsers; when search engine users input keywords to search engine, the software obtains keywords and the search results from search engines. After the users click one of URL in search results, web browsers display a web page but may not display a part of the web page containing the retrieval keywords. The implemented software analyzes the web page, finds a part of the web page containing the retrieval keywords and displays the part of the web page.

This paper is organized as follows; Section 2 discusses the reasons why retrieval keywords are not found easily on searched web pages. Section 3 explains the software that is implemented in this paper. Section 4 evaluates the software by experiments. Section 5 concludes this paper.

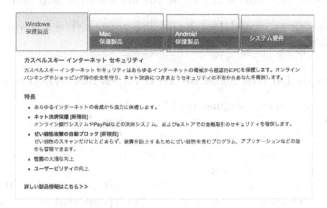

Fig. 1. Sample of tab menu user interface

2   Reasons Why Retrieval Keywords Are Not Found Easily on Searched Web Pages

This section discusses the reasons why retrieval keywords are not found easily on searched web pages. This paper focuses on texts of HTML files but not on

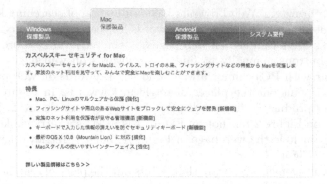

Fig. 2. Fig. 1 that changes by clicking tab menu button

Adobe Flash or images as web page contents. The following is the reasons why retrieval keywords are not found easily on searched web pages.

1. Database that is used by search engine is not up to date.
2. Keywords do not exist on web pages but synonyms exist.
3. Keywords appear separately on web pages.
4. Keywords do not appear on the display areas of web pages.
5. Parts of web pages containing keywords are not in display state.

This paper focuses on second, fourth and fifth reasons. The following subsection explains each of them.

2.1   Keywords Do Not Exist on Web Pages but Synonyms Exist

Fuzzy searching of search engines enables to find web pages that contain synonyms of search keywords but not search keywords. If the users of search engines do not know fuzzy searching, they do not find the parts of web pages that contain synonyms of retrieval keywords and they must be careful to find the parts that are related with the keywords.

One of the solutions for this problem is to use Google Toolbar[10] or Google Quick Scroll[9], which points out the parts of web pages that contain keywords or synonyms of keywords. When web browsers display web pages that are in search results, these two pieces of software give explanation balloons for at most three parts of web pages that are related with retrieval keywords. To click the balloons scrolls web pages to show the part that is related with retrieval keywords. However, the software is available for Google search engine[7].

2.2   Keywords Do Not Appear on the Display Areas of Web Pages

All contents of long or wide web pages are not displayed on web browsers. In this case, the parts of web pages are displayed and scroll bars appear on web browsers. If retrieval keywords do not appear on display areas of the web pages that are found by search engines, the users of search engines must move display areas of web pages to find the parts of web pages that include the retrieval keywords. The longer or the wider web pages are, the more time it takes to find the parts of web pages that are related with retrieval keywords.

This problem can be solved partially by Google Toolbar or Google Quick Scroll, which is explained above. The parts of web pages that the software points out are the parts that Google search engine decides that are related with retrieval keywords. If retrieval keywords appear on several places of web pages, it is difficult to point out the best part that is related with the retrieval keywords.

2.3 Parts of Web Pages Containing Keywords Are Not in Display State

In tab menu web pages like Figure 1 and Figure 2, to view all contents of web pages requires to click all tab menu buttons. Undisplayed contents of web pages are out of scope of web browser searching function. If retrieval keywords exist on undisplayed contents of web pages, it takes much time to find the keywords on the web pages.

There are some researches of the solutions of this problem. One of them gives the way of revising web pages using user operation records on the web pages. However, this solution gives only the way of revising web pages and does not guarantee good revisions of web pages. As far as the authors of this paper know, no research is useful to this problem.

3 Implemented Software

This paper solves the the following problems.

- Keywords do not exist on web pages but synonyms exist.
- Keywords do not appear on the display areas of web pages.
- Parts of web pages containing keywords are not in display state.

This paper implements software to solve the problems. The overview of software is as follows:

1. Obtaining retrieval keywords that are input to search engines
2. Obtaining synonyms of input retrieval keywords
3. Finding parts of web pages that are related with retrieval keywords
4. Checking whether the parts that are related with retrieval keywords are displayed or not
5. Changing the related parts so that they will be displayed if they are not displayed
6. Moving display areas so that the related parts of web pages are in display areas by vertical or horizontal scroll

The following explains the functions that are necessary for the software. This paper implements software as Google Chrome Extension[8].

3.1 Obtaining Input Retrieval Keywords

Input retrieval keywords are contained in query strings of URLs that are sent to search engines. The software obtains input retrieval keywords from query strings. URLs of search results that are sent from search engines also contain retrieval keywords. The software also obtains retrieval keywords from the URLs that are sent from search engines. The software is capable of search results of Google and Yahoo[13].

3.2 Obtaining Synonyms

The implemented software obtains synonyms of retrieval keywords by using Weblio thesaurus[12], which is a web online thesaurus. Weblio thesaurus enables to look up many kinds of thesaurus databases simultaneously. There are several ways of using Weblio thesaurus; Weblio thesaurus can be Japanese-English and Japanese-Japanese dictionaries. The implemented software uses Weblio thesaurus as Japanese-English dictionary because of the following reasons; Weblio thesaurus as Japanese-Japanese dictionary gives too many synonyms of retrieval keywords to select the parts of web pages that are related with the keywords based on synonyms. Weblio thesaurus as Japanese-English dictionary also gives synonyms of keywords and the number of synonyms is suitable to select the parts of web pages that are related with the keywords based on synonyms. Thus, the implemented software uses Weblio thesaurus as Japanese-English dictionary and accesses the URL of Weblio thesaurus [1] to obtain synonyms.

3.3 Finding Parts of Web Pages That Are Related with Keywords

To point out parts of web pages where retrieval keywords exist is not so enough that the parts that the users of search engines would like to view are displayed. If the small number of retrieval keywords are used, there is a possibility that several parts of web pages contains all keywords. However, all parts that contain all retrieval keywords are not related with retrieval keywords. Thus, the software must find and show parts of web pages that are related with all retrieval keywords.

This paper defines the parts that are related with keywords as follows.

- Parts that contain all retrieval keywords.
- Parts that contain all retrieval keywords except one keyword and a synonym of the keyword.

Up to here, this paper uses term "part" of web pages without formal definition. Now, this paper defines the unit of part to be one paragraph on web pages. Concretely, one block element of HTML files is the unit of part[11]. All block elements that contain block elements may be also units of parts, but in this paper

---

[1] http://ejje.weblio.jp/english-thesaurus/content/

the block elements that contain block elements that do not contain retrieval keywords is defined to be units of parts.

Web pages may have many parts that are related with retrieval keywords and it is difficult to select the good part among the many parts. To solve this problem, this paper assigns importance degree to parts of web pages. Importance of the parts of web pages is defined by emphasis of the parts. Web pages are kinds of documents and there are many researches of selecting important parts of documents [2,3,1] and of HTML files[4,5]. The researches for HTML files focus on documents of web pages, but this paper focuses on visual effects of web pages to evaluate importance of the parts of web pages. One of the reasons of focusing on visual effects is that the implemented software is plug-in software of web browsers and is incapable of heavy processes. Analysis of documents of web pages is a heavy process for plug-in software of web browsers, but checking emphasis parts of web pages is a light process.

3.4   Checking State of Display

This paper surveys many web pages before implementing the software. Several web pages are tab menu web pages. As described above, all HTML files of tab menu web pages are considered on search engine databases. If retrieval keywords exist on HTML files of tab menu web pages, the tab menu web pages are listed on the search engine results. Even if the parts of web pages that contain retrieval keywords are not displayed when web browsers obtain HTML files of the web pages, the web pages are listed on the search results of the retrieval keywords. Thus, the implemented software must check whether the parts of web pages that are related with retrieval keywords are in display states. The survey of this paper shows that tab menu web pages are constructed by style sheet, which changes display states of the parts of web pages. The implemented software analyzes style sheets to find display areas of web pages; concretely, the software checks whether display attribute in style information is "none", whether visibility attribute is "hidden" and whether collapse attribute or opacity attribute is "0".

3.5   Showing the Important Parts of Web Pages

As described in Section 3.4, style sheets decide whether the parts of web pages are displayed or not. The implemented software changes display states of the parts of web pages by rewriting attributes in style sheets. The software also moves important parts of web pages on the center of web browsers by horizontal or vertical scroll based on the coordinates of the important parts of web pages.

4   Experiment

This section experiments to evaluate the implemented software and discusses the result of experiments.

4.1   Experiments of Obtaining Synonyms

To evaluate efficiency of obtaining synonyms of retrieval keywords, this paper experiments by using five words, which are "speed", "method", "back somersault", "part time job" and "first" in Japanese. The experiment obtains the synonyms of these words by the implemented software. As a result, Google search engine obtains two synonyms for "speed", two synonyms for "method", one synonym for "back somersault", one synonym for "part time job" and four synonyms for "first". The implemented software obtains one synonym for "speed", one synonyms for "method", no synonym for "back somersault", one synonym for "part time job" and no synonym for "first".

4.2   Finding the Parts of Web Pages that Are Related with Keywords

This paper experiments to evaluate availability of finding the parts of web pages that are related with retrieval keywords in Japanese. The experiment compares the implemented software with Google Quick Scroll as follows; the implemented software and Google Quick Scroll point out the parts of web pages that are related with keywords. The parts that are pointed out by these two pieces of software are compared. The experiment uses the following five keyword lists for the implemented software and Google Quick Scroll.

1. "Banshee"
   "Banshee" is a name of a character in a Japanese comic. The result of the search engine for this keyword includes the following Wikipedia web page.

   "http://ja.wikipedia.org/wiki/%E3%83%A6%E3%83%8B %E3%82%B3 %E3%83%BC%E3%83%B3%E3%82%AC%E3%83%B3%E3%83 %80%E3%83%A0"

   As an important part, Google Quick Scroll points out the upper part of the web page with the balloon that contains "Someone has a popular name Banshee". The implemented software points out the middle part of the web page. This part, which contains caption "Banshee", explains Banshee. The implemented software points out better part than Google Quick Scroll for "Banshee".

2. NVIDIA GeForce GTX 690 Base Clock
   Five words "NVIDIA GeForce GTX 690 Base Clock" are used as retrieval keywords for search engine. The result of the search engine for these keywords includes the following web page.

   "http://www.nvidia.co.jp/object/geforce-gtx-690-jp.html"

   Google Quick Scroll points out the part of the web page where "base" and "clock" are separately placed. Figure 3 shows the displayed web page by Google Quick Scroll in Japanese. The implemented software points out the part of the web page where "base clock" exists. Figure 4 shows the displayed web page by the implemented software in Japanese and "base clock" exists in the frame in Figure 4. This displayed web page is obtained by clicking the second left tab menu button. This part is preferable to the part that Google Quick Scroll points out and this part can be displayed by clicking tab menu button. Google Quick Scroll cannot display this part but the implemented software can.

Fig. 3. Google Quick Scroll

3. "Nagatachoibun" "Ozawa"
   Two words "Nagatachoibun" and "Ozawa" are used as retrieval keywords for the search engine. "Nagatacho" is a name of place in Japan and this place is the center of politics. "Nagatachoibun" is a name of blog for politics. "Ozawa" is a name of a famous politician. Using the words as retrieval keywords for the search engine obtains the list of web pages that are related with politics. The result of the search engine for these keywords includes the following web page.

   "http://ameblo.jp/aratakyo/"

   Google Quick Scroll points out no part of the web page because all parts of the web page are related with the keywords. The implemented software points out the part of the web page where "Ozawa" is a caption. This paper does not decide which Google Quick Scroll or the implemented software is better, but this experiment shows that the implemented software recognizes emphasized parts as important parts.
4. "Yokoo Shunichi" "University"
   Two words "Yokoo Shunichi" and "University" are used as retrieval keywords for the search engine. The result of the search engine for these keywords includes the following Wikipedia web page.

Fig. 4. Implemented software

"http://ja.wikipedia.org/wiki/%E6%97%A9%E7%A8%B2%E7%94%B0
    %E5%A4%A7%E5%AD%A6%E3%81%AE%E4%BA%BA%E7%89%A9
    %E4%B8%80%E8%A6%A7"

Google Quick Scroll points out a part of the web page that contains "Shu-nichi". The implemented software does not find the part of the web page that contains "Yokoo Shunichi" and shows the message that the software does not find "Yokoo Shunichi". In fact, the web page does not have any information on "Yokoo Shunichi". Thus, the implemented software is better than Google Quick Scroll for the search results of these keywords.

5. successful failure "kobo"

"kobo" is an eBook device that is provided by Rakuten, Japanese Company. Using these three words as retrieval keywords for search engine obtains the list of web pages that are related with "kobo". The result of the search engine for these keywords includes the following blog web page.

"http://blog.livedoor.jp/lunarmodule7/"

This blog web page contains three articles for "kobo". Google Quick Scroll points out the part between second and third articles. The implemented software points out the part of the web page that contains the caption of the first article.

4.3   Showing the Important Parts of Web Pages

This paper experiments to evaluate availability of showing the important parts of web pages. The experiment inputs the HTML files satisfying the following conditions to the implemented software and checks whether the software shows the important parts of web pages.

Fig. 5. A web page found by the keyword "DDR3 R-DIMM Frequency transcend"

Fig. 6. A web page found by the keyword "Kaspersky capacity"

– The web pages of HTML files are tab menu web pages.
– Some words that are in the HTML files of tab menu web pages are not
  displayed without clicking a tab menu button.

This paper surveys the web pages on the Internet and finds 47 tab menu web
pages, which are used for the experiment. The HTML files of these tab menu
web pages have display parts and undisplay parts and to click tab menu button
changes display state of each part of web pages. The result of the experiment

Table 1. Time taken to find keywords

Web page \ examinee	A	B	C	D
Web page A	–	175sec	63sec	23sec
Web page B	60sec	49sec	18sec	11sec
Web page C	–	–	26sec	17sec

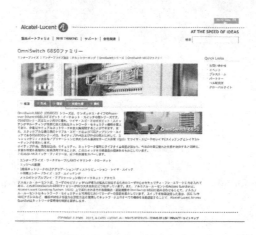

Fig. 7. A web page found by the keyword "Omniswitch 6850 price"

is that the implemented software successfully changes display states in 41 web pages among 47 web pages and does not change display states in 6 web pages. The following is the reason of failure of changing display states in the 6 web pages.

- Tab menu web pages are not constructed by style sheets. Some tab menu web pages are constructed by Ajax and the HTML files of the tab menu web pages do not contain contents that are displayed by clicking tab menu buttons.
- Tab menu web pages are constructed by float attribute and overflow attribute of style sheets. The implemented software does not focus on these attributes.

This experiment uses tab menu web pages, which are the search results for some retrieval keywords. In the case of tab menu web pages by Ajax, if retrieval keywords are words that appear on the parts of web pages and that are not displayed at first, the tab menu web pages are not listed in the search results because the HTML files of tab menu web pages by Ajax do not contain the retrieval keywords. Thus, failure of changing display states does not matter for the implemented software. On the other hand, the implemented software must handle float and overflow attributes in style sheets. This is a future work for the software.

Table 2. Time taken to indicate important parts

Web page \ user	author	software
Web page A	3sec	1sec
Web page B	4sec	1sec
Web page C	10sec	1sec

4.4   Saving Time to Find Important Parts for Retrieval Keywords

This paper experiments to evaluate availability of saving time to find the parts of web pages that are related with retrieval keywords. The examinees in the experiment are two persons who are familiar with computers and two persons who are unfamiliar with computers. The examinees use search engine by some retrieval keywords and view some web page that is in the list of search results. For each examinee, the experiment compares time from viewing the web pages to manually finding the important part of the web pages. The experiment also measures time that it takes that the implemented software points out the important part. The experiment uses the retrieval keywords that satisfy the following conditions.

- One of the web pages in the search results of the retrieval keywords does not immediately display the part that contains the retrieval keywords.
- To display the part that contains the retrieval keywords requires to click a tab menu button.
- It is not easy that the examinees find the part that is related with the retrieval keywords.

Table 1 and Table 2 show the results of the experiment. The examinee A and B are unfamiliar with computers and the examinee C and D are familiar with computers. The symbol "−" in the tables means that an examinee does not find the part that contains the retrieval keywords within 180 seconds. In these tables, Web page A is the web page in Figure 5, which is found by the keywords "DDR3 R-DIMM Frequency transcend". Figure 5 does not include "Frequency", but to click the frame in Figure 5 changes the web page that includes "Frequency". Web page B is the web page in Figure 6, which is found by the keywords "Kaspersky capacity". Figure 6 does not include "capacity", but to click the frame in Figure 6 changes the web page that includes "capacity". Web page C is the web page in Figure 7, which is found by the keywords "Omniswitch 6850 price". Figure 7 does not include "price", but to click the frame in Figure 7 changes the web page that includes "price" below.

Table 1 shows that an examinee does not find the part that contains the retrieval keywords within 180 seconds. The time from viewing the web pages to manually finding the part that are related with the retrieval keywords is different for different people; the examinees that are familiar with computer find the important parts within 20 seconds, but it takes over 60 seconds that examinees that are unfamiliar with computer find the important parts.

Table 2 shows comparison of time between people and the implemented software. "Author" in Table 2 is one of the authors of this paper. The result of Table 2 shows efficiency of the implemented software.

5   Conclusion

This paper implements the plug-in software that solves difficulty of finding the parts that are related with retrieval keywords. The software can handle the difficulty that is caused by the following cases.

1. Keywords do not exist on web pages but synonyms exist.
2. Keywords do not appear on the display areas of web pages.
3. Parts of web pages containing retrieval keywords are not in display state.

This paper also evaluates the software by experiments. As a result of the experiments, the software is useful for search engine users, even if the users are familiar or unfamiliar with computers. As compared with Google Quick Scroll, the implemented software points out preferable parts of web pages that are related with retrieval keywords. The software saves time of finding the parts that are related with retrieval keywords. The future work of the paper is to revise the following.

1. Methods for fuzzy searches
   Current search engines can handle many kinds of fuzzy searches and it is not enough for the fuzzy searches that the implemented software obtains synonyms of keywords. This paper plans to revise methods of obtaining synonyms of keywords.
2. Change of display and undisplay states of the parts of web pages
   The implemented software changes display states of the parts of web pages by using several attributes in style sheets in HTML files, but there are other attributes that are related with display states. This paper plans to revise the software so that it can handle many kinds of attributes in HTML files to change display states.
3. Capability of other search engines except Google and Yahoo
   The implemented software is capable of Google and Yahoo search engines and these search engines are major search engines in the Internet. However, new search engines may become a major search engine and "Baidu" is a major of search engine in China. Major search engines may be different for different countries. Moreover, format of input or output of search engines, such as retrieval keywords or search results, may change. Therefore, the implemented software is expected to have flexibility for change of search engines.
4. Capability of many kinds of web browsers
   The implemented software is available on Google Chrome because it is easier to implement the software on Google Chrome than on the other web

browsers. Google Chrome is one of major web browsers, but the implemented software is expected to become plug-in software for many kinds of web browsers. This paper plans to extend the implemented software for many kinds of web browsers.

We plan to revise the implemented software according to the above points and release the implemented software as free software.

References

1. Hirao, T., Isozaki, H., Maeda, E.: Extracting important sentences with support vector machines. In: Proceedings of 19th International Conference on Computational Linguistics, pp. 342–348 (2002)
2. Okamoto, J., Ishizaki, S.: Evaluation of extraction method of important sentence based on associative concept dictionary with distance information between concepts. In: Proceedings of the Conference of the Pacific Association for Computational Linguistics (PACLING 2003), pp. 315–323 (2003)
3. Otake, K., Okamoto, D., Kodama, M., Masuyama, S.: Information retrieval technology and test collections. a summarization system yellow for japanese newspaper articles. Transactions of Information Processing Society of Japan 43(2), 37–47 (2002) (in Japanese)
4. Sagara, N., Sunayama, W., Yachida, M.: Image labeling using key sentences of html. Electronics and Communications in Japan 89(7), 31–41 (2006)
5. Sunayama, W., Yachida, M.: Panoramic view system for extracting key sentences based on viewpoints and application to a search engine. Journal of Network and Computer Applications 28(2), 115–127 (2005)
6. Cascading Style Sheets, http://www.w3.org/Style/CSS/
7. Google, https://www.google.co.jp
8. Google Chrome Extension,
   http://developer.chrome.com/extensions/index.html
9. Google Quick Scroll,
   https://chrome.google.com/webstore/
   detail/google-quick-scroll/okanipcmceoeemlbjnmnbdibhgpbllgc
10. Google Toolbar, http://www.google.com/intl/ja/toolbar/ie/index.html
11. HTML 4.01 Specification (1999),
    http://www.w3.org/TR/1999/REC-html401-19991224/
12. Weblio English Thesaurus, http://ejje.weblio.jp/english-thesaurus
13. Yahoo! Japan, http://www.yahoo.co.jp/

Author Index

Printed in the United States
by Baker & Taylor Publisher Services